Praise for
Marrow

"Her sister Maggie needs a bone marrow transplant, so Lesser willingly donates hers. But the two end up sharing something even more important. Fearlessly opening up their deepest selves . . . the sisters eloquently school readers about love, self-acceptance, and the truest way to live."   —*People*

"*Marrow* is an unforgettable memoir about two sisters, but it's really about all of us. This is a book about the courage it takes to own our stories, to look truth in the eye, and to write our own bold endings. No one truth-tells with more soul and tenacity than Elizabeth Lesser. Her courage is contagious."
—Brené Brown, PhD, author of *Rising Strong*

"Elizabeth Lesser has reached deep down—down beyond even her bones and into the center of her soul—to write this beautiful book about her sister's struggle with cancer. Every page of this book is rich with love. The love that Lesser describes for her sister is not always the simple kind of love (nor should it be; families are not always easy, after all), but it is love that is just as equally weighted by realism as it is lightened by mysticism. It is real love, and it is powerful, and it is transformative. This is truly a beautiful book, and an important one."
—Elizabeth Gilbert, author of *Eat, Pray, Love* and *Big Magic*

"*Marrow* is a deeply brave, honest, emotional, visionary ride into the scary and liberating marrow of sisterhood. Elizabeth Lesser's years of accumulated wisdom, scorching self-honesty, and stunning insights are on fire here. This book is ultimately a spiritual transfusion, begging us to clean and rid ourselves of any past blood that stands in the path of love."
—Eve Ensler, author of *The Vagina Monologues*

"*Marrow* is wise and raw, vulnerable and funny. Elizabeth's profoundly honest journey to learn what it is to be flawed, to grow, to change, to love, and to let go moved me deeply . . . to my marrow."
—Sally Field, Academy Award-winning actor

"I thought with *Marrow*, Elizabeth Lesser had written a book about dying. But in fact (and miraculously) this is a book that teaches us how to live."
—Jane Fonda, Academy Award-winning actor, activist, and author of *My Life So Far*

"Every human goes through love and loss. Not everyone finds out what matters most. This book is also your story and mine. Read it and you may get to know yourself a little better."
—Deepak Chopra, MD, author of *The Seven Spiritual Laws of Success* and *Super Genes*

"It takes an author of Elizabeth Lesser's extraordinary talent to create a memoir that is as much about the reader as it is about the writer. *Marrow* steers us all into the frightening inevitability of decline and death, then deeper, into the stunning possibility of radiant and irrepressible life. Lyrical, honest, wise, heart-rending, and heart-mending, the story of how marrow connected two sisters—with one another and with the human condition writ large—is a gift that will bless all its readers with bone-deep hope and love."
—Martha Beck, author of *Finding Your Own North Star*

"I am moved to the core by the depth and beauty of this memoir. Like *Broken Open*, this is a book I will reread often as a reminder of what is really essential in life: love and spirit."
—Isabel Allende, author of *The House of the Spirits* and *The Japanese Lover*

"With profound compassion, intelligence, humanity, and humor, Elizabeth Lesser gives us the gift of *Marrow*, a beautiful and wrenching book that is about nothing less than the meaning of love."
—Dani Shapiro, author of *Slow Motion* and *Devotion*

"*Marrow* will take you into the depths of what it means to be a DNA-linked family whose destinies were linked before birth. This beautifully written and evocative book touched me deeply; may it touch you too."
—Christiane Northrup, MD, author of *Women's Bodies, Women's Wisdom* and *Goddesses Never Age*

"Lesser unlocked the goodness of a whole new kind of relationship with her dear sister, and a whole new understanding of her own capacity for love and grief."   —Krista Tippet, *On Being*

"A clear and graceful writer, Liz is adept at describing both the transplant and the emotional process of becoming a sort of joint-entity she calls 'Maggie-Liz.' Readers may recall *My Sister's Keeper* . . . that was a tear-jerker—but this is far more so, a real-life story with no happy ending but many joyful moments."
                    —Sharon Salzberg, author of *Real Happiness*

"*Marrow* shows how the interior of the bone corresponds to the interior of the person. Elizabeth Lesser, whose talent and unusual blend of heart and intelligence I've long admired, pushes far beyond emotions to explore the soul as she accompanies her sister on a long journey with cancer. I've never read a book that so perceptively shows the soul in process. This is a beautiful book that will not only move you, but also show you how to tap into the healing richness of the soul in any serious life-challenge."   —Thomas Moore, author of *Care of the Soul*

"A profound and ultimately uplifting memoir of family love, fortitude, and healing. Readers will be inspired by Lesser's wise and loving approach to both life and death."   —*Publishers Weekly*

"This profound memoir traces the love between two sisters as they travel together through 'thickets of despair and hope,' their bond deepening beneath the bone to the 'soul's marrow.'"   —*Poets & Writers*

"A searching, compassionate, and uplifting memoir."
                                              —*Kirkus Reviews*

"A clear and graceful writer, Lesser . . . brings anecdotes from history, mythology, and philosophy to bear on an essentially tragic story."
                                              —*Washington Post*

Marrow

ALSO BY ELIZABETH LESSER

Broken Open

The Seeker's Guide

Marrow

Love, Loss, and What Matters Most

ELIZABETH LESSER

HARPER WAVE

An Imprint of HarperCollins*Publishers*

A hardcover edition of this book was published in 2016 by HarperCollins Publishers.

P.S.™ is a trademark of HarperCollins Publishers.

The Enlightened Heart: An Anthology of Sacred Poetry, edited by Stephen Mitchell. Copyright © 1989 by Stephen Mitchell. Reprinted by permission of HarperCollins Publishers.

"Days Between," words by Robert Hunter, music by Jerry Garcia. Copyright © 1999 ICE NINE PUBLISHING CO., INC. All rights administered by UNIVERSAL MUSIC CORP. All rights reserved. Used by permission. Reprinted by permission of Hal Leonard Corporation.

FIRST HARPER WAVE PAPERBACK EDITION PUBLISHED IN 2017

Designed by Bonni Leon-Berman

Artwork by Maggie Lake / Photographic prints by Christopher Irion, courtesy of the author.

Library of Congress Cataloging-in-Publication Data has been applied for.

ISBN 978-0-06-236765-5 (pbk.)

17 18 19 20 21   OV/LSC   10 9 8 7 6 5 4 3 2 1

FOR US,

KaLiMaJo

Contents

Prelude

IT STARTS ON AN AUGUST day, above Flathead Lake in Montana, just a few moments before I head to a wedding I am to perform. Not that I have any right to marry people. "I'm a writer, not a minister," I told my young friends when they asked me to officiate. But they didn't care. I have known them both since they were children. Our lives are linked through my kids, who are their close friends, and their parents, who are my close friends, and through a tribe of other friends with many years behind us. And now we are all here, in Montana, to celebrate another link in the chain.

I am standing in the driveway of the house my family is renting, looking out at the enormous lake bordered in the distance by the jagged peaks of the Northern Rockies. As I wait for my husband and sons to join me, I take it all in: the sun illuminating the snow-fields across the lake in Glacier National Park, the big sky, the grand expanses. It's a dramatic, impersonal landscape—the kind of place that takes my New England breath away.

My cell phone rings. I think of turning it off. I'm on vacation. It's a special day. My children are here, my closest friends. Who would I need to talk to? I check to see. A Vermont number. My sister. And so it starts:

"Liz? It's Maggie."

"Maggie?" I ask. Her voice is lower than usual. Dark. My heart jumps a beat. Maggie's voice is never dark. She is one of those people who seem to have descended from hummingbirds. She is tiny and light, and she never lands long enough for you to really know what's going on in her head. Always moving. Always chipper. Here. There. Gone. Back again.

"What's the matter?" I ask.

"I'm sick." That's all she says. A landscape bigger than Montana opens up between us. We both fall in.

"Sick? What kind of sick?"

"Cancer," she whispers. "I'm very sick."

Now it's her words that take my breath away. Finally I ask her what has happened and she tells me a jumbled tale of having weird symptoms, ignoring them, thinking they were one thing, and then finding out they were something quite different. Cancer. Lymphoma. The kind she will die from soon if she doesn't start treatment.

If anyone should not have to get cancer at this very moment, it is my little sister Maggie. After years of being married to the boy next door, the high school sweetheart, the man who has defined her, my sister is quite suddenly a single woman, unattached, on her own. A woman who created a storybook home is now homeless—house-sitting here for one friend, and there for another. Her college-age children are like planets cut loose from gravity. Is it better for Maggie that our mother died recently and our father a few years previously? That she doesn't have to face their worry about her illness, their judgment about her failed marriage?

I feel something pulling at me from across the country, but even more so from deep within. As if there is a buried magnet in my body, quivering to the pull of my sister. What is the deepest part of the body? Is it the blood? The bone? The marrow of the bone? I don't even know what that means: the marrow of the bone. I will find out later.

Introduction

THIS BOOK IS A LOVE story. It is primarily about the love between two sisters, but it is also about the kindness you must give to yourself if you are to truly love another. Love of self, love of other: two strands in the love braid. I have braided these strands together in all sorts of relationships, in varying degrees of grace and ineptitude. I've messed up in both directions: being self-centered, being a martyr; not knowing my own worth, not valuing the essential worth of the other. To love well is to get the balance right. It's the work of a lifetime. It's art. It's what this book is about.

When my sister's cancer recurred after seven years of remission; when we were told her only chance for survival was a bone marrow transplant; when test results confirmed I was a perfect marrow match; when we prepared ourselves, body and soul, to give and receive; when my marrow was harvested; when she received my stem cells that would become her blood cells; when we traveled together through the thickets of despair and hope; when she lived what she said was the best year of her life; when the cancer returned; when she faced the end; when she died; when all of this happened, I took up the strands of myself and braided them together with my sister's strands, and I finally got it right. Although "getting it right" sounds more tidy and final than love ever is. There is no ten-ways-to-get-it-right list when it comes to love. No exact formulas for when to be vulnerable and when to be strong, when to wait and when to pursue, when to relent and when to be a relentless love warrior. Rather, love is a mess, love is a dance, love is a miracle. Love is also stronger than death, but I'm only learning that now.

I must add here that there was another strand that my incredibly brave sister added to complete the love braid and, in doing so, inspired me to do the same. It is the secret strand, the one the philosopher Friedrich Nietzsche called "amor fati"—love of fate. Nietzsche described amor fati as the ability not to merely bear our fate but to love it. That's a tall order. To be human is to have the kind of fate that doles out all sorts of wondrous and horrible things. No one gets through life without big doses of confusion and angst, pain and loss. What's to love about that? And yet if you say yes to amor fati, if you practice loving the fullness of your fate, if you pick up the third strand of the love braid, you will thread ribbons of faith and gratitude and meaning through your life. Some will reject the idea of loving your fate as capitulation or naïveté; I say it's the way to wisdom and the key to love.

When I talk about love, I am not talking about romance. Romance is good. I like it a lot. It's fiery and fun. But it is merely one sliver of the love story. It's a mistake to reduce the whole ocean of love to a little flame of romance and then spend all of one's energy trying to keep that flame from burning out. In doing so, we give short shrift to the vast majority of our love relationships: parents, siblings, children, friends, colleagues, and, of course, mates after the initial passion has mellowed. Trying to sustain fairy-tale romance is a foolish quest. But you can sustain a different kind of love across a lifetime with a whole motley crew of people. It takes guts to love well, and it takes work to sustain important relationships, but I promise you, it is possible, and it's what our hearts are really longing for.

You may be thinking of dulled or bruised or ruined relationships in your life as you read this. You may be thinking, she doesn't know *my* sister, my brother, my ex, my kid, boss, friend, mate. And you may be right—it is not possible to heal or sustain every relationship. Sometimes we have to end things, or do the work of healing on our own. But I propose that most of our significant relationships can be mended, sweetened, enlarged. And I propose that deepening one relationship can unlock all sorts of goodness in your life—with other people, with your work, with your fate.

I propose this to you because my sister and I had a relationship comparable to most human relationships. We were imperfect people, with qualities that both supported and eroded our abilities to love. We were similar in some ways, yet also different enough to misunderstand each other, to judge each other, to reject each other. Sometimes we were close, and sometimes we were strangers. And like most people—and certainly like most siblings—we carted around with us bags of old stories and resentments and regrets. We dragged those bags from childhood into adulthood, into other relationships, into our work, into our families. We believed the stories in the bags—the tales we had heard about ourselves and told about each other. We had never unpacked those bags and showed each other what was in them.

Until we had to.

IN THE YEARS between my sister's first cancer diagnosis and her last recurrence, she lived a remarkably full life. She re-created a home for herself and her new man; she rededicated her life to her children and her work and her art; she overcame several serious health crises; and she learned to manage the fear and pain that come with being a cancer survivor. Her life stabilized, as did our relationship and my own life. During that time I did what many writers spend their time doing: I started several books, but never finished them. With my first two published books, I had used my own life as the story line. But I was sick of talking about myself. So

I decided to write a novel. That way, I could hide my story (and the stories of the poor people who have the misfortune of being related to me) behind created characters. But fiction is a different beast, and I couldn't wrestle a novel to completion. I started a fable and then a collection of essays, but nothing gelled.

The book I most wanted to write was about authenticity—the idea that beneath the chatter of the mind and the storms of the heart is a truer self, an essential self, a core, a soul. Call it what you like, but life has brought me to the point where I know that the striving and insecure ego is not the whole truth of who I am, or who you are. More and more, in glimpses caught through meditation and prayer, through acts of kindness and courage, and sometimes just by having a cup of coffee in the morning or a sip of wine with friends, I find myself quite suddenly in touch with a fullness of being that wakes me out of slumber. It's as if God is calling roll and I shoot up my hand, saying "Here!" This can happen at the oddest times. I'll be wheeling my cart through the grocery store or driving home after a long day at the office when grace descends and I am relieved of the illusion that I am merely a cranky, imperfect, overextended person. Instead, I sense a more dignified being hiding behind the assumed roles—a noble soul, riding faithfully through the human experience, related to everyone and everything, aware of the splendor at the heart of creation.

I wanted to write a book about *that* self—the soul self, the authentic self, the true self. I wanted to explore why we forget who we are, and how we can remember. I'd been thinking about this book for a long time, at least for as long as I have worked at Omega Institute, the retreat and conference center I cofounded in 1977, when I was still in my twenties. Through my work I have been exposed to a wide array of people—hundreds of thousands of workshop participants from all over the world, and the noted authors and artists, doctors and scientists, philosophers and spiritual teachers who come to Omega to help people heal and grow. It's been a good place for me to work because I'm an unapologetic voyeur. I've never doubted my purpose in life: It's to watch people. It's to ponder what the hell works here on Planet Earth and why it's so hard to put seemingly simple instructions for living into everyday actions—instructions like the Bible's "Love your neighbor as yourself" or Shakespeare's "This above all: to thine own self be true."

When you get down to it, the most widely accepted adages that have guided human beings across the ages all focus on the same ideas: to love the self, to give of the self, to be true to the self. But there's a problem with these guidelines: They presuppose you know what that self is. Someone forgot to mention the long process of uncovering the shining seed at the center of your identity. Being true to that self involves sifting through the layers of bad advice and unreasonable expectations of others. It requires seeing through your own delusions of grandeur or your fear of failure or your impostor syndrome or your conviction that there is something uniquely and obviously screwed up about your particular self.

My first job in life was being a midwife. I delivered enough babies to know that every one of us comes into this world in possession of a radiant, pure, good-to-the-core self. I witnessed this each time I touched the skin and looked into the eyes of a brand-new baby. I saw his self. I saw her soul. I sensed in each baby an essential self like no other self before it—a matchless, meaningful mash-up of biology, lineage, culture, and cosmic influences we can barely fathom.

And then we grow up, we become adults, and we spend so much of our time uncomfortable in our own skin—almost embarrassed at being human. We devalue and cover the original self, layer by layer, as we make our way through life. I wanted my next book to be a travel guide through the great journey of uncovering. "There is something in every one of you that waits and listens for the sound of the genuine in yourself," the civil rights leader Howard Thurman wrote. "That is the only true guide you will ever have." What better thing to write about than the act of listening for and then following *the only true guide you will ever have*?

But something was stopping me as I put fingertips to keyboard. Perhaps it was my ambivalence about much of the literature of "authenticity." There's a nagging narcissism to it. A book about being true to the self can read like a manual for joining a cult of one. Try to write about it and you're smack-dab in the middle of a perennial paradox: how knowledge of self, and love of self, and esteem of self go awry if they don't lead ultimately to understanding and respect and love of others.

And then there's the sticky question of "What is the self?" Is it merely a bundle of neural impulses held together by flesh and gravity for a tiny flash of time? And when the flash burns out, does our body turn to dust and our personal ego dissolve into the cosmic soup? Or is each one of us more substantial than that? Are we spiritual beings having a human experience? Does our soul continue once released from the confines of body and ego? And when, as human beings, we listen for guidance from our authentic core, is it really the eternal soul whose song we hear?

Even though I knew I would never definitively answer these questions (since no one ever has), I wanted to dive as deeply as I could into the mystery. The questions may have no firm answers, but the search for them brings us closer to the kind of life each of us yearns for. I may not be able to answer the big questions, but I do know a few things for sure: I know that people who have tasted the dignity and goodness of their own true nature are more likely to see and respect the dignity of others. I know that if I have an authentic self that is noble and sacred, then you have one too. This may sound like a no-brainer, but it's one of humanity's biggest stumbling blocks—this sense of me against the other. Instead of traveling side by side, helping each other as we fall and being inspired by each other as we rise, we defend ourselves; we attack; we try to go it alone. Instead of reveling in one another's shining authenticity, we compete, as if there is a limited amount of shine in the world, as if the only way to see the shining self is against the backdrop of a diminished other.

This became my most compelling reason to write about authenticity. To link up the liberation of the genuine self with the healing of our relationships and the mending of our human family. For all of the marvelous technological ways of connecting to each other, there's still so much loneliness, misunderstanding, and disconnection in the world. Connection is a basic human need. We want to be understood, seen, accepted, loved. We want to matter to each other. We want to relate, soul to soul.

And so I fumbled around, trying to craft a book that could shine a light on the path that leads to the authentic self, a self that defies description yet begs to be revealed. "One can't write directly about the soul," Virginia Woolf lamented in her diaries. "Looked at, it vanishes." Still, I wanted to look.

WHEN I WON the cosmic lottery and tested as a perfect match for my sister's bone marrow transplant, I did what I often do when I'm scared: I became an amateur researcher. I do not like to bury my head in the sand. Rather, I like to arm myself with knowledge, even if in the end the knowledge can become its own form of sand in which I bury myself. But in this case, the research I did into bone marrow, stem cells, and the miracle of transplant went way beyond the acquisition of knowledge. And what my sister and I experienced was much more than a medical procedure.

My research revealed to me that bone marrow transplants are fraught with danger for the recipient. For months after the procedure my sister would face two life-threatening situations. First, her body might reject the stem cells that would be extracted from my bone marrow and transplanted into her bloodstream. And, second, my stem cells, once in my sister's body, might attack their new host. Rejection and attack. Both could kill her. The medical professionals were doing everything they could to ensure neither would happen. What if Maggie and I could help them? What if we left the clear sailing of the bone marrow transplant up to the doctors, and conducted a different kind of transplant? What if we met in the marrow of our souls and moved beyond our lifelong tendency to reject and attack each other?

People have said I was brave to undergo the bone marrow extraction. But I don't really think so—you'd have to be a miserable, crappy person to refuse the opportunity to save your sibling. But getting emotionally naked with my sister . . . *this* felt risky. To dig deep into never-expressed grievances, secret shame, behind-the-back stories, blame, and judgment wasn't something we had done before. But my sister's life hung in the balance. And so, over the course of a year, sometimes with the help of a guide but mostly on walks and over coffee, just the two of us, and sometimes with our other sisters, we opened our hearts, we left the past behind, and we walked together into a field of love.

What I learned from both transplants—the bone marrow transplant and the soul marrow transplant—is that the marrow of the bones and the marrow of the self are quite similar. Deep in the center of the bones are stem cells that can keep another person alive, perhaps not forever, but for a time and, in the case of my sister, for what she called the best year of her life. Deep in the center of the self are the soul cells of who you really are. Dig for them, believe in them, and offer them to another person, and you can heal each other's hearts and keep love alive forever.

Here's one more thing I learned. You don't have to wait for a life-and-death situation to offer the marrow of yourself to another person. We can all do it, we can do it now, and there's a chance that the life of our human family does indeed depend on it.

And this is how I finally came to write a book about authenticity and love.

Throughout the book you will find snippets from my sister's journals—"field notes," as she called them, from the varied layers of her life. Besides being a nurse, mother, farmer, baker, musician, and maple syrup producer, my Renaissance sister was also an artist and a writer. Her artwork evolved over the years into exceptional botanical pieces and prints that hang in people's homes all over the country. Her writing took the form of journals, hilarious letters and e-mails, illustrated children's books, and a memoir she dreamed of writing called *Lower Road*. She said there were enough things written about taking the higher road; she wanted to write about taking the lower road and finding higher ground the hard way. There was a long dirt road in her area with the actual name of Lower Road—a single lane that hugged a mountain and led into a hollow flanked on one side by marshes and ponds and on the other side by rusty trailers and old farmhouses. When she was a young visiting nurse, her work for the state of Vermont often took her to Lower Road. The book

Lower Road was to be a chronicle of her relationship with her patients who lived there: the teenage mothers, the veterans with PTSD, the addicted, the abusive, the abused. The forgotten rural poor whom she cared for with a no-bullshit form of tenderness.

When Maggie's computer became her journal, she began e-mailing me entries: excerpts from the always changing *Lower Road*, field notes from the clinic she ran, funny stories about people she met at craft shows, joyful rants about her new home, about the wildness of the woods in springtime and the sweetness of the sugarhouse on dark cold nights when the maple sap ran. And when she got sick, her field notes came from the loneliness of her hospital bed and the window seat in her home. She wrote quickly, in run-on sentences, making up words, switching tenses all over the place. She never used capital letters and she bent grammar rules. She wrote like a hummingbird would write if it stayed still long enough to gather its thoughts and put them into words.

I had always planned to help Maggie craft a book out of her hummingbird words. She wanted me to, and that's why she sent me a whole mess of disorganized computer files. We began working on them when she was recovering from the transplant. But when her energy waned, I asked her how she would feel if I included some of her field notes in the book I was writing. I had been showing her early segments of my book, and she had a wistful appreciation for it—a sense of humor and also grief that she would not be around to see how it ended. Together we decided to include some of her words in my book, and so I scattered them throughout—a trail of Maggie's truth crisscrossing mine.

Part One

THE GIRLS

You are born into your family
and your family is born into you.

—ELIZABETH BERG

PHONE BOMBS

WHEN I WAS A KID, telephones were stationary objects. Most houses had one, or at the most two of them—one bolted onto the kitchen wall and the other on a bedside table, rarely used. When I became a teenager, my friends got phones in their rooms. Princess phones, they were called, usually pink, with push buttons instead of a dial, and a long cord so you could walk around or lie in bed and chat under the covers. The princess phone never made an appearance in my family's home. My sisters and I were barely allowed to talk on the phone at all. Why would we need one of our own?

Phones became omnipresent later on. First, cordless phones made their debut, and then of course came the cell phone. The cell phone changed everything. But before there were cell phones, what changed my relationship with the telephone was becoming a parent. Having children turned a benign object—the phone—into a time bomb. When it rang, I worried, and often my worst-case scenarios came true: a failed test, a bloody nose, a broken arm. One of my sons got suspended from middle school for giving away answers to an exam. During high school, another son was pulled over for speeding and the cop discovered pot in his pocket. I remember where I was when those calls came in.

Things I never thought would happen also traveled through the airwaves and into the phone like little bombs. *Ring!* My father died. *Ring!* Colleague quit. *Ring, ring!* Trade Towers blown to bits. And then there was the phone bomb from my sister at the wedding in Montana. On that day I learned to do something many people are born knowing and then spend years in therapy trying to unlearn: I went into denial. For a whole day. This was revolutionary for me, someone whose heart stays unreasonably open most of the time.

Like all of us, I have several characters living within me—there's my vigilant rational self who lives in my head, my wild emotional self lodged in my heart, and a deeper self that some call the soul. That deeper self is always there, wiser than worry, vaster than fear, quick to see through the eyes of love. But the rational self is a bossy guy that crowds out the soul on a regular basis. Sometimes the rational self is right on the money, but often it is small-minded and tyrannical and it leads me into a cul-de-sac of overthinking. And my emotional self can spin out of control like a crazed dervish, throwing off sparks of joy and wonder, anger and despair. Round and round, I follow my mind and my emotions. The human experience is dizzying if we can't find the still point in the midst of the turning.

The still point is there. It is always there. I know it. I have found it again and again, even within the most turbulent whirlwinds. It may take me a while, but at least now I know there is a still point, and that the storm will pass and the center will hold. When I am in the grips of too much thinking, too much feeling, when I am frightened or ashamed, judgmental or paranoid, self-righteous or jealous, I know to wait, I know to pray, I know to trust. And sometimes, when there's just too much noise—when my emotions whip up a storm, or my overactive mind chatters like a jackhammer—patience and prayer don't cut it. That's when it can be helpful to take a brief denial time-out.

Which is what I did in Montana after receiving the phone bomb from my sister. I locked up my emotional creature, turned off my repetitive mind, and went to the wedding without them. I mingled with the crowd; I oohed and aahed at the tent set in a wheat field under the big sky; I performed the ceremony as if I had done such a thing hundreds of times before. All the while, I kept the news of the phone bomb in some kind of top secret vault. Then, copying the behavior of partygoers throughout the ages, I downed several drinks at the reception so as to be able to make small talk and eat and dance. Denial! Where had you been all my life?

The next morning, I left the family behind and got on a plane. It was nearly empty. I had a row of seats all to myself—a good thing, because the minute I buckled the belt, my heart reopened on its own accord. I let the feelings come. I gave over the reins to my emotional self. She took off right away.

"Maggie's too young to die," I cried. "This is so unfair."

"There's no such thing as fair," rational self interrupted, making a predictable comeback.

"Well, it's terrible nonetheless." Now I was weeping. "She's in the middle of a divorce; she doesn't even have a home; her kids ..."

Rational self was unmoved. "No such thing as terrible, either. It is what it is."

Emotional self and rational self went on like this for a while until I tired of their either/or banter. I closed my eyes, and noticed that my shoulders were up around my ears. I dropped them down, softened my whole body, and breathed my way toward the still point until I could hear the voice of my soul.

And there she was, telling me the truth: "Have faith," my soul said. "You'll see—your sister will grow from this; she'll rise to meet it. And you will too. You'll grieve and you'll learn, you'll rage and you'll worry, but through it all you will grow deeper and deeper into the truth of who you really are. You will, Maggie will, all who travel with her will uncover surprising treasures because of this path her soul has chosen." When soul speaks, there's really no arguing. Everyone else just shuts up and listens. The bigger story sparkles in the silence. What needs to be done is revealed. Mind and heart join hands and vow to work together.

For the rest of the plane ride I rested in the rare peace that the soul brings. It was as if I was being filled with fuel for the long journey ahead. I didn't know what would come. I didn't know how long a voyage I was embarking on. I didn't know that I would be brought all the way into the actual marrow of my bones, and deeper still into the holy marrow of my true self. I only knew to pray for the soul to be my guide.

The next day, driving from my home in New York to my sister in Vermont, worry and grief took over again. My heart filled with sadness. And not just for Maggie. Not just for the fearsome treatments she would have to go through and the unknown outcome and the ways in which nothing would ever again be the same for her. My heart also broke for us—for our family, for our story, for who we had always been and who I foolishly expected we would always be. "The girls," my heart whimpered, holding on tight to my three sisters, to the configuration of my childhood, to my known place in the world. I cried the words aloud: "The four girls."

"Oh, stop it," my mind snapped, sounding quite like my mother.

THE GIRLS

I WAS BORN INTO A family of girls, the second of four daughters. My sisters and I were known as "the girls." Or just "girls," as in "Girls! Time for supper!" My mother yelled that line several thousand times over the years of mothering four daughters. We also heard this line a lot: "GIRLS. Stop bickering or I'll wallop you!" My father was famous for that one, threatening us with "wallops" as our family made its interminable car trips from New York to Vermont. My father's work as an advertising man who represented the ski industry took him—and therefore us—from his office in New York City to the mountains of Vermont all winter long. Why my parents insisted on bringing all four girls with them every weekend befuddles me to this day, but complain as we might, come Friday afternoon, we would cram ourselves into the station wagon for the four-hour drive north—vying for the window seats, cold and uncomfortable, tired and bored—until we finally fell asleep against each other.

Despite his threats, my father only came close to walloping one of us once, in all his years of being outnumbered and exasperated by "the girls." I cannot remember what drove him to attempt to deliver on his threat. I do remember, as do my sisters, the scene: Something I have done to provoke my father has caused him to chase me up the stairs of our house, swinging at my behind with my mother's purse. My sisters run after us, laughing. My mother stands at the bottom of the stairs, helplessly yelling, "Girls! Girls!" By the time my father catches up to me, he has lost his steam. He drops my mother's purse, throws up his hands, and, mumbling something about "the girls," stomps back down the stairs and escapes outside.

An advantage to having siblings is that the pressure is off any one child to live up to all the dreams of the parents. It's nearly impossible for one kid to do it all—to be well behaved *and* courageous, bookish *and* athletic, cooperative *and* original. And so siblings fill in for each other. But there's a disadvantage as well. Without advance agreement, siblings are assigned a role that can brand one for life. Show a tendency in one direction, and that becomes who you have to be all the time. This one's the saint, and that one's the rebel. This one will go far; that one will stay close. It can take a lifetime to escape the narrow boundaries of a fixed family identity.

This was certainly the case in my family. Where one of us was thin and athletic (my older sister), the other (me) was chubby and introspective. Where one excelled in school (me), another brought home bad grades (again, older sister). Where one stood up to our father's authority (me), my younger sisters were the quieter ones, the identified pleasers, intent on keeping the peace. And so we settled into those roles, hearing and telling stories about each other, branding ourselves and dragging those branded selves into the rest of our lives.

There were constant reminders—expressed or implied—of the characters we were to play on the family stage. My mother wouldn't allow me to take ballet lessons because I was not as "coordinated" as my sisters. She would drop off two of them at the little dance school taught by a teenager down the street, and then explain to me I couldn't go because my body was "anatomically incorrect" for ballet, but that shouldn't bother me because I was smart. She'd shame my older sister for her poor school habits, even as she giggled with her about my knock-knees and the way I looked in a bathing suit. Maggie, my younger sister, was the "good" one—the well-behaved girl, the one my mother could depend on. And our shy littlest sister was Daddy's favorite, overrun by her big sisters, forever locked into being the baby.

Like the pantheon of gods and goddesses in Greek mythology, siblings take on archetypal roles—roles that solidify one's sense of self long after childhood is over. In our pantheon, I was the bossy one, the agitator—"the princess," they called me. Somehow I got it in my mind, even as a little girl, to challenge my father's power. It struck me as outrageous that in a family of women, my father got to call the shots. I wondered why my mother deferred to him even though she seemed more astute, and was certainly as educated and worldly. But these were the 1950s and '60s, and although my mother had graduated college with honors, my father established the family values, determined how we spent our time, and, when he was around, enforced what we did and didn't talk about.

The fact that we were four little girls didn't stop my father from including us in his adventurous activities, most of which were inspired by his time spent in the army, in the 10th Mountain Division—the ski troops—during World War II. It's not that he felt girls should have the same opportunities as boys. Rather, he didn't seem to notice we were girls. Or maybe he did and just preferred not to accept the fact that all of his offspring were female. We certainly were never asked if we wanted to join his regiment. It was just assumed.

In retrospect, I am grateful to my father for dragging us along on treks up New Hampshire's Mount Washington, with our heavy downhill skis strapped to our backs, or for insisting we trudge for miles to find a spot on a Long Island beach where we could escape the lifeguards and swim in the dangerous surf. We were never told we couldn't do something because of our gender. But all of us, including my mother, were ridiculed if we acted "like a girl." Small talk, gossip, worry, idleness, vanity—these were all signs of feminine weakness, according to my father, and if we demonstrated those behaviors, we risked his scorn. My mother metabolized and enforced the official policy: work hard, be strong, keep busy.

My parents were typical of many Americans raised in the "Greatest Generation." The Depression and the war molded their characters. They were vigorous, frugal, and civic-minded people who rarely complained. In their day, self-reflection was a waste of time and psychotherapy was for crazy people. And parenting? It was not yet a verb. People had children, fed and clothed them, sent them to school, made them do chores, and pretty much that was it. Sure, some parents took their kids to Little League or piano lessons, but mostly they left us alone. We played in our suburban neighborhood without adult supervision, helmets, or sunscreen. Rarely did my mother help us with homework, even though she was a high school English teacher who cared intensely about education. It was our task to excel, not hers.

My sisters and I spent an enormous amount of our childhood together, more so than many siblings. We competed not so much for our parents' approval, but more for each other's. We were constant and creative playmates, but we also were competitive and adversarial. As we grew up and became women, we grew further apart in some ways and stayed deeply connected in others. But always, just below the surface, unexplored and unexpressed, were those roles we had assumed in the family, those stories we had been told and believed, those conclusions we had come to about each other and ourselves.

AGAINST THE TIDE

MY PARENTS WERE SOCIALLY MINDED intellectuals who regarded religion as a lower rung on the evolutionary ladder. At the bottom of the ladder were one-celled amoebas, then came dinosaurs, then superstitious cave people, then superstitious religious people, then came the Renaissance and Galileo and the birth of science, and everything else smart and forward-thinking came after that. That was history as taught to us by our mother, who had a particularly bitter taste in her mouth from the religion of her youth. She hailed from a devout Christian Science family that held closely to the scriptures, especially those about the body being an illusion and illness being a sign of what the church called "mental error." According to Christian Science doctrine, if you prayed diligently, you would be healed of all sickness and even death. Therefore, giving credence to the aches and pains of your body or going to a doctor, God forbid, amounted to desertion of the faith. My grandparents withheld medical care even when my mother and her brothers were seriously ill, even if other members of the church died from a similar illness. When my mother showed any weakness—physical or emotional—she was told to "know the truth," code in Christian Science to snap out of it.

My mother renounced her religion in her twenties, but she never got over the shame of having a body and the trepidation of caring for it. While she didn't overtly preach Christian Science doctrine to her daughters, she did repeat some well-worn phrases from time to time, especially when we were sick. "Mind governs" was one of her favorites—a quote from *Science and Health*, the most revered Christian Science text. We had no idea what "Mind governs" really meant, but we absorbed my mother's interpretation: your body is a figment of your mind's imagination, so if you complain of pain or illness, you're a hypochondriac.

My grandfather remained a practicing Christian Scientist until the day he died in his late nineties. He was a strong presence in my childhood. In my memory, he is always sitting in the same wingback chair in our living room. His pipe rests in an ashtray on a little table, and he's reading *Science and Health* for what must be the seven thousandth time. I still have his copy of the book. Almost every sentence is highlighted or underlined, and there are comments in the margins on every page. My mother mocked my grandfather's piety, but I recognized him as a fellow seeker, although as a child I didn't have the words to engage with him, to ask him some obvious questions. It wasn't until I was in college, a few years before he died, that I began to talk to my grandfather about spiritual issues. This is why I have his tattered copy of *Science and Health*. He gave it to me after I got up the courage to talk to him about a nagging contradiction I noticed in his philosophy.

"If the body is an illusion," I asked him, "then why do you eat?"

His answer was the book. He handed it to me with a half-smile. I have come to recognize that smile from conversations I have had with other religious people who take scripture literally. It's a smile both condescending and worried. It says, "All questions will be answered in this book, dear child." But it's also a plea: "Don't scratch the surface too deeply. Don't unravel the threads or the whole thing might fall apart."

My father came from an equally devout Jewish family. He was forced into attending services, eating kosher, learning the prayers. But the faith never stuck. He put down his foot after his bar mitzvah, and by high school was freed from his religious duties. He never set foot in a synagogue again. I didn't experience him as Jewish; I didn't experience my mother as Christian. Rather, both my parents were as zealously unreligious as their parents had been pious.

If my parents adhered to any sacred text, it was the *New Yorker* magazine, and if they worshipped anything, it was the trinity of the great outdoors, social justice, and literature. My mother was an English teacher. She read us Greek myths and American poetry and cared deeply about grammar. My father was a nature-lover and, incongruously, a Madison Avenue ad man. Every morning, he took the train from the still-wooded north shore of Long Island into New York City, where he wrote ad copy and jingles. Every night he'd come back home and test his work on his family as we sat around the dinner table.

Meanwhile, I was born with a spiritual ache in my bones. As early as I can remember—maybe four or five—I would lie awake at night, my heart pounding to the deafening beat of the big questions: Where did I come from? What's the point of all this? Where do we go when we die? My mother's remedies to my existential worries were to offer dire insights from Jean-Paul Sartre and Virginia Woolf. Or she would quote Charles Darwin or Dr. King as a way of pointing me in a different direction—away from self-examination and toward science or social action.

My father had nothing but impatience for anything that smacked of soul-searching. His answer to whatever ailed anyone was to go outside and tramp around in the woods. Even though he was born in Brooklyn, and we lived on Long Island, and he worked in Manhattan, his heart was set on returning to his soul's homeland, his Jerusalem: the state of Vermont.

When I think of the time and the place of my childhood—the 1950s and '60s in suburban America—and then I think of my parents, I have to laugh. Whereas most adults were trying to be Ward and June Cleaver, my father and mother were aiming for Henry David Thoreau and Rosa Parks. They may not have been the warmest and fuzziest of parents, but I was proud to be their child, even though I felt there was something insufficient in their overarching worldview. I didn't know exactly what was missing, but I was determined to find out. I was a mystical little kid adrift in a family of cynics—a seeker in a boat with no oars. I tagged along with neighbors to Catholic Mass and bought gospel records on the down low. After President Kennedy and Dr. King were shot, I hung their photos on my bedroom wall and prayed to them in the cover of night.

Whenever I would pray, I would put my hand over my heart and breathe into a spot that felt like a gaping hole. If I could stay with it long enough, the hole would fill slowly, like water rising in a well, and I would feel a temporary sense of peace, a quelling of the questions, and a slightly embarrassing emotion: the rising water felt almost romantic. I had no words for this feeling, and I had no one to ask about it since sentimentality was nearly criminal in my household.

I remember the first time I heard the phrase "God is love." I was still in grade school. My mother was performing her nightly ritual of cooking dinner while listening to the news on the radio. My sisters and I were sitting at the kitchen table, doing our homework. An item came on the news—it was the anniversary of a legendary

Easter Sunday performance by the opera singer Marian Anderson. My mother listened with rapt attention. Then she turned off the radio and told us the story of Marian Anderson with the same reverential tone that followers use to tell the parables of their faith. "Do you girls understand the real meaning of Easter?" my mother asked us, knowing full well we didn't since we had no religious training of any kind. "The real meaning," she continued, "has nothing to do with eggs or bunnies. The real meaning is that God is love." And then she told us how the Daughters of the American Revolution—the reviled DAR—declined to book Marian Anderson into Constitution Hall in Washington, DC, because she was black. That caused First Lady Eleanor Roosevelt—the Godhead of my mother's nonreligion—to resign from the DAR and arrange for the concert to be held on Easter Sunday, on the steps of the Lincoln Memorial.

"The sun was shining," my mother said. "And seventy-five thousand people of all races came together to hear one of the world's greatest artists sing 'America.' That's what Easter is all about—the resurrection of love. If you want to know what they mean by 'God is love,' well, that's what they mean."

"God is love?" I asked my mother. "That's what I think too!" My sisters rolled their eyes.

"Well, that's what they say," my mother snorted.

"Who? Who says that God is love?" I asked. I suddenly recognized in those words the feeling I had when I prayed.

"People who go to church say that. But it's just something they mouth. They're parrots," my mother said. "They don't walk their talk."

"But maybe they feel it when they pray," I said. My mother gave me a quizzical look and turned the radio back on, indicating the topic deserved no more attention. But it was too late. I was intrigued. It appeared I wasn't alone in my heart-pounding, well-filling, love-feeling prayers. Others had felt the same thing and probably were talking about it somewhere.

As I entered adolescence, I fantasized about belonging to a church more than I dreamed about going on a date. I continued going to Mass with my best friend. I weaseled my way into the confession booth; I knelt at the altar; I tasted the body and blood of Christ, which seemed swooningly amorous to me. When I came home one Wednesday afternoon with a smudge of ash on my forehead, my mother was appalled. My sisters fell on the floor laughing.

After the famous Ash Wednesday incident, my mother made a point of showing me the April issue of *Time* magazine. It was 1966. I was thirteen. The cover was black and featured three huge words in screaming red ink: "IS GOD DEAD?"

"See?" my mother said.

I was concerned but not deterred. I made trips to the library and took out books by authors like Thomas Merton, a Catholic monk, whose autobiography, *The Seven Storey Mountain*, filled me with hope. Merton was raised without religion, and he was now a monk! When I went off to college, I was excited to be going to the same school that Merton had attended several decades previously—Columbia University in New York City. I was at Barnard College, the women's school across the street from Columbia. It was also my mother's alma mater, and a hotbed of political activity. While I got involved with antiwar and civil rights causes, I also took the subway to churches mentioned by Merton in *The Seven Storey Mountain*. Like him, I would enter a church and sit alone in the cool and the dark, full of angst, praying for direction.

From the moment I pushed off the shore of childhood, I began rowing toward the land my mother and father had deliberately sailed away from. I dropped out of Barnard at the end of my sophomore year and went to California, searching for a guru. It was the 1970s and Eastern meditation teachers were washing up on the shores of America. I wanted one. I was nineteen. Most young people in my generation were leaving the ethos of the '60s behind, looking to start a family or a career. But that didn't interest me; I was looking for God. It was like walking in the opposite direction of a stream of people on a crowded sidewalk. I pushed past the norm of my upbringing and the culture at large, with an intensity I did not understand. I felt the intensity most when I went home, not only in the presence of my parents but also with my sisters. And especially with my younger sister Maggie.

CONDITIONS OF WORTH

MAGGIE AND I WERE BOTH born in August, two years and eight days apart. Overwhelmed by four kids, my mother killed two birds with one party, and year after year Maggie and I celebrated our birthdays on the same summer day. This was not either of our choices. In my mother's picture albums, you can see the roles we assumed in the family system—me the dissenter, and Maggie the peacemaker. In one photo, when I was eight and she was six, I scowl at the camera as little Maggie dutifully blows out the candles on the cake.

Little Maggie. She was a tiny, adorable creature. My first memories of being her sister are of wanting to protect her. She seemed too small and scraggly to be able to make it in the world of school buses and gym class and neighborhood games where the big boys bullied the little kids. But Maggie never wanted anyone's help. She compensated for her tiny stature with a tough and stubborn stance. She'd have none of it when grown-ups called her cute, or her friends tried to carry her around like a doll. She developed a dirty mouth at a young age, and a desire to stand up for the underdog as she grew older. She valued self-reliance in herself and other people, but was also the consummate caregiver. She worried about everyone else's feelings, as she kept her own needs and fantasies in a secret place. This made her alluring and inaccessible.

I, on the other hand, was an open book, an oversharer, confrontational and deep—often too deep for my own good. I wanted contact and meaningful conversation. Even as children, I over-whelmed Maggie and she withheld herself from me. She was too little and I was too much. We danced this dance all through child-hood; it took different forms at different ages. Sometimes we met in the middle and were friends, but more often we kept to our own corners—corners of the house, the Monopoly board, the neigh-borhood, the schoolyard. My bigness scared her, especially when I stood up to my parents. Her smallness aggravated me: Why couldn't she say what she meant, ask for what she wanted, share her secrets? By the time we got to high school, we had made our own worlds. I couldn't figure her out, so I ignored her. She couldn't quiet me down, so she avoided me.

For many years, Maggie and I orbited each other in ever widen-ing circles. Months after I graduated from high school, our house was broken into and the intruder tried to violate my youngest sister. My mother quit her job; they sold the house and left Long Island and moved "back to the land"—to a tumbledown farm in a tiny town in Vermont. Maggie and my youngest sister were still in high school. They went back to the land too. This was the direction we all were supposed to take; the direction the whole world should take, according to my father. Lord knows if my mother wanted the life of a rural homesteader—there's a chance none of us ever knew what my mother really wanted. But she professed to want it. In fact, not wanting it—not wanting to leave the sordid, so-called civilized world and head north to the woods—was tantamount to treason. If you were a good person, a moral person, you would counter the ills of our consumer society by never again driving on a freeway or owning a television or showing your face in a shop-ping mall.

Maggie and I absorbed the family philosophy in different ways. As I was protesting the Vietnam War in the streets of New York City, she was studying botany at Antioch College in Ohio. While I was hitchhiking to California, in search of a guru, she was in Wyoming with my older sister, hiking and skiing the big peaks. When I joined a spiritual commune, she went to nursing school. And then—surprising us all—Maggie moved back to our parents' tiny town to marry her high school boyfriend. She one-upped my parents. It was like getting a green card, marrying into a Vermont family. Her husband's New England roots connected her to generations of Vermonters. My parents would always be "flatlanders," refugees from New York, slightly suspect outsiders forever branded by their cosmopolitan past. But Maggie had leapfrogged her dodgy heritage; now she belonged. Under her husband's tutelage, she learned the skills of farming, slaughtering and butchering animals, logging, building, maple sugaring, and living off the land and off the grid. She created the life for herself that my father had always wanted. Thus proving she was the good girl—the one who followed the tide back to shore—and I was the defector, the one who went her own way, which was not the correct way.

By the time we were all grown women, with families of our own, I was the only sister who didn't live in Vermont, who didn't split and stack her own wood, who watched television and, on occasion, purchased unnecessary plastic objects for her kids at the mall. Coming home for holidays was often an exercise in losing myself. Everything from my clothes to my car, from where I lived to where I worked, felt wrong. My life was too big, too connected to the outside world on the one hand, and to the weird inner spiritual world on the other. Maggie's life fit the family picture better.

She and her husband had built a log cabin on the banks of the Saxtons River, down the road from my parents, in a classic little town, in the pristine homeland of Vermont. It was a rugged and real existence. In comparison, mine felt soft and wimpy. I wasn't chopping the heads off chickens or jumping in an icy swimming hole after a wood-fired sauna on a star-studded night. No one ever accused me of being a wuss to my face, but that's what I felt like when I would watch Maggie wielding a hammer or scraping honey from the frames as bees swarmed around her head. It all seemed heroic to me.

Back in my own life, it wasn't as if I was a slacker. I was leading a large organization; I was writing books; I was being a single parent. I was making grown-up decisions about difficult things. Some of those difficult things were so difficult that I went into therapy—which also took courage, but not the kind valued in the family. Psychotherapy was most assuredly not part of my parents' code. It flew in the face of everything they held sacred: grit, emotional restraint, and self-sufficiency. Carl Rogers, one of the founding fathers of American psychology, wrote about "conditions of worth"—the standards of behavior children believe they must follow to receive love and avoid criticism. Children internalize conditions of worth and then use them as instructions for living. Once on the shores of adulthood, you spend your life either blindly living out those conditions of worth or, if you're lucky, sifting through them and choosing which fit you and which you've outgrown.

Conditions of worth aren't necessarily bad things—families and societies need some agreed-upon standards. When a child bites another kid and the parent expresses displeasure, the child begins to understand that he'd better not bite other children if he wants to be an acceptable member of the clan. We may long to give and receive unconditional love, but it's almost impossible to pull off—unless you're a saint, or a hermit who never has to test the theory on real people. What *is* possible is to be mindful of when we impose excessive conditions of worth, or when those conditions are just our own unexamined opinions and habits that don't necessarily jibe with another person's inner compass. Conditions of worth can be part of a healthy value system, but they also can squelch the uniqueness right out of a kid. They can hobble dreams and compress the soul.

My parents' conditions of worth ran the gamut from the wise to the ridiculous. Both my mother and father had high standards when it came to social justice. They expected their daughters to be informed, to care, to do something of value for the world. It wasn't enough for us to merely go to school, play with our friends, help around the house. Even as kids we got the message that our lives were not just our own—that when we confronted suffering or prejudice, we had a duty to do something. This was one of my parents' conditions of worth that I cherish. In trying to live up to their expectations, my sisters and I gained the courage to take a stand for the things we believe in.

But even the wisest conditions of worth come with their shadows. For people who preached tolerance, my parents were astonishingly intolerant. My mother was a snob when it came to almost everything—how the neighbors overdecorated their houses at Christmas, how teenagers were degrading the English language, how the real opiates of the masses were television and Disneyland. My father took the despoiling of the natural world personally. He resented the neighbors who lived in the newly constructed suburban homes across the street from us. Their lifestyle was *wrong*—the way they washed their cars with the garden hose (waste of water), or their choice of "gaudy" landscape plants (hot-pink azaleas in particular), or the plastic lawn chairs they proudly displayed on their weed-free (toxic) lawns. Both of my parents went into mourning when a shopping mall was built on one of the last remaining farms near us. If that wasn't bad enough, it was named the Walt Whitman Mall because of its proximity to the little house where Whitman was born. The confluence of the sacrilegious desecration of farmland and the dishonoring of an American poet united my parents in their outrage.

I take pride in my parents' reverence for justice and for their protection of nature. They were ahead of their time. I have tried to carry their torch forward. On the other hand, I also inherited their intolerance. Mother Teresa said, "The problem with the world is that we draw the circle of our family too small." Widening the family circle to include those with bad grammar, different political views, and plastic lawn chairs has been a lifelong effort for me—grinding the gears in the opposite direction of my parents' conditions of worth.

See, here's the thing: We can offer our children treasured beliefs and customs without demonizing those other "bad" people across the street or across the globe. And we can start by lightening up when our kids show inclinations or interests that may conflict with our own conditions of worth. But being a parent is the world's hardest job. In the daily rigor of family life, we all blindly impose a myriad of conditions on our kids. Some we drag with us from our own childhoods. Some we ladle out without examining their validity because they are drummed into us by church or state. You can pin a whole slew of common mental ailments—depression, anxiety, confusion, anger, procrastination—on what happens when our very human need to be accepted bumps up against the equally compelling longing to be true to thine own self.

When I went into therapy in my early thirties, I began to identify the conditions of worth that were running my life without my consent. Did I really believe that in order to be a good person, to be loved, to be valued, I must always show grit, emotional restraint, and self-sufficiency? That I must live a certain way, in a certain place, and only with certain kinds of people? At first I was terrified to explore these questions, as if just by asking them I'd be unlovable. Slowly, though, I began to untangle the threads of my adult self from the threads of childhood, and to define my worth for myself. It was a liberating experience. And it not only freed me to be me. As I accepted the exiled parts of myself, I became more accepting of other people—all kinds of people.

But nothing could bring me back to square one more than visiting my family. Driving down Maggie's dirt road, I could feel parts of my fledgling self-worth drop away, as if the back of the car was open and pieces of luggage were falling out. Walking up the rough stone steps to her house, I felt stripped down to everything I was not. I was not a rural, self-sufficient, do-it-yourselfer. I was not Laura Ingalls Wilder, the heroine of our childhood. And worst of all, after I did the unthinkable and got divorced, I was no longer a self-sacrificing married woman. Maggie was happily and righteously all of the above. Or so I thought.

I know now that Maggie feared losing parts of herself in my presence too. That she secretly admired me—my courage to examine my life, to say what I wanted, and to stand up to the powers that be at work, at home, in the world. I didn't know then that being around me both inspired and threatened her. She was intent on being the good girl in the eyes of my parents and her husband and the doctors she worked for. If she let go of that rigidly held identity—the happy, energetic, good girl—what might happen to her life? I know now it was fear that kept us from being the kind of friends we became later on. We loved each other dearly, but she was afraid to get too close. I was a bad influence; her life might descend into chaos if she opened herself to me. And I was afraid to confront her resistance. What if her judgments of me were correct? What if I had made all the wrong choices?

I mourn those lost years. And even more, I mourn what it took for us to finally find each other.

WHAT THE SOUL SAID

THE PHONE BOMB EXPLODED IN Montana with the news of Maggie's illness in August during that week between our two birthdays when as little girls we shared one party. We were no longer little girls. We were, as Maggie called us, grown-assed women. I had just turned fifty-four, and she was about to turn fifty-two. The two of us had recently begun to weave our lives more closely together. Things had changed to set the stage for a new kind of sisterhood. Our parents had died—first my father, in a way that so matched the way he lived it was like the punch line to a great story. He was eighty-five and in better shape than most people are at twenty-five. He went skiing one day, came home, had dinner, got into bed, reread a chapter of his favorite book, *War and Peace*, turned out the light, went to sleep, and never woke up. Then, a few years later, my mother died, also in a way that fit the way she lived. She had been hiding a secret from us; she was seriously ill with a treatable disease that she had not treated for years. By the time we found out, it was too late to help her. The death of our parents left huge holes in our lives that my sisters and I tried to fill with each other.

And then, just months after our mother died, Maggie left her husband. She too had been hiding a secret. Her marriage, which had always seemed as wholesome and sturdy as her log house, was in fact deeply troubled. As the story leaked out, I was reminded of how little we know about the deepest heart of those closest to us, how their reality is often different from what we imagine it to be. There had been trouble in paradise for a long time, trouble that Maggie had been too ashamed to reveal and too afraid to leave. But leave she did—walking away from the home on the river, the gardens, the animals, the bees, and the studio where her art had supported the family for years. Her kids were both in college. Our parents had died. It was time. And so she spun out of the solar system of the little town, and the gravitational pull of her parents, and her in-laws, and her husband.

Right before this happened, only months before my mother died, my second book was published. My mother was proud. But she was also embarrassed. The book's opening story is about my session with a psychic in a trailer park. My mother had been one of the early readers of the manuscript. Most of her critiques were grammatical, but she also begged me to lose the story about the psychic. She seemed to have no problem with my writing about sex or divorce—it was the psychic story that "cheapened" the contents. She also crossed out the word "soul" frequently, and suggested using the lowercase when referring to God. ("Think of it as a proper name, like Bob," I said, trying to appeal to her inner English teacher.)

The story about the psychic stayed, and as it turned out, it's the one that meant the most to Maggie. I never expected Maggie to even crack the book's cover. She was an avid reader, but her taste did not include anything that smacked of self-help. She liked novels or nonfiction books about beekeeping and bread baking. Then my mother died and Maggie left her marriage, and there's nothing like trauma to change one's reading habits. There was one paragraph from the story about the psychic that Maggie hand-copied onto a note card and kept in her car. For a long time the car was all she had. It's what she drove away in and where she kept her stuff, including the note card in the glove compartment.

Sometimes the terror and guilt about the end of her marriage and the loss of family and home eroded Maggie's resolve. As she drove the back roads as a visiting nurse, she would feel the car turning itself back toward her home on the river, as if it knew where to go better than she did, and she would pull the car to the shoulder, reach into the glove compartment, and read the excerpt from my book: " 'It is time for you to answer the call of your soul,' the psychic said emphatically. 'It's calling, but you're too scared to listen. You think you know what's important, but you don't. You think it's important to keep things safe, but that's neither here nor there. What's important in this life is to learn the soul lessons.' "

Sitting at the side of the road, Maggie would argue with the card: "What do you mean, 'the soul lessons'? What lessons could possibly be more important than an intact family, or a marriage vow, or a home? And what do you even mean by 'the soul'?" She said her arguments were directed at the psychic, but later she admitted she was also talking to me. "I'm trading everything for *this*?" she would ask aloud, regarding the car crammed with the remains of her life—boxes of patients' charts, crates of flower specimens that she picked and dried and pressed for her botanical prints, garbage bags stuffed with winter coats and boots.

The soul's voice, though vast, is not loud. Other voices are louder—the voice of fear, the voice of blame, the voice of guilt, or denial, or despair. Sometimes I think the voices in the head are like an orchestra gone rogue. Trumpets blaring and percussion booming, drowning out the poignant violin solo, the little song of the flute. Without the knowing hand of the one who grasps the whole piece of music, without the conductor, it is just noise.

The soul is the conductor. "Put your soul in charge of your life," the psychic had told me. This was back when I was in the desolate middle of my own divorce; when I was changing everything for the sake of something I could barely describe, even to myself. What was that call I was hearing that seemed to come from an ache deep within? I was going to put that in charge of my life? I too argued with my soul for a long time before I came to know it as my wisest self, my compass that would direct me to a different kind of safety, an inner stability that far surpassed anything the noise in my head could imagine. Getting quiet enough to hear the voice of the soul became my practice. Learning to distinguish what was soul from what was dread, or guilt, or pride—that became my purpose. To dig for the soul, and then to gather the courage to put it in charge of my life.

I began to search for people whose soul seemed to be in charge. They had a certain look. A certain stature: strong yet humble, sober yet funny, striking yet ordinary. They looked determined and self-assured, and at the same time you got the sense they'd drop everything if you needed them. When I met Dr. Maya Angelou backstage at a conference, I found my icon of soulfulness. She's who I think of now if I've lost touch with my own soul. I conjure up an image of her tall self, striding to the lectern, with her red high heels and even redder lipstick. And her dignified posture. That's what I remember most—how she carried herself as she walked onto the stage and began her talk with the first stanza from her poem "Caged Bird":

A free bird leaps
on the back of the wind
and floats downstream
till the current ends
and dips his wing
in the orange sun rays
and dares to claim the sky.

That is what happens when you put your soul in charge of your life. You dare to claim the sky. That sky is different for everyone. For one person, maybe the sky is having a baby, being a parent, growing a family. But for another it's never having kids; it's traveling the globe; it's saving the world. Your sky might be leaving a job, whereas another's might be fighting for it. Your claim to the sky could be an act of surrender—that moment when you finally learn how to love another. Or your claim to the sky might be when you finally learn how to love yourself; when you walk away from a relationship that demeans the soul, and you lay claim to your freedom. You know your sky. And if you don't, it's because you haven't listened closely enough. You are arguing with your soul instead of putting it in charge of your life.

Maggie's argument went on for many months, and actually many years, because even after she made a modicum of peace with claiming her own sky, still she often could not hear the voice of her soul, and when she could, she barely believed she deserved to listen to its call. One year after she told the truth about her marriage, one year after being uprooted and homeless, one year after standing on her own for the first time in her life, Maggie's body went haywire. The genes within the DNA of one little bone marrow cell mutated and became an aggressive cancer cell and spread rapidly through-out her body.

The day after I returned from Montana, on Maggie's birthday, I met her at the Dartmouth Medical Center in New Hampshire, where she was diagnosed with stage IV mantle cell lymphoma. My only clear memory of that day is listening to the doctor tell Maggie that she would die—and soon—if she didn't start treatment that afternoon. As he described the regimen—chemotherapy, radia-tion, months in the hospital, a year of isolation—Maggie fainted and slipped off the examining table. I lunged to catch her. Sitting on the cold hospital floor, holding her in my arms, I felt my parents holding me in their arms. And right then and there I vowed to them I would do what I could to help my sister.

The first year of Maggie's treatments was a race between what would kill her first, the cancer or the medicine. But she was as tough as she'd ever been, and eventually she won the race; she went into remission. She returned to her work as a nurse practi-tioner, serving her rural community, where she was known and loved as Dr. Maggie. She resumed her artwork, collecting and pre-serving plant life and turning it into masterful botanical prints that she sold at craft shows and galleries. But best of all, she had a home again, and a wonderful partner—Oliver—a man she had fallen in love with before her diagnosis, and who shepherded her through every gruesome treatment. The word "cured" began popping up during her increasingly infrequent hospital visits.

Often during those first years of remission I would think back to the plane ride home from Montana, and I'd hear my soul admon-ishing me to have faith.

"You'll see," my soul had told me. "Your sister will grow from this; she'll rise to meet it. And all who travel with her will uncover surprising treasures because of this path her soul has chosen."

"Yeah, yeah," I would say to my soul. "Easy for you to say with your big perspective and sense of meaning."

But growth *did* happen, and gifts *were* given. So much so that as the years went by—first one year and then two, and then five, then seven—I figured the growth was sufficient, the treasures unearthed. I figured this path her soul had chosen had ended at a plateau of health and stability and well-deserved happiness. And so, as she rebuilt her life, I went back to mine.

Part Two

THE MARROW
OF THE BONES

There is nothing but mystery in the world,
how it hides behind the fabric of our poor,
browbeat days, shining brightly,
and we don't even know it.

—SUE MONK KIDD

THE MATCH

AND THEN, QUITE SUDDENLY, AFTER seven years of remission, the cancer comes back. Or rather, it never fully succumbed to the treatment. A few little cells (and maybe even just one) have been hibernating. Now they are awake and duplicating in Maggie's blood, her lungs, her lymph nodes. She caught it fast, but it's spreading faster, and the only way to beat it this time is with a bone marrow transplant from a genetically matched donor. Before that can happen, a match must be found. But even before that she has to take a potentially lethal dose of chemotherapy. And this time she also has to take the bullets of full-body radiation—so that her cancer-laden blood cells are eradicated to make way for cells from the donor, should one be found. I've never liked the way war jargon is applied to cancer treatment, but in this case it seems appropriate. I don't mention this to Maggie, but I've recently learned that chemotherapy was developed after World War I, when changes were observed in the bone marrow cells of soldiers exposed to mustard gas.

At first Maggie refuses treatment, even when her doctors tell her that without it she will live only a few weeks. The thought of what happened the last time hits her like a truck; it barrels down the road and slams into her dignity. All she can think of is vomiting and hallucinating and losing her hair and living like a ghost as the whole world passed her by.

"I will not go through that again," she tells the doctor as we sit in his examining room on a freezing February day, in the Dartmouth Medical Center in New Hampshire, horrified to be in the same room again seven years later, the same doctor, the same nurse, the same questions, the same lack of conclusive answers. We pepper the doctor with questions: Will a transplant work? *For some people.* Will she survive the treatment? *Many people do.* What's the survival rate? *Those kinds of statistics aren't helpful.* How long do people live after transplant? *That depends on a lot of factors.*

Maggie's daughter holds her mother's hand. She's crying, but Maggie isn't. Instead she looks like a trapped bird, her head turning from me to the doctor to Oliver to her kids. Wanting out. Out of the room, out of her body, out of life if this is what life has become. But the doctor convinces her that she can start the chemotherapy and stop at any point. And while she begins treatment, they will search for a bone marrow donor. They will test each of the sisters—not her children or other relatives—because siblings present the best chance of finding a "perfect match," one where all the genetic markers line up. The closer the genetic markers, the more successful the transplant. There's only a 25 percent chance of a sibling match, and a smaller chance of the match being perfect. If none of the sisters are a close enough match, they will search the international donor bank, where there's an even lower likelihood of getting a high-degree match.

If a match is found, and if Maggie tolerates (code for survives) the high-dose chemotherapy and radiation, and if it can rid her body of the lymphoma, she can choose to go ahead with the transplant. But for now, all she has to do is start the chemo, and all the sisters have to do is get our cheeks swabbed and wait for the results.

Maggie nods her head OK. That's her level of buy-in for now. But it's enough to begin. We go straight from the doctor's office into the maze of the hospital for her first chemo treatment. I sit with her in the infusion suite. That's what the chemotherapy area of the hospital is called—the infusion suite. All around us, fellow refugees from normal life lie huddled in heaps of bedding and tubes. Others rest in lounge chairs, under warmed blankets that the angel nurses replenish frequently. Friends and family make quiet conversation, or stare out the windows as the New Hampshire sleet pelts the glass.

I watch Maggie watching. A young man in the bed next to hers is receiving his first chemotherapy infusion; he practically vibrates with anxiety. An older woman—a chemo veteran—sits alone in a reclining chair, reading. She's bald and sunken-eyed, with an expression of wry acceptance. I smile at her and she winks. A nurse carries a tray with food to a man on the other side of the suite. The smell of soup lingers and mingles with the antiseptic odor of cleaning products. I take my sister's small hand, cold under the warmed blankets, and pat it until she falls asleep. The chemo ticks like a clock, dripping into her veins. I sit until it begins to grow dark.

Before I leave, I gather up my courage and tell Maggie I'm thinking of going on a vacation to the Caribbean. Saying the words "vacation" and "Caribbean" in the chemo suite seems cruel; I feel like one of the evil stepsisters going to the ball, leaving Cinderella behind to pick lentils out of the fireplace.

"I won't go if you don't want me to, Maggie," I say.

"No! Go," she pleads. "I want you to live your own life. At least one of us should. Promise?"

"OK. I'll go. I'll enjoy it for the two of us."

"Well, don't enjoy it too much," Maggie says.

And so my husband and I decide to do something millions of

people do: escape winter for a week and go somewhere warm. But this is rare for us. The two of us are work- and family-obsessed people for whom leisure travel feels like an act of treason. We procrastinate about where to go and then convince each other that neither of us has the time to take off.

But this has been a difficult year and a cold winter. And so here we are, in the Miami airport, changing planes, heading to a Caribbean island. As I sit next to my husband in a row of orange bucket seats, I already feel my body uncoiling. The warm sunlight streams through the tall airport windows. Maybe I will be able to do what Maggie begged of me—to forget about her for a few days. I lean back and exhale.

The announcement that boarding will begin soon for our plane comes over the loudspeaker.

"I'll be right back," my husband says. "Watch my bag, OK?" He pushes his backpack in my direction.

"I will not watch your bag," I reply. My husband has a maddening habit of disappearing minutes before it's time to depart, overcome with the sudden need to purchase a pack of gum. While we have never missed a flight, we've come close, and we've come even closer to my flying off without him. I think that's why he asks me to watch his bag.

"I will not watch your bag," I repeat, "and you will not leave." I hold onto his arm. "See?" I point to the travelers gathering at the gate. "We're about to board the plane. We need this vacation."

At that very moment my cell phone rings. I take it out of my purse, see the name of the hospital, and brace for awful news. I show the caller ID to my husband. He sits down.

It's the bone marrow transplant coordinator calling to tell me that the lab results for all the sisters have come back. "I have good news!" the nurse says. She seems overjoyed to be the bearer of positivity. I can only imagine how rare this is for her.

"We found a match for Maggie," she exclaims. "Are you sitting down? It's you!"

I'm too stunned to reply.

"And there's even better news," the nurse continues. "You're a perfect match! All ten genetic markers lined up with Maggie's." She begins explaining the science of genetic tissue testing, but I tune her out. My mind goes in several directions at once: Did I imagine I would be perfectly matched with Maggie? No, not really. If I had to guess, I would have picked one of the other sisters. I wonder if they'll be jealous, or maybe they'll be relieved, or probably both. I wonder if it's dumb luck that we're perfectly matched, or is it fate, kismet, karma? It feels preposterous—like a science fiction story. Or maybe it's a miracle. I'm not sure who gets to determine such things, but this feels like a miracle to me. I wonder what Maggie thinks.

"Does Maggie know?" I ask the nurse.

"Yes. I just spoke with her. She says you should go on vacation and call her later."

I sense the presence of someone behind me and turn around to see who's there. No one. But then I feel it again. I look, but no one is there. Everyone else has lined up to board the small aircraft. I finish the call, take my husband's hand, and we follow the others across the tarmac and into the plane. We find our seats, the plane takes off, and my husband leans back and closes his eyes. But I just sit there, hearing the transplant coordinator's voice replaying in my mind, over and over: "I have good news! We found a match for Maggie! It's you!"

"Wow," I whisper to myself. "Wow." That's the most I can come up with.

And then I feel it again—as if someone is behind me, trying to get my attention. I turn and look over the top of the headrest. The seats behind us are empty. So I turn back, lean against my husband, and close my eyes too. And that's when I see them—my parents. As clear as if they were on the plane with us, I see my mother and father. They smile at me and nod their heads in some sort of silent agreement. They were never ones to dole out praise or thanks, and they don't do that now. They do something better—they dare me to hope.

I keep my eyes shut and remain as still as I can. I don't want my parents to go away. I want them to tell me something, to explain their sudden presence, to explain the bone marrow match. I wait. They remain with me. And then I imagine words floating out of their spirit mouths.

"We loved you girls into being," they say.

"Our love gave Maggie her life the first time," my father says.

"Your love can give her a second life," my mother says.

And then I understand. I may not know for sure about fate or karma or miracles, but I'm sure about love. My eyes fill with tears.

"Wow," I whisper to my father and mother.

"Wow," they whisper back.

---

field notes • march 1

my 3 sisters were tested for the possibility of being a match for a donor stem cell transplant. the possibility of this happening was low—25%. each sister had to scrape her inner mouth cheek with a tongue blade, and send that sample off to a lab. a sibling donor's cells have a better chance of engrafting and being accepted into one's bloodstream and marrow than a non-family member's. the nurse at dartmouth called me today with the news that liz and i match 10/10. a perfect match. i felt my spirits notch up on the hope scale. but i'm suspicious of hope. it has fooled me before, and i don't even know what i'm hoping for anyway. a year? 2 years? a cure? i'm afraid to read the statistics; afraid not to. afraid to hope; afraid not to. liz called me from vacation. i told her i was afraid to hope. so she told me a greek myth about the spirit of hope. everytime i talk to her she quotes walt whitman or talks about a greek god. i think she's turning into our mother. or maybe i just need a mother now.

ELPIS

IN GREEK MYTHOLOGY HOPE WAS a spirit known as Elpis. She and other gods and spirits were kept in a jar by Zeus and entrusted into the care of the first woman, Pandora. Overcome by curiosity, Pandora opened the vessel. She lifted the lid, and out rushed the gods and spirits. The gods soared into the sky, abandoned the mortals, and went back to Mount Olympus. But the evil spirits remained on earth. Envy, toil, hate, disease, and all of their cranky and cruel cohort flew to the four corners of the world. Realizing what was happening, Pandora hastened to close the container. Too late! All had escaped, except for one. Hiding in the vessel was Elpis . . . hope. It is said that Elpis remained in the jar to help human beings now that evil had been unleashed. Whenever the world seemed too much to bear, we humans could open the lid and call on Elpis for faith and optimism.

I call Maggie from the porch of our little cottage overlooking the Caribbean Sea. I expect to hear a more hopeful tone in her voice since the last time we spoke in the chemo suite. I know she has heard from the nurse that our marrow matches and transplant is now possible.

"Is this Maggie-Liz?" I say into the phone. We'll end up using our combined blood-sister name all through the transplant process, but at the moment she's in no mood for lighthearted banter. She's not ready to sign on for the transplant, she says. She's not sure she can bear to continue the treatment. Her hair is falling out. She's constantly nauseated and can't eat. Her fingers feel numb. She's lost her fighting spirit, she says. Why keep fighting when all signs point to defeat? Why hope? Hope only makes it worse when things fall apart.

"And they will fall apart again," she says. "I'm sorry to sound so morose, Liz."

I tell her the story of Elpis. I tell her how the Greeks depicted hope as a young woman carrying flowers in her arms. Elpis was said to bear the energy of spring, of green sap rising in the veins of trees, of the smell of rain on dry earth. Her opposite, Moros, spirit of hopelessness and doom, was a hunched man cloaked in black.

"Who do you want to hang around with?" I say into the phone. "A girl with flowers, or a really depressed guy named Moros?"

"You know I love flowers," Maggie says. "But I hate when people tell me to have hope. As if everything's going to be OK if I just have a positive attitude."

"But that's not what hope is about. It's not about everything turning out OK. It's about being OK with whatever happens."

"Easy for you to say."

I have noticed how quickly Maggie angers when anyone glosses over the rigors of the transplant and goes straight to its potential success. I think she feels abandoned when others spout hope. She thinks we don't understand the depth of her fear, the truth of the risks, the looming mountain of physical pain and exhaustion. That we have left her all alone to scale the mountain. That hope in the face of such a daunting task is dumb.

"Elpis was no dummy, Maggie," I say. "She knew the evil spirits would get under our skin and convince us the world is doomed, that we are doomed. She stayed behind in the jar so we could take swigs of optimism when we needed it. Because hope is energizing, and despair is crippling. You need the energy of hope right now. It will help you make a decision. It's like drinking coffee. Suddenly the clouds part."

I never know if I'm saying the right thing. I never know if Maggie is even listening, or if I'm stating the obvious or grating on her nerves like some Pollyanna evangelist.

"So what should I hope for?" Maggie asks, her voice dulled by grief. "That the transplant won't kill me? That if it saves me I won't feel like crap for the rest of my life? That the rest of my life is more than a few months?"

"You can hope for the strength to handle whatever comes. Maybe it will be a cure. Maybe it will be pain. Maybe it will be death. Nobody knows what will happen next—not the doctors, not the websites, not you. We don't even know what *should* happen. Life is more mysterious and meaningful than our pint-sized brains can fathom. That's what hope is for me—trusting in the mystery." I almost whisper those last lines. It takes some hubris for a well person to wax spiritual to a sick person.

"OK, now you sound like Walt Whitman," Maggie says. "Or like Marsh quoting Walt Whitman." (Throughout our childhood, my sisters and I never called our mother Mom. We called her by her name, Marcia, or her nickname, Marsh.) Maggie assumes our mother's English teacher voice and quotes Whitman: " 'And to die is different from what any one supposed, and luckier.' "

"Yeah, like Walt said," I laugh. I don't care if she's making fun of me. At least I know she's listening. She may even be taking

Whitman's words to heart. I take a risk and say, "You know, to live is pretty lucky too. And to live with hope until you die—that's the luckiest."

Maggie doesn't say anything. A breeze lingers on the porch where I am sitting. It smells like lemon blossoms. I feel the hot, tropical air on my bare skin. I close my eyes and imagine Maggie in bed, under the covers, weary and worried, looking out at the gray sky and frozen fields.

"You still there?" I ask.

"Yeah, barely." And then she says, "It's kind of amazing we're a perfect match, isn't it? I didn't think any of the sisters would match. But I really didn't think it would be you." I hear the life returning to her voice. I hear energy and humor. And I hear the old, edgy stories of our sisterhood.

"I know," I say. "It's a shock. But it also isn't. It feels like a privilege for me, Maggie. And it feels like our destiny."

"Really? Destiny? But we're so different. I thought it would be one of the other girls."

"I'm gonna try not to take that personally," I say.

"No, I don't mean it that way, Liz. It would be an honor to get your marrow. To spend the rest of my life as Maggie-Liz." Now I hear wonder in her voice, and terror and tears.

"Well, I want you to know I'm one hundred percent in," I tell her. "If you say yes to the transplant, I will too—with all my heart. But you also don't have to go through with it. Whatever you choose to do, I'll stand by you every step of the way. We're in this together now."

Already I can sense a new person taking form as we speak: Maggie-Liz. The love child of our willingness to give and receive,

to lay down the past and pick up something new, to say no to fear
and yes to hope.

"Here's to Maggie-Liz," I say, pouring hope from the jar and
offering a glass to Maggie across the sea.

"Here's to hope," Maggie says.

field notes • march 5

now that it's a possibility, i have to decide about the transplant. i feel
trapped with no way out. damned if i do, damned if i don't. i am frozen
in place. my hair is falling out, i'm down to 95 pounds, i hurt everywhere. in my body and my heart. today i saw my daughter. we were
driving down the road with the intention of going shopping. my only
goal for the outing was to stay positive. but as i drove, i began to break
down and we pulled over when i could no longer contain my crying. i
was tired of performing like i was stable. like everything was gonna be
alright. i was exhausted from being perky, from hiding my hurt that i
probably won't be around to see my kids' weddings, their homes, their
children. i won't be there to help them. as i wept, i told norah, i don't
know if its appropriate for you to witness this part of your mother's
process. she held me and we cried together. after we cried, we just sat
there, until she asked me to consider going through with the transplant
so we could have more time together. even a short time. i felt something
move inside my heart. i felt the presence of hope. maybe this was that
spirit liz was talking about. elpis. for the first time i really considered giving the transplant a try. it made me weep again, but this time because
i felt a lightening of the deep grief. i felt the presence of something—a
tiny flicker of a fighting spirit, a tiny flicker of hope.

BLUE HOLES

WE MEET UP WITH FRIENDS in the Caribbean. They like to snorkel, so we hire a boat and travel an hour out into the open sea to a blue hole. A blue hole is like a vertical cave—a circular, steep-walled chasm layered with striking shades of blue water. Dark inky blue down in the deep hole, and light-infused aqua closer to the surface. Fish are drawn to the plant growth around a blue hole. And not just colorful little fish, but also hammerhead sharks and giant groupers and stingrays.

I am terrified. The boat anchors at the rim of the blue hole. Everyone else in the group swims right into the yawning cave, cavorting with the fish and motioning to each other when they spot something "interesting." I lurk at the edges until I see a fish too big for my liking, and then swim back to the boat, fast. I rationalize that if we were supposed to see underwater life, God wouldn't have hidden it in a deep, dark hole.

Sitting on a long bench in the boat, alone except for the driver, who is sleeping in his captain's seat, I think about hidden things. Hidden life under the sea, under the ground, under the skin. The buried marrow in my bones and the secret stories in my heart. What are we supposed to see and hear, show and tell? Are things hidden for our own good, or is the human journey about going into the shadows and searching for the deeper truths about ourselves and each other, about life itself?

When I was a midwife, I taught childbirth classes to the mothers- and fathers-to-be. As I delivered more and more babies I discovered that the people who transcended their squeamishness and paid close attention during the anatomy lessons were the ones who had speedier, easier labors. To encourage them to get comfortable with the inner workings of the female body, I would assign the same homework at the end of each class: fall in love with the uterus. This didn't appeal to a lot of people—women and men alike. Even after I explained that the uterus was gorgeous and extraordinarily intelligent, they didn't want to peer too closely at the pictures of a glistening red organ shaped like a pear and located between the bladder and the rectum. It was all too graphic and intimate.

I promised the women they would be less likely to need drugs or other interventions if they could visualize the uterus and understand the mechanics of the cervix—that little muscle that must stretch from a clenched fist to the size of their baby's head. If you fight the pain, if you resist the contractions, you cause even more pain. I told them that labor is like life and life is like labor: sometimes the most painful experiences deliver the best things—new life, unexpected insight, the chance to stretch and grow. This was the greatest lesson I learned in my years of delivering babies: don't strain against pain; learn its purpose; work *with* it and the energy of the universe will assist you.

And so I would bring to class medical charts and models, and show videos of the uterus in labor, but the queasy and the anxious would cover their eyes as if I were showing a horror film. The insides of the body were as foreign to the couples in my childbirth classes as the fish in the blue hole are to me. I look across the span of water and watch my husband and friends enjoying the splendor of what lives beneath the sea. I'm jealous of their courage. I know my fear is irrational. No one has ever been attacked snorkeling in this blue hole. I'm probably more likely to die of sunstroke in the boat. I'm denying myself the elation of this once-in-a-lifetime experience. I move to the side of the boat and prepare to jump back into the water. But I'm too scared.

Instead, I stretch out on the bench, close my eyes, and think about Maggie, and about being her marrow match. I put my hands on the middle of my hips and push hard with the heel of my palms until I feel the big bones beneath the layers of skin and fat and muscle. Those bones are only inches from the body's surface, but they seem as far away and unfathomable as the bottom of the sea. Suddenly I want to learn everything there is to know about bones and marrow, blood and stem cells. If Maggie says yes to the transplant, I want to fully participate without fear. Just as I encouraged my pregnant couples to fall in love with the uterus, I want to fall in love with the marrow of my bones. I have to laugh—I've walked around in this body for more than fifty years and I have no idea what goes on in the hidden blue hole of the bones. Time to change that. If getting to know the uterus helps ease a baby into the world, learning about marrow might help ease my sister into new life.

I may not be courageous enough to explore a hole in the ocean; I may not want to fall in love with hammerhead sharks. But I am ready to excavate the marrow of my bones and expose the marrow of my soul for my sister. Bobbing in a boat in the middle of the sea, I feel a fierce kind of love for Maggie that takes me by surprise. I knew I loved her, but not like this. We've spent most of our lives circling around each other, each of us feeling imperfect in the mirror of the other's life. Now my parents' words come back to me: "Our love gave Maggie her life the first time. Your love can give her a second life." So this is what they meant. They weren't talking about throwaway proclamations of affection at the end of a phone call. They were talking about going deep. And not just into the bones, but also into anything hidden and unhealed between us.

I hear the others swimming toward the boat. I sit up and wave to them. They will have stories to tell me about life in the underwater caves. And if all goes well, I will too. Maggie and I will swim together into the blue holes of our bodies and souls and bring back tales from the deep.

MOTHER CELLS

A FEW WEEKS LATER, I buy a big hardcover book about cell biology and try to carve some new neural pathways in my brain in order to understand the most basic information. Paying attention to the text requires my blasting through a mountain of mental resistance. Math and science have always been a struggle for me. If I were a child now, I'd probably be diagnosed with a learning disability. It sure felt that way all through school. I had my first experience of math-induced brain freeze in elementary school when confronted with long division, and full-on mental paralysis in junior high when it came time to memorize the periodic table of the elements. But now I am motivated to fall in love with bone marrow and stem cells, so I stay up late every night, reading *Essential Cell Biology*.

I discover that although bones seem as dead as rock, they are actually super alive. They are like living layers of geological sediment protecting a molten core. The core of the bones is the marrow, and in the marrow are the stem cells, the source of life. Stem cells are also called mother cells because they have the potential to create many types of new cells that your body needs in order to live.

The human body is composed of one hundred trillion cells—give or take a billion—with each cell assigned a specialized function, like skin cells, blood cells, muscle cells, organ cells, brain cells. Specialized cells do not live very long, so the body needs to replace them continuously. I used to think of my body as a constant—a trusty chariot that would cart me around till death do us part. But in actuality, my body today is not what it was yesterday or what it will be tomorrow. Humans shed and regrow skin cells every twenty-seven days, making almost a thousand new skins in a lifetime. Each day fifty billion cells throughout the body are replaced, resulting, basically, in a new chariot each year. Every second, 500,000 cells die and are replenished. Red blood cells live for 120 days; platelets live for only a week; white blood cells live for a mere eight hours.

And then there are the stem cells that live deep within the bone marrow. Unlike specialized cells that die and must be replaced, stem cells are self-renewing—they divide in unlimited numbers and become new cells. Some of those new cells remain stem cells, and some leave the bone marrow and flow into the bloodstream, magically morphing themselves into whatever kind of specialized cells the body needs. A stem cell is like a mother. She sends her children out into the world to become who they were born to be.

When doctors harvest bone marrow from a donor, it's the stem cells—the mother cells—they are after. The premise is pretty simple: Destroy the bone marrow in the cancer patient and replace it with several million healthy stem cells from a donor. Then do everything possible to help those donor stem cells engraft in the cleaned-out cavities of the patient's bones. If all proceeds according to the plan, the mother cells make themselves at home in the new bones and begin to self-renew, building a new bone marrow factory where baby blood cells are produced and sent into the bloodstream, bringing the patient back to life.

Sounds like a good plan, but it's also a dangerous one, because

in preparing the patient for the transplant with high-dose chemotherapy and radiation, healthy cells are collateral damage. The patient must endure a near-death experience in order to live. Sitting
in the dark quiet of my house, underlining sentences in *Essential
Cell Biology*, I can almost feel the river of life and death, change
and rebirth, flowing in my bloodstream. I shut the book and close
my eyes and say a quick hello and thank-you to my stem cells just
in case we'll be calling on millions of them soon.

field notes • march 20

i have always said i want to come back in my next life as an eggplant. a
big stupid purple lump languishing in the sun, oblivious to the complex
messes us humans make. until i met denise. now, i am considering
withdrawing the eggplant request and asking for reassignment; i might
want to come back as a human again. i had another round of pre-
transplant radiation at the hospital today. on the way home, we stopped
at lou's restaurant for lunch. wearing my saliva-smelling, hot, steamy
mask, we sat at the counter and i fell apart, letting the tears soak the
mask. denise, my waitress, a cancer survivor herself (who knew?),
came to my rescue. one look at my bald head and my mask, and she
came right over, first with a hug. then a quick lesson in breathing: in
through the nose, out through the mouth, then a pep talk, then she
gave me a book of quotes. then a caramel cupcake. denise pointed
out this quote from gilda radner: "if it wasn't for the downside, having
cancer would be the best thing and everyone would want it." i used to
hate when people said things like that. but it's true. this disease teaches
you what's important, and as it turns out it's the things you already
have. your kids, your mate, your home, a good meal, a good friend, a
good day. but here's my favorite quote from the book, by roger ebert,
who has a terrible, face-eating kind of cancer: "i believe that if, at the

end of it all, according to our abilities, we have done something to make others a little happier, and something to make ourselves a little happier, that is about the best we can do. to make others less happy is a crime. to make ourselves unhappy is where all crime starts. we must try to contribute joy to the world. that is true no matter what our problems, our health, our circumstances. we must try."

so, i will try. i will try to proceed with good cheer because "to make others less happy is a crime." i don't want to be a criminal! "to make ourselves unhappy is where all crime starts." that's something i am just beginning to understand. i hope i'll get some more years to live by those words.

THE MYSTERY

ONCE AGAIN WE TRAIPSE INTO the cancer ward at the hospital to meet with the oncology team. Their team: one doctor; one nurse; one transplant coordinator. Our team: Oliver, Maggie's partner; Norah and Hayden, Maggie's kids; me; and, of course, Maggie, her clothes hanging off her tiny body, her eyes looking even larger and darker than usual. The teams wear uniforms. The nurses are in light green scrubs; their masks hang below their chins. The doctor wears his white coat, his white hair neatly trimmed. Team Maggie is a motley crew. I've come straight from New York and I look like it—black pants, black sweater, black boots and coat. Maggie's son, Hayden, is a forester; he's dressed in a red wool sweater, canvas pants, and steel-tipped boots. When I hug him, he smells of pine trees and chainsaw grease. Her daughter, Norah, owns a large working farm; I've always admired the way she still dresses like a college girl in whimsical outfits, even though she spends her time fixing tractors and feeding pigs. We crowd into the small, antiseptic examining room. We are talking and joking, happy to be with each other despite the jittery circumstances. Our noise and textures and odors bring the forbidden mess and germs of the world into the hospital. We seem completely out of place, until I remind myself that this is what the place is made for—the mess and germs of being human.

It's time for Maggie to decide. We take our seats. There are so many of us I double up with my nephew and we hold onto each other. The doctor reviews the options: if Maggie chooses not to proceed with the transplant, she will die soon, and if she chooses the transplant, it may kill her. Of course, he doesn't come right out and say this—he never does—but that's the hidden message in his vaguely worded script. And if she survives the transplant, we ask again, are there any numbers of months or years to hang this decision on? Again, vague answers that we have already heard.

Although people surround her in the crowded room, I know Maggie feels alone, wrestling with conflicting magnetic pulls. The pull to live for as long as possible, here on earth, with us. To experience the softness of another spring, the humid heat of summer, the winter's shocking cold, the joy of love, the sadness of loss, the beauty, the pain, the mess. And then, the other pull—the pull to die, to surrender, to say no to more chemotherapy and radiation and transplant and months of drug-induced nausea and isolation and the unrelenting anxiety that the cancer may return. To say good-bye now, to leave with some dignity while she still can. I don't know which path I would choose or she should choose. I reach over, stroke her arm, and silently pray.

I say "silently" because prayer is not something Maggie relates to; that's putting it mildly. Last week, our born-again cousin e-mailed and pronounced she was praying for Maggie's health. This infuriated Maggie, as if without asking our cousin had conscripted her into the faith. Maggie called me immediately to rail against the stupidity of religion. I proposed that our cousin's beliefs might not be what she imagines them to be—that intelligence and spirituality are not diametrically opposed. That you can be a legitimate, thinking person and still listen to Christian music on the radio.

"This is why I'm surprised you and I are a perfect genetic

match," Maggie replied. "What if I become more spiritual if we do the transplant? If my blood is your blood?"

"Yup. Before you know it, you'll be speaking in tongues," I say.

"No, really, Liz. Will I suddenly believe in God? That might not be a bad thing at this moment. What do you believe in anyway? Maybe I should know this before I sign on the dotted line." She's never asked me this before. It's not an easy question to answer, but this would be a good time to try.

I tell her what I don't believe first. I don't believe our brains can fully fathom God, or come up with iron-clad answers to the big questions—like who we are and why we are and where did we come from and where do we go? We can't think our way through any of those questions. We can try. I love the way we try— science, art, religion, wine, mountain climbing, whatever. But so far, no one has definitively answered anything. So I say to Maggie, "When I pray, I pray to just settle down and trust the mystery. Prayer for me is relaxing into the mystery."

"Really? That's what prayer is?"

"Well, maybe not for everybody, but it's not my business how other people pray. To me, prayer is letting go of fear and relaxing into the vast, eternal mystery. I don't care what you call that mystery—God, consciousness, universe, spirit. Those are all made-up names for the unnamable. All I know is there's nothing better than that wide-open, opinion-busting, all-things-are-possible, everything's-OK feeling of prayer."

What I want to say but I don't, because it's probably not the right time, is this: "Who knows, Maggie, if you decide to forgo the transplant, maybe you're the lucky one—maybe you're being called out of this world for glorious reasons, leaving us fools behind to slog our way through another day. Maybe it's not a tragedy for your kids. Maybe they'll spin their grief into strength, maybe you will help them flourish from the other world. Or maybe you'll choose to go ahead with the transplant and you'll outlive us all and prove that miracles are possible. Maybe this is all happening for you to finally stop doubting yourself and to step boldly into who you always were meant to be. Maybe you'll become a world-renowned artist, or you'll wander away and become a monk. We just don't know. That's what I believe. I believe we dwell in mystery, and although that mystery often seems to suck, when I pray, I wake up, and I know that it's all for something, that nothing is wasted, and it's all good."

Now we're here in the examining room, and I'm taking deep breaths and calling on that mystery as we wait for Maggie to make up her mind.

"What's it going to be, young lady?" the doctor asks, putting his hand on Maggie's shoulder. "Shall we prepare for transplant?"

And without missing a beat, Maggie looks around the room at us, her motley team, takes a sharp breath in, and says, "OK, let's do it."

We drive away from the hospital. It's one of those early New England spring days that can't make up its mind. It's raining in the parking lot, but by the time we get onto the highway it's snowing. Oliver is driving. I am in the passenger seat. Maggie is stretched out in the back. I turn around and ask, "How are you doing?"

"Shhh," she says, putting her finger to her lips and closing her eyes. "Shhh, I'm relaxing into the mystery."

REJECTION AND ATTACK

TO PREPARE FOR BEING THE bone marrow donor, I have been getting every test known to humankind: blood tests, stool tests, urine tests, chest X-ray, electrocardiogram, gynecological exam, mammogram, HIV test, even a test for syphilis. And a long health interview that poses intimate questions about everything from my sexual history to my mental stability. They want to know if I have ever had or have now any medical problem that would make it difficult for me to undergo the donation process or that could result in my cells infecting Maggie with a disease. She will have no immune system by the time my stem cells are transplanted into her bloodstream. I must be as healthy as possible to be a donor. They take so much blood for the tests I wonder if any will be left for the transplant.

Donor stem cells can be harvested directly from the bone marrow or from the peripheral blood, which is the blood flowing in the veins. "Harvest": that's what they call the collection of stem cells. I like that word. It has a homegrown ring to it. This helps me shift my imagery away from a television hospital drama to one of those Italian films where gorgeous people sit at a rustic farm table on a late summer evening, eating food from the fields.

After my tests come back, it is determined that the stem cells will be harvested from my peripheral blood. I read the literature given to me by the very kind transplant nurse at the hospital. We agree that it would help to have a PhD in cell biology to understand the information sheets. As best as I can tell, this is what they say: A successful stem cell harvest results in the harvesting of at least two million stem cells, although the preferred number is five million. This is a huge amount of stem cells compared to the number normally circulating in your bloodstream. To stimulate cell growth, the donor is injected with a growth factor every day over a period of five days before the harvest. This causes a rapid increase in cell production, so much so that the bone marrow is forced to push millions of stem cells out of the marrow and into the blood. On the fifth day the donor returns to the hospital, an IV is placed in a large vein in the arm or chest, and for up to six hours the blood is cycled through a machine that separates the stem cells from the other blood cells. The stem cells are retained, while the rest of the blood is returned to the donor through the same catheter. During the process the donor's entire bloodstream is circulated over and over through the machine. The process can be completed in one day, but often needs to be repeated daily for a few days until enough stem cells have been collected.

For now, I ignore the parts of the information sheets that describe the painful side effects and potential risks of the procedure, and focus on the more miraculous aspects of marrow and cells and blood. I am becoming a devotee of blood. I feel like a vampire, but a nerdy one. A few weeks previously, one of the doctors administering my tests told me, "After Maggie finishes all of her chemotherapy and radiation, she will no longer have any of her own stem cells. And after the transplant, your stem cells will keep her alive. They will become the source of her blood, and your blood will be her blood for the rest of her life." I hadn't really understood what the doctor meant. Now I do.

As I continue to read, I zero in on two big risks Maggie will face after transplant: failed engraftment and graft-versus-host disease. Failed engraftment occurs when the infection-fighting system of the patient recognizes the transplanted donor stem cells as being different and rejects them. Graft-versus-host disease occurs when the transplanted donor cells regard the recipient's body as foreign and go on the attack. Both complications could lead to Maggie's death.

"Rejection" and "attack": those two words appear in all the literature about bone marrow transplants. They seem so familiar, those words, especially in the context of my relationships with Maggie, with my other sisters, in all my relationships—in all human relationships, for that matter. Rejection and attack, that's what we so often do when we see each other as different, when we feel threatened, out of our safety zone, or just clueless about how to share the human experience. We interpret difference as danger, and in covert or obvious ways, we reject or attack otherness. Sometimes we pull back, we protect, we shut down, we reject. Other times we try to control the other, bend the other, and when we can't, we give in to our fatal attraction to aggression—we attack. Even when we adore each other, even if we know better, even if we make it our moral practice to tame the tendency to reject or attack, these are difficult instincts to overcome.

They're certainly difficult instincts for me to overcome. Whether it's the way I want to excommunicate my husband for taking up golf, or my knee-jerk animosity to those with different political opinions, I spend my days self-correcting the instinct to reject or attack. We all know there is a better instinct, a bigger perspective, a deeper pull: to accept, to embrace, to lay down the arms, to take the first step toward tolerance or forgiveness. Raise your hand if you've mastered this. Certainly as a species we haven't. On the bigger stage, rejection or attack starts as a small act of otherizing and explodes into feuds and war. In our daily lives, most of us aren't literally violent, but we do violence to each other's souls when we shut each other out or attack each other's personhood. How interesting that even at the smallest cellular level there is both the urge for peaceful coexistence and the instinct to reject or attack.

If after the transplant my stem cells become the source of Maggie's blood, and have the responsibility of keeping her alive and well for the rest of her life, it seems to me it might be good to do something to bolster my cells' urge for peaceful coexistence and mellow out their instinct to attack. And Maggie too—her body will be on high alert for alien invaders. Can we do something— psychologically, emotionally, spiritually—to assist the medical aspects of the transplant? Multiple studies (some done at the very hospital where our procedures will be performed) have demonstrated the power of the mind and emotions in healing—in lowering blood pressure and stress hormone levels, relieving pain, improving immune functioning, and helping patients reverse serious clinical conditions. Surely these findings suggest that Maggie's chances for a good outcome could only be increased if she and I paid attention to our peace of mind and emotional openness before the harvest and transplant.

I leaf through the information sheets, looking for anything that comes close to this line of thinking. Maybe some suggestions on how to talk to each other about our feelings or fears, or the ancient baggage we may want to drop before exchanging blood? But there's nothing there. We'll have to make it up ourselves—figure out a way to hold our history up to the light and move beyond our lifelong tendency to reject or attack. Is there a way to help me generate abundant and willing stem cells, and to help Maggie receive the cells with openness and trust?

Perhaps if Maggie and I can sit together and, with the help of a therapist, retrace our years of sisterhood and clear up old wounds or misconceptions, we can affect her body's willingness to accept my cells. We can call on my cells to make a peaceful passage into her bloodstream. We can go into the medical procedures better able to give and receive, having put down never-expressed grievances, secret shame, made-up stories, blame, or judgment. Before the bone marrow transplant, we could try for a soul marrow transplant—each of us setting aside the old stories that have kept us separate so that a more truthful intimacy can grow.

I look for a way to describe my intent without using words like "therapy" or "ritual." I don't want to scare Maggie off. I find the perfect way of introducing the idea in my parents' holy text, the *New Yorker* magazine. I clip a cartoon out and send it to Maggie. This is something both my parents did, mailing us girls carefully scissored *New Yorker* cartoons, sometimes with comments, sometimes just a clipping in an envelope. The cartoon I send Maggie shows two women talking to each other. One says, "I've never forgiven him for that thing I made up in my head." The other looks on, knowingly.

Maggie calls me. "What was that cartoon all about?"

I tell her my idea of helping the stem cells make a peaceful advance into her bloodstream, about the possibility of rejection or attack, and of the mind-body studies that prove the connection between what we think and how we heal. "We've made up a lot of things in our heads about each other," I explain. "Maybe if we talk about those things, maybe we'll find some stuff to let go of, to forgive, to clean up and clear out before the harvest and the trans-

plant. What if we come out of hiding and go for the deep stuff?"
I fully expect her to reject or attack the idea. As it turns out, that's
just a story in my head.

"I love that idea," Maggie says. "I'm in."

Before we choose a therapist Maggie and I come up with a list of
questions we want to explore in our first session:

> Here are things I have done that may have hurt you. Will you
> forgive me?
> Here are ways I have felt hurt by you. Can I safely tell you my
> truth?
> Can I be myself with you?
> Will you accept me?
> Will you love me?
> Will you make a place for me, all the way down to your marrow?

In framing the questions and speaking them aloud to each other,
we feel the answers rushing in, like waves coming to shore.

"See," Maggie asks, "who needs a therapist?"

Part Three

❧

THE MARROW
OF THE SELF

The authentic self
is the soul made visible.

—SARAH BAN BREATHNACH

BESHERT

THERE'S NO WORD IN ENGLISH that quite captures the meaning of the Yiddish word "beshert." It sort of translates as "predetermined," but that word doesn't have the same oomph as "beshert." When used by matchmakers, "beshert" means the one person you are destined to be with, your soul mate or, as one rabbi put it, the other half of the broken eggshell.

"Beshert" is also used to describe synchronicities—like when you think of someone you haven't seen in ages and then you run into that person that same morning, walking to work on a street you rarely take. Why were you thinking of that person? And why did you take that street today? And what if you—or your friend— had left the house at a different time? You don't know the answers to these questions, but they make you wonder who's directing this show anyway. That's another meaning of "beshert": something that seems to have been predestined by something you do not understand, and yet still, you trust it was meant to be.

That's how I feel about the bone marrow transplant. That it was meant to be. Not something we ordered, not anything we agreed to, but it came anyway, and therefore, it is beshert. Would I go back in time, alter destiny, and undo the need for the transplant? Smother the wildfire before it started spreading throughout my sister's body? Of course. But I can't, and so we must go forward, trusting that in bringing together the broken eggshells of our love, there is something beshert—meant to be—for both of us.

What might that be? For Maggie, it might be a long life. For me, the privilege of helping her live. But I think the cosmic Cupid has some other things in mind too, and maybe we can touch on those things in the therapy session. In reuniting the Maggie-Liz eggshells, and in revisiting the stories that have kept us separate, maybe we can also heal other broken places in our lives. Because those stories we all drag around with us from childhood, unexplored and unforgiven, get deep into our psyches and become who we think we are. Meanwhile, the marrow of our selves is kept concealed, and our souls are left untapped.

It takes courage to dig for the soul with another person. I've done most of my soul-searching on my own—on the secluded islands of meditation and therapy. It's less challenging to examine myself—warts and all—in the privacy of my own head, or in a room with a therapist who keeps all confidences. It always surprises me how hard it is to lay bare my most vulnerable authenticity to my husband, with whom I have lived for almost thirty years, or with my closest friends and colleagues.

We crave intimacy with others, and yet we fear it. We want to be seen and loved for who we are, yet *we* don't know who we are! This is the tragedy and the comedy of being human. Afraid to look too deeply into our own selves, and afraid to ask others, "Who am I to you?" we circle each other, harboring old stories, many of which are not even true. I've been a brave person all my life. I've traveled to dangerous places; I've delivered babies; I've given speeches to large crowds and intimate gatherings; I've stood my ground at work and in the world. But being brave one-on-one with another person—to me, that takes the most courage. It seems that intimacy should be easier—that we should have been born knowing, or at least taught, how to bare our souls honestly to the people in our lives. That instead of rejecting or attacking, we would move toward the other with curiosity and warmth, even when feeling shamed or hurt or angry or afraid. But we don't do this easily, we humans. We need help in learning how.

In his masterpiece of a book, *The Art of Loving*, Erich Fromm writes that love is an art that must be learned, but that "in spite of the deep-seated craving for love, almost everything else is considered to be more important than love: success, prestige, money, power—almost all our energy is used for the learning of how to achieve these aims, and almost none to learn the art of loving." My aim in going to see a therapist with Maggie is for both of us to practice what Fromm considers the first step in the art of loving— what he calls relating "from center to center." He writes, "Love is possible only if two persons communicate with each other from the center of their existence . . . If I perceive in another person mainly the surface, I perceive mainly the differences, that which separates us. If I penetrate to the core, I perceive our identity, the fact of our brotherhood." And, in this case, the fact of our sisterhood.

SISTERS OF THE REVOLUTION

I'VE BEGUN TO PILFER MY mother's photo albums. She and her brother—my crazy psychiatrist uncle—were the family photographers. You can tell which pictures my mother took: group shots of the family at the beach, on hikes, in the neighborhood. My uncle's photos are artsy shots of individuals with moody expressions in low-lit rooms. Over the years, my mother carefully glued the photographs into twenty big black books. When my mother died, my sisters and I divided up the collection. I put my five black books on a high shelf in a closet, but I take them down now, and even though I can feel my mother's dismay as I dismantle the system, I unglue pictures of Maggie at different stages of her childhood and line them up chronologically on my desk.

There she is, a bundle in my mother's arms—the third baby girl brought home from the hospital. And there I am, eyeing her dubiously, wondering what to make of this little interloper. In another picture, she's two and I'm four. We're paddling around in the shallow waters of the Long Island Sound. I have two long braids and short bangs, and I'm staring straight into the camera with a satisfied expression on my face. Maggie has a pixie haircut that makes her look like a tousled little mouse. She keeps her eyes on the water with an earnest and anxious look. In another picture, we're having a tea party, sitting on the sidewalk. I am serving. Maggie is waiting with her hands in her lap. Here she is at seven or eight, standing under a blossoming apple tree, playing the violin. She's tiny and adorable. She was always tiny and adorable. Then she turned into a teenager. She stayed tiny but became stunningly beautiful. There's the photo of her at eighteen leaning against the dock at the beach—her sun-bleached hair falling below her shoulders, her flashing dark eyes, her soft smile. No wonder all the boys were in love with her. No wonder they still are.

Everyone loves Maggie—that's what we have always said in the family, and if I say it to her friends, they agree right away. What is it about her? Her bright hummingbird energy? Her love of what's wild—the forest, wildlife, her own wild nature? She's an unusual mix: part wild child, part worrier, part warrior. She's flown on seaplanes into the Alaskan tundra in wildflower season, scavenging for her artwork, and camped there, alone among the glaciers and grizzly bears. Yet she's also stayed close to home, living for years in our parents' Vermont town, marrying the boy next door, taking care of everyone but herself. She's fought battles for her patients, yet when it comes to fighting for her own well-being, she's scoffed at the whole idea—putting up with people who treat her badly, not paying attention to her body's warning signs. She's danced all night with unabashed joy at concerts, done endurance swimming around islands in Maine, and made me laugh so hard I've wet my pants. And yet she spent way too many years hiding her bright light so as to not outshine anyone else. She made a big impression on others, but kept herself small.

Sometimes I think Maggie stayed small because by the time she was born, my older sister, Katy, and I had already taken up a lot of space. Katy came barging into the world with a double dose of energy. My mother didn't know what to do with her. Neither did the conformist teachers in the elementary schools of our day.

At parent-teacher conferences my mother would tell the teachers, with a hopeful and worried tone, that perhaps Katy was a "late bloomer." Perhaps she would settle down and conform later on. She never did, and the world's a better place because she didn't.

When I was born, Katy was four years old. I must have taken one look at the fraught relationship she had with my mother and decided right then and there to do things differently. I was calmer and more introspective than Katy, but I was just as strong-willed. The two of us seemed to know from an early age that we had things to do and places to go. In those days, powerful little girls were called "bossy." It was not a compliment. Katy and I were bossy.

Maggie and our youngest sister, Jo, took a backseat to their older sisters. They were the good girls. Maggie was a people pleaser, a nervous sprite, someone who kept secrets, including her own. Jo was the little one, "the least of the Lessers," as she says now. We left her out of a lot of our games and adventures because she was the baby. She was shy and barely talked for the first years of her life. Everything had already been said. Both Maggie and Jo said less than the big girls.

Until they became teenagers. Then, all four of us became creatures of our times. Just about every aspect of American life was in upheaval when we were teenagers. We spoke up against the Vietnam War, and for civil rights. We wore miniskirts and skimpy shirts. We had sex, smoked pot, and listened to rock and roll that broke the sound barrier. We called each other "sisters of the revolution." Our poor parents.

In the middle of the line of photos of Maggie, I place a few of the four girls. Katy, Liz, Maggie, Jo. My father called us KaLiMaJo. Here's a picture of us in navy-blue sweatshirts at the beach, hoods pulled up and tied beneath our chins. Here's one of us at a cousin's wedding, in matching Easter dresses, lined up in size order. And here we are as young women, long hair, happy smiles, arms around each other, striding down a dirt road in Vermont. In some ways, we were a united front. We were the four Lesser girls. We were KaLiMaJo. But in other ways we were rivals. We kept each other locked in the roles we had been assigned as children, even as we grew out of them in the rest of our lives. The places we lived, the men we married, the jobs we took, the families we created, the choices we made: they served as ways of both uniting and separating us. Never did I feel more connected to other humans than with my sisters, and yet at the same time, never did I feel as insecure or judged or hurt or pissed off. Would I ever be released from the role of the bossy one, the princess, the hot-shit city slicker who had left the state of Vermont and therefore the state of grace? Would any of us ever see the other without the blinders of family branding? And who would we be to each other without the attached stories?

Although we grew up in the same house, with the same parents, each of us four girls tells a different version of the story of our sisterhood. From the moment we could think, we began forming stories—about our mother, our father, each other, and how all the pieces fit together. All siblings do this; all humans do it. This is the great mystery of our shared existence—how what each one of us calls reality is only one small rendering of a vast and complex story. Take two siblings, or any two people, and ask them to describe an important event. What you'll get are two distinctive and sometimes conflicting accounts, each spiked with strong opinions masquerading as fact.

Memoirists confront this phenomenon all the time; they cleave to as true a tale as they can, but their own bias gets in the way at every turn. Anaïs Nin, one of the great memoirists of the twentieth

HIDING SOMEWHERE NEAR US

ALTHOUGH SHE AGREES TO VISIT the therapist, Maggie warns me not to get too excited. "It's too late for me to change who I am, Liz," she says.

"Why would you have to change who you are?" I ask her.

"Isn't that the point of therapy?"

"Actually, it's the opposite," I say. "You don't try to change yourself. You try to know yourself, and then to *be* yourself—your real self."

"What does that even mean, 'your real self'?" Maggie asks. "I feel pretty real these days."

"Words are going to fail me here," I say, preapologizing for the inadequate words at my disposal. "These are hard things to talk about without sounding like a moron."

"Try me," Maggie says.

"What I mean is we're all born exactly who we are supposed to be, but we take these weird detours in order to fit in, or please others, or get our way, or just get by. We suffer wounds and build up scar tissue. You know how Shakespeare said, 'To thine own self be true'? Well, for most of us, the voice of 'thine own self' gets harder and harder to hear because other voices take over. Therapy is separating out the voices in your head, and deciding which ones to listen to and which ones steer you away from your real self, your real purpose, what you love, what you value. There's power in naming the voices in your head: This one's my father's voice, that one belongs to a sister, that other one to a teacher, a husband, a wife, the culture, the country. Ah, and this one, this one rising to the surface, this one is mine. My own self. Can I trust that voice? Can I be true to it? That's therapy."

"That doesn't sound moronic," Maggie says. "But do people really ever figure all that out?"

"Well, it takes some time," I say.

"But we've only got a couple of hours."

"Yeah, and we have the ticking time bomb of the transplant. It will motivate us because we're doing it for each other," I say. "We have a compelling reason to get down to the marrow of ourselves."

"This above all, to thine own self be true." My English teacher mother was quick to point out that Shakespeare put those famous words into the mouth of Polonius, the least true-to-thine-self of all the characters in *Hamlet*. It was the Bard's ironic way of saying that, while the key to life is authenticity, most of us pay lip service to the idea, never really biting into the gold kernel of truth at the core of the self. Never really having the support, the know-how, the guts to mine the gold and live the gold and give the gold. That's the tragedy at the heart of *Hamlet*. And it's a tragedy in all of our lives until we summon the courage to dig deep, to say our truth, to be our truth.

There is a gold kernel of truth within each of us. It is the marrow of who you really are. It's right there—your true self, your soul self—shimmering and powerful, free of fear, clean of envy, clear of purpose. And yet, at the same time, it's tantalizingly out of reach, hidden under layers of crappy things said and done to you; discounted or even threatened because of your gender or class or race; drowned out by the noise of your own anxieties and shame

You may be walking to work, passing the same store windows you do every day, but today, grace descends and your true self comes out of hiding. You see your reflection in the window, and for a minute you just know that by some mysterious and purposeful design, you belong right here, right now, in your body, in your life. You look around at the people rushing in both directions, and instead of your usual mix of annoyance or isolation, jealousy or judgment, you love them, you feel one with them, you want the best for them. You're not sure where this equanimity of spirit comes from, but it feels like the truth of who you are; it feels like your soul. You'd like to capture and harness it. You'd like to put it in charge of your life. You see all of this in your reflection in the window as you rush to work. But then you arrive, and you go into a meeting where you swallow your opinion, or you defend your position. You say something you later regret, or you don't say what you really wanted to. Your soul self swiftly goes back into hiding.

Or maybe you're driving your kid to school, distracted and overwhelmed as usual. Your eye catches the face of your son in the rearview mirror. And for no reason whatsoever your heart softens and you cheer up so fully that you are suddenly and blessedly free of striving, of rushing, of ruminating. It doesn't matter that you're late or that the remains of breakfast are encrusted around your son's mouth. It doesn't matter that it's winter and you are ten pounds overweight or that your boy writes his name backwards. You look at his face, and something comes over you, and in that moment you taste the delight of "enough." Your son, just as he is, is enough. He's more than enough! And you are enough. You slip through the keyhole into a vast realm of freedom—the freedom of knowing and loving without apology exactly who you are.

I live for those moments. I've gone to great lengths to experience them—to make contact with my true self. I don't necessarily recommend everything I've done. I've tried some weird therapies and chancy adventures—all-night ceremonies, dubious teachers, exotic healings. All to find what isn't even lost. All to uncover what is barely beneath the surface. All to reveal what seems uniquely mine, and yet is part of the same fabric of what is uniquely yours.

And why, you may ask, spend precious time searching for something as elusive as a soul? Why not leave it where it hides—near to us, yet so difficult to find and sometimes dangerous to follow? There are two reasons: First, you search for the soul for the sake of your own life—for purpose, for meaning, for strength, for freedom and peace and love. Second, you search for your soul for the sake of everyone else. You do it for your family, your children, your coworkers, the whole world. The world needs your originality, your ideas, your humor, your creations. All of this is alive and well within you, hiding somewhere near you, beneath the layers, down, down, down, into the soul.

WHAT IS THE SOUL?

IT'S ONE THING TO WRITE about the marrow of the bones—there's a lot of research out there to back me up when I'm describing bones and blood and stem cells. It's another thing to write about the marrow of the self. The marrow of the bones is home to your stem cells. The marrow of yourself is home to your soul, although there are no clinical studies I can quote to prove this. There are traditions and ceremonies, poetry and music, mystical conjecture and luminous experience. But any discussion of the soul is subjective. I offer you here my own definition. It may differ from yours. That's OK with me. I have no argument with multiple ways of defining the soul or spirit or God. The more the merrier.

What is the soul? In the deepest part of each of us, we are one and the same. My essence and your essence are the same liquid light, poured from the great ocean into the small vessel of an individual body with its singular personality and purpose. Words alone cannot describe our essential, eternal, spiritual nature. But words are what I have. Musicians can sing of the spirit, and artists can paint its incandescence. I only have words. I use the word "soul" to describe how eternal essence is bent like refracted light through the prism of our human nature. Soul is essence filtered through genetics and gender and ancestry and upbringing and the times in which we live.

Your soul here on earth is uniquely yours. It is different from my soul, although eventually all streams lead back to the great ocean. Some people call that ocean God, some call it spirit, some don't call it anything—they just experience it as a vastness, or a question mark, or an abiding sense of love and light. In the vastness our distinctions and differences melt into Oneness, but while we are here, we are meant to express the uniqueness of who we are, each one of us a snowflake fallen from the essence down to earth. We are meant to take pleasure in our individuality, even as we remember our essential unity. The soul is the bridge between pure essence and human individuality.

When the soul bridge is in place, we can go back and forth between essence and ego, unity and diversity. We remember how we all come from the same place, but have different purposes while here. We realize how spectacular a chance we've been given to bring heaven to earth. When our egos get puffed up, or when our rational minds dominate, or our emotions and senses overwhelm, the soul retreats. The bridge draws up; we are stranded in separateness.

But the soul can be wooed back. Sit tall and still. Close your eyes, drop your shoulders, soften your belly. Breathe. Now, tell your overwrought mind, shhhhh. Breathe, shhhhh, wait. There! That quietude you feel, that relaxed presence, that openness, that peace. That is your soul. Even if you sense the soul for a split second, even if you have to wade through restlessness and boredom for that one taste, even if you barely believe in what you are doing, it is wise to woo the soul. To learn her language. To let him guide you.

GENIUS AND JUNO

HERE'S ANOTHER WAY OF SPEAKING about the soul. The Greeks believed that each child was blessed at birth with a personal daimon—a spirit guide, a golden thread connected to one's brightest purpose and ultimate destiny. We don't have an adequate word today for the daimon. "Soul" works for me, but it has connotations that turn some people off. "Guardian angel" might work for some, but others will take the words literally and scoff at the idea of an immaterial being capable of holding back a truck as you cross the street. That is not what the Greeks meant. To them, your daimon—your spirit guide—lived within you. You were born with it; you came into this world with your daimon embedded in the body, like the grand oak already present in the acorn—a kind of spiritual DNA that already knows who it is, what it should do, how it should live. Greek philosophers spoke of the responsibility to put the daimon in charge of your life. If you didn't—if you tried to live someone else's life, if you covered your light, if you squandered your purpose—you would deny others the fullness of your gifts.

The Romans, who appropriated many Greek concepts, called the daimon your Genius. Each person (well, in Roman times, each man) had his own Genius. We've reduced the meaning of the word "genius" to intellectual prowess, but its original meaning was the unique indwelling character of each person. To the Romans, everyone had an essential character and therefore a distinctive calling. Places, objects, and events had indwelling natures as well, including your house and the street you lived on, cities and mountains, seasons and festivals. The Genius was often represented by an image of a vital and youthful boy, meant to symbolize the ageless, eternal soul that had temporarily taken up residence in the person, place, or thing.

If you were a woman in ancient Rome, you got to have a Genius too, but it was called your Juno. Juno was Rome's presiding goddess. She was symbolized by a woman sitting under a verdant fig tree, holding a resplendent peacock. The month of June was named after her. She was life in its fullness—sweet but also fierce. She protected life, and was known to throw thunderbolts if crossed (a useful skill to embolden in your own personal Juno).

The job of the parents in ancient Rome was to help the child know and trust her Juno, to discover and follow his Genius. I am not sure how many of the ancients actually put this into their parenting practice. I imagine they were as flawed as we are. But theoretically, they believed it was not the role of the parent to unduly influence a child's sense of self, or to overdirect his steps in the world.

Most of us today were parented and socialized in such a way that, by the time we reach adulthood, our Genius is so covered over with shoulds and shouldn'ts that we often don't know where to look for our Juno, our Genius, our authentic self. In fact, the whole notion seems questionable. Is there really such a thing as an "authentic self," a "real self"? I say yes. Perhaps it is suppressed or scuffed up, but it can be liberated; it can be polished. I have personally experienced this. After years of trying and failing, and then trying more and succeeding by fits and starts, I know now that when I get my small ego and my frightened reactivity out of the way, my authenticity, my soulfulness, will rush in and fill the confines of my being. It will guide my steps and gratify even the toughest times with a sense of meaning.

Your Juno or Genius must be courted. Although it is strong and luminous, your guardian spirit is unassuming and even shy. It responds to persistent yet kindly biddings. Once awakened, it outshines everything false within you and in your life. But it needs room and time to stretch as it stirs. Your Juno, your Genius, they know who you are—they know you suffer from a case of mistaken identity. But they are not the argumentative types. They're not as loud as some of the other voices in your head. But that doesn't mean they aren't there.

It takes some work to make contact with your Juno or your Genius. You may need some help. Psychotherapy can be helpful. So can meditation. Both are good for taming the voices in your head—the ones who bark bad directions at all hours of the day and night.

It's not that difficult to know where to look for help. Seek out helpers in the form of therapists or teachers (or books or systems) who seem to be following their own Genius or Juno. How will you know this? Those in touch with their authenticity share similar traits. They are gentle and strong in equal measure. They are not overly concerned about what others think of them, and yet they are greatly concerned about the well-being of others. They are so in touch with themselves that they are open toward everyone. They have tasted the sweetness and the bitterness of their life and declared it all good; they want you to taste your own life too. They don't want your allegiance; they want your liberation. They won't come after you; you must seek them out. And when your work with them is done, they will give you wings to fly away.

And then the real work begins. The daily commitment to being genuine in everything you say or do. The courage to be vulnerable, to express who you are in a world that wants you to conform, to be bold and loving toward those whose own genuineness is so blocked that they will feel threatened by yours. It's a lifelong road trip, this reclamation of your authentic self, but it's worth it. Through it you come home to a dignified and grateful ground of being.

How will you know your own Juno when she arrives to greet you? How will you recognize your Genius's face? You'll feel a sense of at-homeness, a lack of pretense, nothing overproduced, a wholeness. You'll know her as the "genuine article"—like an apple picked right from the tree, or that cracked teapot that belonged to your grandmother, or your leather jacket that no one else likes but you do and you always have because for some reason it's meaningful, it's expressive, it's you. That is your Juno. That is your Genius. Eventually, you will come to know with all your brain cells that your authentic self is the one thing you can trust the most.

AUTHENTICITY DEFICIT DISORDER

IT NEVER CEASES TO ASTONISH me how much we all suffer from ADD. Not attention deficit disorder. The ADD I am talking about is *authenticity* deficit disorder, a condition you won't find in the *Diagnostic and Statistical Manual of Mental Disorders* because I made it up. But still, it's real. And like many disorders, authenticity deficit disorder manifests along a spectrum. Some of us have a mild case. We go through the day with a low-grade embarrassment at being human, hesitant to show our true face with all of its odd and magnificent irregularities, reluctant to look inside, do some housecleaning, and get to the marrow of the self. Others of us fall on the more serious end of the ADD spectrum. Our sense of inadequacy and shame is overwhelming and crippling. Serious ADD can take the form of depression, anxiety, fear, isolation. It can hold us back from living fully. It can make intimacy impossible.

Most of us fall in the middle of the ADD spectrum—sometimes pleased about who we are, sometimes ashamed. Sometimes clear about our path in life, other times befuddled and stuck. In the privacy of our own nutty heads, we imagine everyone else got the instruction book, but not us—in fact, we suspect there may be something uniquely wrong with us. But we keep that insecurity to ourselves; we keep it a secret. And then we try to cover it up with all sorts of facades and defenses that over a lifetime become habitual. We try to look the part of someone who's got it all to-gether. Depending on what we think the world wants from us, we try to sound cool, act strong, be smart. Or maybe we hide behind a macho mask, or a good-girl persona. Maybe we act the good-girl part when what is called for is to be the rebel, or maybe we act the rebel part even when there's nothing to fight. Meanwhile, back in the marrow, our shining soul is what the world really wants. But we don't believe that. We believe the opposite—that if we looked too deep or shared too much, our basic unacceptability would be found out.

And so we relate to each other on the surface because we're afraid if we reveal too much, if we show all our cards, we won't be loved, we won't be accepted, we won't belong. We'll be taken advantage of. We'll be judged and excluded. But that is a supreme misunder-standing. If we only show to each other our surface scars—our defenses, our reactivity, our false intimacies—then that's what we get back. Show me your surface and I'll show you mine.

Here's the real truth: Underneath the facades and scars and coping mechanisms, you are good to the core. You are not perfect. But you are good. When we show each other our whole selves—scars and all—we get down to the marrow, to the soul. This isn't the easiest thing to do with another person. Sometimes it means admitting that you're scared to go there, that you don't trust the other person, that you have been hurt in the past. But if you can do that, you'll inspire truthful intimacy in the other. It's not a perfect equation—some people are hard nuts to crack, and some people will never break open to you, but it is always worth the effort. Always.

It's in the depth that we're given the chance to lay claim to each other's goodness and to bring it up into the relationship. This may sound way too laborious, way too risky. But I think it's riskier and more labor-intensive not to do it—not to come home to your own goodness, not to seek out the goodness in others. We spend so much time and anguish circling each other's inauthentic, wounded selves. It's shockingly liberating to break the cycle of authenticity deficit disorder. And a first step in doing so is to realize how we all suffer from ADD.

In my many years of working at Omega Institute, I've been like a spy in the inner sanctum of the human potential movement, trying to get to the bottom of what really helps people heal their wounds and uncover their gifts. What helps people heal physically? Psychologically? What helps them drop their unhappiness and anxiety, and develop self-love and self-worth? What helps them grow spiritually, trading a small, fearful vision of life for a vaster consciousness? And most importantly, what helps people turn self-healing into a gift for our hurting world? I've sat in classrooms and auditoriums, listening for the answers to these questions. I've interviewed healing practitioners, spiritual teachers, business leaders, Nobel laureates, artists and futurists and scientists—all so I could chart this journey of how human beings can recover from authenticity deficit disorder.

People often ask me, "Wow, you've hung around such amazing teachers, what are they like? What's the most enlightening thing you've taken away from all this? What's the big secret?" I hope my takeaway doesn't disappoint you. The big secret is this: every teacher or author or leader or artist I've worked with is an ordinary human being—every single one of them. That's the big secret. Yes, they are wise and they are profound, but they are also just like you and me. They eat, they go to the bathroom, they forget where they put their keys, they quarrel with family members. They try to live up to their noblest ideals, and sometimes they do, and sometimes they don't. They have their heartbreaks and blind spots and contradictory behavior. From sitting backstage with some of the most brilliant scientists and wise rabble-rousers and calm healers, I can tell you, without a doubt, that everyone has weird neuroses and surprising insecurities, and everyone has moments of befuddlement just about being human. We look to them for answers, but they too are still searching. This realization has ground into me the truth of what has been said across the ages, but somehow we never really believe: that the answers are within you; that you, yourself, are the answer.

In my early years at Omega, when I was in my twenties, I found it disconcerting when teachers started falling off their pedestals. Like discovering over dinner that a renowned relationship expert was getting divorced, or hosting a retreat for peace activists and finding out they were very angry people. Or meeting the depressed happiness researcher. Or the monk with a big ego. At first this upset me. But as the years went on, it liberated me. It made me more tolerant of all people's inconsistencies, and it made me more compassionate toward myself. It showed me that no one is living the exact life you think they are, so if you compare your life to another person's, you're usually comparing it to a fantasy of your own making. Seeing the imperfect humanness of my teachers side by side with their genius has helped me stop expecting perfection of myself. My close encounters with the wise ones have helped me relax and lighten up. I've let go of the goal of perfection and taken up the goal of authenticity.

The end of authenticity deficit disorder is not a glamorous new personality. It's less exciting and more wonderful than that: You become more fully yourself. You become more present, more awake, more alive. You uncover a natural intelligence that knows what you need in order to fulfill your destiny. You look less and less outside yourself for validation and direction. Your life becomes who you are, and not what you do.

Eve Ensler, the activist and playwright who wrote *The Vagina Monologues*, has been a frequent speaker at Omega. She once came to Omega straight from being in a war zone in Africa. She told me a story about marching into a meeting with government officials and giving them a piece of her mind about the appalling prevalence of violence against women. I asked her, "How do you find the courage to speak truth to powerful people like that?" And she said, "Because I know everyone is just making it up as they go along, including presidents of countries. Wherever I go, it's just people making things up. So I figure, if they can make it up, I can too. And you can too. Make up something from your deepest truth, and put it in the service of love."

People like Eve Ensler have shown me that work on the self is not an act of selfishness. To develop kind regard for oneself can become an act of kindness for the world if we turn the light outward as well as inward. When you get to know your own goodness—your core self—you wake up to the obvious yet startling realization that other people also have a core self that deserves to be known and loved. And therefore, the act of uncovering the true self is not a solitary one, for to know oneself is to be compassionate enough to really know the "other," and to be brave enough to be known.

THE CERTIFIED HUMAN
PARENTING MANUAL

MY FIRST HUSBAND WAS A doctor. He trained me in midwifery, and I assisted him in home births. I was only twenty when I scrubbed into my first birth; my husband wasn't much older. We were babes ourselves. He was doing his medical internship in a hospital in San Francisco and I was finishing college. I had gone back to school not because I wanted to but because if I didn't I'd break my mother's heart.

We were living with that guru I had been searching for and found in California. He wasn't your run-of-the-mill guru. He was an erudite religious scholar who had grown up in France, fought for the allies in World War II, and moved to the United States when young Americans began showing interest in Eastern spirituality. His father was a revered Indian mystic; his mother was American. She was the niece of Mary Baker Eddy, the founder of Christian Science—a coincidence I found compelling.

By day, I was halfheartedly going to college in San Francisco. When my classes were over, I'd cross the Golden Gate Bridge to where we were living in Marin County and wholeheartedly apply myself to my education in meditation, Eastern religions, Western religions, all kinds of spiritual traditions. And midwifery. The academic education I was receiving in college paled when compared to the spiritual instruction I was receiving from my teacher, and the medical training from my husband. I was learning about the inside of things—the inner spiritual life, the insides of a woman's body, the guts of the human experience. Finally.

The body, as it turns out, is as mysterious as the cosmos. For all we know, it's a mirror of the cosmos. The secrets of the universe dwell within us, from the marrow in the bones to the tips of our fingers. Did you know that there's a one-in-sixty-four-billion chance that your fingerprint will match up exactly with someone else's? And that those little ridges and whorls on the tip of each finger are formed from pressure on a baby's developing hands in the womb? No two people have ever been found to have the same fingerprints.

When I was a practicing midwife, we followed a strict checklist after the birth of each baby, a list that included heart rate, skin tone, reflexes, and other markers and measurements of infant health. After completing the checklist, I would take the baby's little hand and examine the stamp on each tiny finger. It was like reading the baby, reading the fingerprint of its soul. In greeting so many babies in their first minutes of life, I became convinced that our only purpose here is to study the fingerprint of our own soul, to get to know it, to love it, to live it.

There's a problem, though. From the moment we begin to reveal to the world our soul's fingerprint, family and society offer conflicting directions. If you're an energetic kid, you'll be told to calm down from an early age. If you're shy, you'll be pushed to connect; if you're quiet, you'll be encouraged to talk; if you're loud, shhhh. "You're too _____(fill in the blank: aggressive, passive; social, withdrawn; wild, timid; messy, prim . . .)," say the parents and the teachers. Of course this implies a comparison to the perfect human being who does not actually exist. All those other kids we're told to be more like—the siblings and the cousins and the friends—are busy being compared to their siblings and cousins and friends. No wonder we're all so confused.

The babies I delivered never looked confused to me. Their gaze was steady and clear. Before I swaddled each one and gave him or her to the parents, I always whispered a quick and easy welcome-wagon speech in their ears—something like "Hello! Hooray! We've been waiting for you." Infants look to their first earthlings—mother, father, siblings, tribe—for signs that they are welcome here. They search the first faces they see with intense curiosity, as if they are saying: "Here I am! This is who you got! Let's get to know each other. Let's belong to each other." And to the best of their capabilities, parents try to welcome their new little human with joyful acceptance.

But it's a tough job being a parent; no one is quite prepared for it. If mothers and fathers were handed a script to read to their newborns from a Certified Human Parenting manual, it might go something like this:

Welcome, little one! We are glad you have come here. We want to know everything about you—down to your marrow, down to your fingerprint. Please show us who you are. We'll listen closely to what your soul needs and what it longs to express. But we also will teach you the ways of this earth. There are some things here that cannot be changed, but there are many things that can and should be changed. We will help you figure this out because we know you have come here to make a difference; we will help you find that purpose.

You will cross paths with many "others" throughout your life, and they too will be sorting out their unique purpose and plans. This will be your greatest challenge: staying true to your marrow while honoring the truth of others—their values, their backgrounds, their wounds, and their strengths. If you have siblings, they will be your first teachers in this arena. They will serve you a confusing cocktail of care and competition, friendship and rejection. Please forgive them for mistaking you for an invader.

And please forgive us—your parents—if we give you conflicting instructions; if we push you toward individuality and also insist you play well with others. Somewhere in between those two impulses is the holy middle path. To be true to yourself and to be good to others. Our greatest gift to you will be to walk that middle path ourselves, because we know talk about the path is cheap. We promise to try to walk the talk.

That's what should have been said to us, and what we should say to our kids, and they to their kids. But even if a script like that were hammered out in the United Nations and then handed out at every birth around the world, it would still not guarantee any kind of universal success. Babies wear down even the strongest among us. Not to mention toddlers and teenagers and adult children. The Certified Human Parenting manual should really include the shocking information that the job never ends, and that one needs to follow the script year after year. Someone forgot to tell us that.

Also, someone forgot to tell us that our own journey never ends. There is no finish line. There is always more to uncover, more to know, more to heal, more to love, more to give. Being true to oneself is a rough-and-tumble ride, full of challenges and wonders. The Jungian scholar James Hollis writes, "We are not here to fit in, be well balanced, or provide exempla for others. We are here to be eccentric, different, perhaps strange, perhaps merely to add our small piece, our little clunky, chunky selves, to the great mosaic of being. As the gods intended, we are here to become more and more ourselves."

MY MOTHER'S FACE

YEARS AGO, BACK WHEN I was spending a lot of energy "trying to fit in, be well balanced, and provide exempla for others," my courageous ex-husband dragged me to a notorious personal growth workshop called the est 6-Day. We were in our thirties; our marriage was ten years old and faltering; we had two little kids, a stressful business, and a shaky future.

The tactics of the est program were similar to those of the military: Gather a group of people together, take away their personal belongings, and allow no contact with the outside world for an extended period of time. Then, during that time—in this case, six days—from early morning till late into the night, bombard the hundred or so participants with nonstop instruction, group process, and extreme physical exercise, while offering a restricted-calorie diet and a piped-in soundtrack that included the theme song from the movie *Rocky*. The premise was that the intensity of the schedule and the rigor of the program would clonk us over the head with wisdom so that we would, in the words of the 6-Day, finally "get it" and "stop having an argument with reality."

It sounded great on paper. My husband and I were in the middle of a huge argument with each other and with reality. The reality was we were married. The argument was we didn't want to be married anymore. He had broken my trust and my heart; I had returned the favor. Would the 6-Day put an end to our argument?

Would it help us slink back into the marriage with our tails between our legs and make peace with reality? I wanted it to. But I was dubious about the whole thing. First of all, there was an aggression to the organization I didn't like. Even if I was having an argument with reality, I didn't see how anyone was going to argue me out of it. And secondly, I didn't want to have the argument in front of a group of strangers. It felt dangerous to me. My husband and I had Band-Aids all over our hearts. I was afraid the 6-Day might demand we rip them off, taking the marriage too.

On the other hand, we needed to do something. We were too young to accept a bitter marriage, but old enough to have a lot at stake. And so I tagged along with my husband to the 6-Day, complaining all the way. The literature said the program started the minute you signed up for it, and that you could prepare for the experience by listening to your real feelings and jotting them down. But that was the whole problem right there! I didn't know what my real feelings were, and even if I did, I wouldn't have listened to them. I didn't understand then what I know now: that my own precious self was worth listening to, that what I wanted was of value, and that telling the soul's truth is not something best done in a military setting.

It certainly would have been better if I had known how to let the truth set me free in a more gentle way than what happened during the 6-Day. My memory has erased most of what my husband and I said to each other during interminable exercises and brief, calorie-restricted meals. I do remember saying—or was it yelling?—"I never really loved you." Well, that certainly was not true. I loved him as well as someone who didn't love her own self could love.

But human beings learn in strange and broken ways. We venture far astray to find what we already have. Does that mean I could have uncovered my genuine self without the journey, without the ragged circling, the painful losses, and the unkindness hurled and received? The lucky among us may be able to ride high on a cloud through the storms of life. That has not been my experience, nor the route I have noticed most mortals taking. Sometimes it is in the eye of the storm where we find the eye of the heart—the genuine self, the marrow of what really matters.

And so, off we went to the 6-Day, both of us determined to patch up our leaky ship. I can remember only a few of the actual strategies employed by the "trainers," as those leading the 6-Day were called. During the week, we did one exercise where a trainer had the whole group follow his command to stand up or sit down for hours until finally, way past midnight, everyone had complied and was performing in harmony; we had our hair cut and restyled by professionals hired to help us shed our old identities; we ate lightly and we ran several miles each day. All the while, we sat in our group and were encouraged to spill our guts.

I knew what the training was trying to accomplish. I respected the goals. But I resented the martial methodology. For whatever reasons, I had always been the kind of person for whom spilling one's guts came easily. I was actually trying to go in the opposite direction. I needed to put some boundaries up between me and other people. The more everyone else cooperated with the regime, the more I refused to go along. I was central casting's angry resister. I was brought into the head trainer's office when I demanded I be allowed to call home and check up on my children. I told the trainer I wanted to leave, that I wasn't getting anything out of the program except missing my kids and feeling pissed off. He told me that my resistance to the program was no different than my resistance to life itself, and that the more I fought, the further I got from the truth I so dearly desired to know.

I'll never forget a line he said to me, a line that had been repeated throughout the 6-Day: "You are already in Baltimore but you don't know it, so you keep trying to get to Baltimore."

"But this isn't Baltimore," I answered, exasperated by the psychobabble. "This is upstate New York!"

The trainer looked at me with compassion. "Sweetheart," he said, "YOU are Baltimore. OK? We are trying to help you get to Baltimore."

And so I hung in there, because, indeed, I did want to get to Baltimore. The final exercise of the 6-Day took place after dinner on the last night, and went "as long as the last person gets it." My intention going in was to fake "getting it," whatever that meant; I didn't want to be the one keeping the whole exhausted group up half the night. The exercise consisted of lining up in front of a wall-length mirror, each of us sitting in a chair, facing the mirror. We were told to stare at our face, to look into our own eyes, to take in our features, to scan our body. To look and look and look, and to really see.

All around me I heard people laughing or crying or yelling. But soon all the sounds in the room dimmed and I was only aware of my face in the mirror. Only it wasn't my face. It was my mother's. I kept blinking and looking away, not wanting to see my mother's face, not wanting to see her features in mine—her high cheekbones, her brown eyes and bushy brows, her funny smile, her fine hair. She looked like me. Feelings of revulsion welled up within me, and then revulsion turned into rage. I did not want to look like my mother. The more I allowed myself to feel my real feelings, the more shame I felt. And then in a flash I remembered a conversation with my mother that had occurred several years after my parents moved from my childhood home on Long Island. In her typically impulsive way, my mother got rid of everything she didn't want to take to the house in Vermont, without inviting "the girls" to claim our belongings. This included dolls and toys, keepsakes and schoolwork—the debris left on the shore after children move out into the world.

In high school and college I had studied sculpture. I loved the damp smell of the classroom, the quiet poses of the model, the texture and temperature of the clay. I loved molding emotions into form. I was usually surprised by what my hands chose to make. Perhaps I thought I'd fashion the clay into mermaids or horses or gods. But inevitably I'd lug home busts and figurines of girls and women—sisters, mothers, daughters. The primary images of my young life.

My favorite piece was a life-sized head I made in high school that looked strikingly like my mother. I had no intention of creating such a statue; the model in class looked nothing like her. But there was no denying it—there it was, my mother's face made out of clay. After I fired it in the kiln and mounted it on a piece of driftwood, I gave the head to my mother. She swore she loved the statue, but she put it on a low shelf in the living room behind the piano where no one could see it. And there it stayed, until my parents moved.

After the move I looked for the statue in the Vermont house.

"Where's the statue of you, Marsh? Where's that statue of your face? The one I made in high school?"

"Oh, it's no fun to look at your own face," she answered. "I sold it in the garage sale."

"But Marsh! I made it. I gave it to you. You should have asked me. Maybe I wanted it."

"Well, it was my face and I don't like looking at my face, so I got rid of it."

Now—a decade later—I was sitting in front of the mirror at the 6-Day, seeing my mother's face and hearing her say, "I don't like looking at my face." In my exhausted state, I began talking out loud to her:

"Why? Why don't you like your face?"

"No one really likes her own face," my mother's reflection said back to me.

"Why not?"

"Because it's a map of everything that's wrong with you."

"Like what? What do you think is wrong with you?"

"All the things I should have done but didn't do. All the things I did do but shouldn't have done. All my flaws. All of my mistakes. All the bad things from childhood."

"What bad things? Tell me about them."

"No, I can't. It's self-indulgent to relive the past."

"No, it's not! Talk about it! Tell me. Don't be ashamed. Then you'll see the good things too. And maybe you'll love your face."

"It's too late for me to love my face. Love YOUR face. You do that for me."

By that time I was crying. I was sitting in a chair, facing a wall of mirrors, talking to myself and weeping. A part of me knew I was making the whole thing up—my mother would never have talked to me like that. And yet a part of me knew I wasn't making it up at all.

"Marsh! Love your face," I kept saying, over and over, heart-broken that my beautiful, talented, charming mother was unable to see her true self—the face of her goodness, her uniqueness, her soul. I knew that if she would explore her perceived errors and her unhealed wounds, she would come to the shining center of herself. But she shook her head and said again, "It's too late for me. You love your face."

"It's never too late, Marsh," I cried. My heart ached for her. I closed my eyes and put my hand on my chest and sat still for a long time. When I opened my eyes again, my mother was gone and I was looking at myself. "It's never too late," I said to the girl in the mirror. I stared at my face. I saw parts of my mother, parts of my father; I saw my ancestry, my culture, my tribe, my times. I saw both love and anger in my eyes. I saw my familiar, imperfect features—nose, lips, eyebrows, chin, arranged in a way unique to me. This was my face, my heritage, my gift to either celebrate or reject.

And suddenly, I got it: This was my Baltimore. This was the way home. This was the reality I had been arguing with. My very self—all this time I had thought I was struggling to love my husband when really I was struggling to love myself. This was the argument I needed to put an end to.

The next morning, at the closing gathering of the 6-Day, we sat in a large circle. The leaders asked each of us to sum up the entire event in three words. By then, everyone knew that "three words" meant exactly that: three words. After a week of endless talking and sharing and processing, I was happy for the brevity of the exercise.

When it was my turn to say what I was taking home from the experience, I didn't hesitate.

"My mother's face," I said.

READING *ANNA KARENINA* FOR
THE THIRD TIME

MY FATHER CLAIMED TO REREAD the entire Russian novel *War and Peace* every year. I don't usually read a book a second time, but following his lead, I set out years ago to reread Tolstoy's *Anna Karenina*. I figured if my father could get through 1,500 pages of Tolstoy's *War and Peace* on an annual basis, I could reread *Anna Karenina* at least once.

The very first time I read the book was over Christmas vacation during my sophomore year of college. It had been assigned in my comparative literature class at Columbia University, where I was pretending to be a New York City intellectual but was actually spending more time marching for civil rights in Harlem or learning to meditate at a Tibetan Buddhist center way downtown.

At Christmas break, my boyfriend (who would become my first husband) and I escaped the gray and grunge of a New York City winter and sought refuge on a low-rent Caribbean island where they allowed camping. I had visions of skimming through a semester's worth of reading while lazing under a palm tree. Instead, we pitched our tent on a sunbaked, bug-infested beach and fended off skinny dogs that begged for food all day and night. There were only two places to get away from the bugs and the dogs—either in the crystal blue water just steps from where we were camping, or inside the moldy, sweltering tent.

I chose the tent. I picked up *Anna Karenina*, described by my professor as the most important book in the Western canon. Within less than an hour of our first morning on the island, I committed to Anna and the tent for the rest of the vacation. If I stayed inside, if I stuck with Anna, if I didn't abandon her, perhaps she might avert the impending tragedy that clung to every sentence, every word.

And so, as my boyfriend snorkeled, I rode through a nineteenth-century Russian winter in a horse-drawn sleigh alongside Tolstoy's cast of characters: the beautiful Anna, who risks social exile and the loss of her children for love and authenticity; her duty-bound, patriarchal husband, Karenin; Vronsky, Anna's dashing, idealistic, and narcissistic lover; and the moral compasses of the book, Levin and Kitty. I followed the long path to Anna's destruction and rooted for her even though she behaves so poorly, even though I knew she was doomed. Her tale grabbed me in my gut. It filled my young sails with hope and anger. It brought to the surface of my consciousness feelings that needed the traction of words.

When I finished the book, I was enraged. Why did it end that way? Why didn't Anna rise up against social convention? What kind of messages were women left with—that putting personal fulfillment over social duty leads to ruination and death? That when a woman deviates from her prescribed social responsibilities she's damned, yet when a man deviates from his, he is pardoned, and even envied? And why was this "the most important book in the Western canon"? I was so frustrated by the ending (and by being in a tent for a week) that on the final day of the vacation, I walked to the edge of the sea and tossed the moldy paperback book into the waves.

WHEN I READ *Anna Karenina* for the second time, I was thirty—a young mother caught in the undertow of her own doomed marriage. This time, I identified with Anna, and I read the book as a cautionary tale. I was horrified with myself. I had made a mess of my life, and if I didn't clean up my act, I wouldn't necessarily end up like Anna—(spoiler alert) under a train—but I might wreck my family. As Anna's life unraveled with every page, I vowed to piece my marriage back together. I would stop behaving like Anna; I would try to conduct my life with less drama and more dignity. Wasn't that the message Tolstoy was trying to relay? Didn't society need each one of us to hew to an agreed-upon moral code? What would happen to this world if we all just did what we wanted? If we put the shaping of our own destiny ahead of what was good for the whole?

I didn't throw the book away at the end of the second reading. I placed it in the bookshelf, and every time I passed it I felt my heart harden into a nut-sized nugget of resolve: *I will be good. I will be good. I will be good.* Of course, none of this happened. My marriage dissolved and my life became a train wreck, but unlike the unlucky Anna, I survived, and more than that, I transformed the trauma into a treasure of the utmost worth: my own self, my true goodness, my soul.

Poor, dear Anna. Everything and everyone—including she herself—conspires against her. She is unable to consummate the real love affair of the book: the love she should have felt for herself. If she could have come home to a sense of inner validation, a path toward freedom would have revealed itself to her. She could have carried her cherished children with her down that path. As she matured into her own destiny, she could have reconciled with Karenin, or stood her ground with Vronsky, or found someone else, or none of the above. It wasn't until my third reading of *Anna Karenina* that I came to understand this. I am not sure that Tolstoy would agree. He was a creature of his times, and in those times women were not assumed to be capable of taking the classic hero's journey toward selfhood.

One of my feminist icons, the mystifyingly overlooked historian Gerda Lerner, wrote about the particular challenge women have in defining and taking their own hero's journey. "Since the female experience has usually been trivialized or ignored," Lerner says, "it means overcoming the deep-seated resistance within ourselves toward accepting ourselves and our knowledge as valid. It means getting rid of the great men in our heads and substituting for them ourselves." You know that classic interview question: "What two people—dead or alive—would you most like to be seated between at a dinner party?" No one has asked me that yet, but if any one ever does, I'll answer, "Gerda Lerner and Leo Tolstoy." I'd ask them to come up with an alternate ending to *Anna Karenina*, after Anna has overcome her deep-seated resistance toward her own self-acceptance and validation. After she's replaced all the great men in her head with herself.

For the past couple of months, on my long drives to and from Maggie's house and back and forth to the hospital, I have been reading *Anna Karenina* for a third time courtesy of an audio version read by a man with a voice I imagine to be Tolstoy's. Once again I lose myself in the Russian winter, even as the greening hills of Vermont flash by the car's windows. I am now older than Tolstoy was when he wrote *Anna Karenina*. I think I finally understand the book. Now I am able to empathize with all of the characters— Anna, Karenin, Vronsky, Kitty, Levin, all of them. Each plays a role in the story, just like each one of us plays a role in our own family system and social system. Liberation from those roles is hard-won. And only the greatest storyteller is able to express the real drama of a human life, which is the arduous journey toward claiming one's authentic destiny. All of the characters in *Anna Karenina* in their own way attempt that journey. But only one consciously casts off the roles he was expected to assume, and eventually lives by the edicts of his soul. That character—Levin—is said to be Tolstoy himself.

To be the Levin of your own story, to risk everything for the marrow of the soul, to lay claim to your Genius or your Juno—is this not at the core of every great story, from Jonah in the whale, to Joan of Arc, to Levin and Anna, to you and me?

Today, as I near Maggie's house, the audio book comes to an end. The man with the Russian accent reads the last few paragraphs. Levin stands on the balcony of his home and looks up into the heavens and finally understands that the soul at the core of his life is good, that he is goodness itself, and that his real job in life is to bring that goodness out into the world.

Later on today, Maggie and I will drive to the hospital where I will begin the process of the bone marrow harvest, receiving the first shot to stimulate stem cell production. After that, we'll meet with the therapist. We will dig for our goodness and harvest the marrow of ourselves for each other.

Part Four

❧

THE TRANSPLANT

Out beyond ideas of wrongdoing and rightdoing,
there is a field. I'll meet you there.
When the soul lies down in that grass,
the world is too full to talk about.
Ideas, language, even the phrase "each other"
doesn't make any sense.

—RUMI

THE FIELD

THE THERAPIST WE HAVE CHOSEN comes recommended by Maggie herself. Which is all the endorsement I need. I call him and set up an appointment. Because suddenly everything is happening at once. The medical team wants to proceed quickly. Maggie is receiving a new type of chemotherapy, and as soon as the treatments are finished and her tests come back cancer-free, she must receive the transplant. The doctors can't afford to leave the window open for the tiniest sliver of time. Even a crack, and the cancer can come back. They need my stem cells. I have rushed through and passed all my tests. I am cleared to proceed with the harvest. Step one—the first injection of a drug that encourages stem cell growth—will occur on the morning of the day we are scheduled to see the therapist.

Some people are naturally inclined to ask for help before their lives fall apart. But most of us drag ourselves (or we're dragged) to the doctor or the healer or the gym or the therapist only when we're desperate. Before Maggie was first diagnosed with lymphoma, our older sister, Katy, practically handcuffed Maggie and delivered her into the hands of a therapist. Maggie had backed herself into an untenable situation—finally finding enough courage to take a stand in her marriage, but too stuck and scared to make a move. Maggie approached therapy as a short-term fix, as opposed to a way of changing long-held beliefs and habits. The therapist helped her build a little boat to carry her safely out of the marriage, and that was enough for her. She landed on the shore and went her own way.

I know it breaks some unwritten law to choose a therapist who has previously worked with only one member of a duo, but I don't care. We are not your ordinary duo. And this is not an ordinary situation. The urgency of the transplant has made us as giddy as skydivers. We are going to jump out of the plane without having answers to some important questions. Questions like: How can one three-hour session possibly get to the core of a lifelong relationship? What exactly are we expecting the outcome to be? What if it doesn't work? What if it makes things worse? Is this guy up to the task? I don't know, but I figure if he's brave enough to jump out of a plane with two sisters strapped to his back, I am going to trust that he can land us in a clearing, in that field the poet Rumi talks about.

"Out beyond ideas of wrongdoing and rightdoing, there is a field," Rumi writes. "I'll meet you there." That was the way I described to Maggie what I hoped we might achieve with the therapist. "I want to meet you in a field of love," I told her. "And maybe that will encourage our cells to do the same." The lines from Rumi cinched the deal, and we quickly set a date for the session to coincide with the start of the marrow harvest.

On this spring day I set out to Maggie's house as the sun is rising. The trees are leafing out, waving their bright green flags in the morning light. Each hour of driving north sets spring back a week. When I get to Maggie's, it's chilly and the trees have barely a halo of green. I leave the car idling and run into her house to get her. We have two important things on our agenda today: First stop is the hospital, where I will receive an injection of Neupogen. After that we'll head to the therapy session.

Maggie wants to drive. "You're the invalid today, Liz," she says, thrilled to be in the driver's seat with me as the designated patient for a change. My Neupogen shot is the first of five I will receive as an outpatient over the next five days. It's administered in the same chemotherapy suite that Maggie has visited so many times. I watch her body tense as we walk down the familiar hospital halls. Only this time, it's my body that will be poked and shot up with a chemical substance. And this time, I'm the one the nurse asks the questions I've witnessed Maggie answer over and over: "Date of birth?" "Are you aware of the risks involved in this procedure?" "Allergies to any medications?" And then the shot, and it's all over until tomorrow. We head back to the parking lot. Maggie takes the wheel again and I lean back in the passenger seat.

As we get closer to the town where the therapist has his office, Maggie says, "Tell me again why we're doing this?" She says she doesn't really subscribe to the whole notion of self-examination. Whereas Socrates believed "the unexamined life is not worth living," Maggie thinks examining one's life is an expensive and self-indulgent waste of time.

"But didn't the therapist help you when your marriage was in such turmoil?"

"Yeah, he did," Maggie concedes. "He helped me a lot."

"How? How did he help you?"

"I guess he helped me figure out what I really wanted. He helped me see it was OK to . . . to . . . want something for myself," she mumbles, barely able to say the words. "To want what was true . . . for me."

"Well, that would be an important thing this time around too," I say. "To know what you want; to say what you know is true; to say it loud enough for me to hear, and my cells to hear, and your cells to hear."

"I know," Maggie says. "That's why I'm doing it. But I don't really like spending time examining my life. Especially now. I'd rather just be living it."

I, on the other hand, have spent a lot of time examining my own life and everyone else's too. I can't imagine taking this confusing human journey on automatic pilot. I need help! It's quite obvious we all need help—parents, children, workers, bosses, Congress, countries. How about just admitting that we have no idea how to get along, how to communicate, how to heal from the past and move on into a better future? How about requiring some rudimentary training in self-examination around the same time that people are required to take algebra or French or driver's education? There's an enormous vault of wisdom to draw from. The modern psychotherapeutic version is just one way of self-examining. The study and the healing of one's motivations and desires and behaviors dates back to the ancient philosophers—the Taoists in China and the yogis in India, the Egyptians and the Persians and the Greeks—and to prehistory, to the indigenous cultures whose shamans and witches were the world's first therapists.

In all of these settings—East and West, North and South, sacred and secular, ancient and current—the best of the philosophers and witch doctors and shrinks have always been what shamanic cultures call "wounded healers." Wounded healers are comfortable with people in dark and troubled places because they too have been there and have found their way out. They may not have perfected the human experience, and they may be a little strange from frequent sojourns into the underworld, but they do have eyes that can see in the dark, and faith in the return of the light.

So it doesn't bother me when Maggie and I climb the rickety narrow stairs to the second floor of the old building in an old town in Vermont and enter the eccentric office of the therapist. The waiting room is a tad unusual—just a landing with nowhere to sit. So we stand there, waiting. I look at Maggie. She is mostly bald and alarmingly thin. She looks at me. I am pale and woozy from the Neupogen shot. We start to laugh, and then we become uncontrollably hysterical. We've done this throughout our lives in a variety of inappropriate settings, including our mother's choral concerts, stores and theaters, weddings and funerals. Just one look at each other can set us off, and it's still dangerous to sit next to each other during public events.

The door opens and the therapist finds us doubled over in laughter. It doesn't seem to faze him. He leads us into his office. He looks less like a doctor and more like a cross between an aging rock star and a court jester, with long silver hair, a short silver beard, rumpled pants, and a T-shirt. There's a goofiness about him that matches the decor of the large room. A collection of teddy bears and other tchotchkes adorn the shelves and tabletops, while degrees and state licensing certificates hang crookedly on the walls. There's a refrigerator and a hot plate in one corner, and filing cabinets and storage boxes pushed into another. Three mismatched couches that one might find in a college dorm are lined up against a wall, and a sagging chair is set facing the couches. The room smells like pickles—slightly sour, slightly sweet.

The therapist motions for us to sit somewhere on the row of couches. Maggie and I perch next to each other on the middle couch, like two birds on a long wire. The therapist takes his place in the sagging chair. He stares at us for a while. Then he lays out a loose plan for our three-hour session, stopping every few sentences to ask if we are OK with it. We bob our heads, two birds on the wire. Every now and then we giggle and stop ourselves from all-out hysteria. He ends the introduction with "I will be making myself tea and maybe a snack during our time together. And maybe feeding my dog." He motions to a furry heap in the corner, next to the filing cabinets. As if on cue, the dog wags his tail.

I am glad Maggie already knew what she was getting herself into; otherwise I would be distracted, worrying about her reaction to the room, to the dog, to the smell of pickles. But since she seems at ease, I am too. I have met plenty of other nonconformists in the healing professions. My line of work would have dried up a long time ago if the ability to help or heal required pressed pants and a neat office. And so here we are, two sisters sitting across from a modern-day shaman, about to jump out of a plane. My heart is pounding. This surprises me. Intimacy is always an exposure; truth telling can be downright scary, but I hadn't realized I was this scared. Suddenly it feels more daunting to drill deep into my relationship with my sister than to have my bone marrow extracted. I take Maggie's hand and squeeze it. She squeezes back.

The therapist asks what each of us wants to get out of the session. I fish in my purse and find the questions we came up with when we first decided to have the therapy session. I hand them to the therapist and wait for him to finish reading. Then I explain how I have just begun the process of the stem cell harvest. I describe the pitfalls and dangers of the transplant. There's the chance I won't produce enough cells, and even if I do, there's the possibility of attack and rejection once the cells are transplanted. I tell the therapist I want to do whatever I can to encourage my cells to proliferate and then to willingly separate from my body and become one with Maggie's. I want to check out if there is anything within me—in my thoughts and my feelings and my memories and my body, all the way down to the marrow of my bones, to my tiniest stem cells—that might interfere with the success of the transplant. And if there is, I want to examine it, hold it to the light, and let it go.

Maggie says her reason for being at the session is pretty simple. She wants to live; she wants the transplant to work; she doesn't want to reject my cells or to let my cells get too pushy once they are in her. She admits she has a tendency to judge and reject me and, at the same time, to let herself get pushed around by me. But now she wants us to be a team, to become Maggie-Liz, to work together to save her life. She says she is ready to look at whatever we need to look at in order to be that team.

"What's that poem, Liz?" she asks me. "That Rumi poem about the field?"

" 'Out beyond ideas of wrongdoing and rightdoing, there is a field. I'll meet you there.' "

"Yeah, that's what I want the session to be about. I want us to meet in that field—out beyond wrongdoing and rightdoing," Maggie says. She starts to cry. She puts her hands over her face, and the tension of the past weeks and months gather like rain clouds behind her hands and she weeps. I put my arms around her. I gaze at the therapist. Now he looks like Saint Francis, his eyes brimming with empathy, a halo of late-afternoon light streaming in from the window behind his head.

"So," he says. "Let's start at the beginning."

He leads us back to when we were little girls. We bring up incidents and images from different eras of our childhood—wrongdoings and rightdoings. It's like flipping through my mother's picture albums, providing text to go along with the photos. I've been in couples counseling before. But this feels different. The more we talk, the more stories we share, the more I feel some magical kind of lubricant easing the gears of our communication. Instead of get-

ting stuck in the past—instead of using the stories as implements of
blame or self-recrimination—we move quickly through the years.
I don't know if it's the life-or-death nature of what brings us here,
or the skill of the therapist, or help from unseen forces, but it's as if
we are on a swiftly moving river, flowing fast into the field beyond
wrongdoing and rightdoing.

We remember the pleasure we took in being sisters—the fun,
the adventures, the hysterical laughter, the cocoon of belonging.
And we dredge up stories of rejection or attack. I pat my thigh
bones and tell the stem cells to pay attention—to the love and to
the conflict. Maggie's stories of rejection and attack focus on being
one of the insignificant younger girls—discounted and invalidated
by the older sisters, "the runt of the litter," as she says. In my stories, I am misunderstood and judged by all the sisters, accused of
being self-important and confrontational—"the princess" or "the
Big Shit," as I've heard myself described (or imagined being called
behind my back).

The therapist, sitting across from us in the sagging chair, keeps
us on track. He encourages us to listen to the other without defensiveness and to tell the truth even if it's hard to bring the stories out
of the mute and secret places. We scroll through the years: neighborhood games, long car rides, family gatherings, school projects,
shared birthday parties, pulling hair, stealing toys, triangulating
with the other sisters, all the way up to high school. I am surprised
by some of Maggie's stories; she is surprised by mine. I find myself
wanting to interrupt her, to set her straight. I see her wanting to
interrupt my stories too. But the therapist holds up his hand. "Just
listen," he says.

So I listen. Underneath every story of rejection or attack, I begin
to hear a common tune, the shadow theme song of our relationship:

I am too much; Maggie is not enough. After a while, the therapist tells Maggie to face me and ask me something she's always wanted to ask.

"Why did you always have to stand up to Dad?" she says with uncharacteristic boldness. "Why couldn't you just let him run the show without always having to confront him? The conflict scared me. And it made me mad at you." She says this without attack. I can tell that she only wants to understand and be understood. This allows me to answer truthfully.

"I always felt like I was doing the dirty work for everyone in the family," I say. "Meanwhile, you pretended everything was OK, and then you snuck around and did what you wanted anyway. What's the point of that? Why not confront things head-on? I thought I was standing up to Dad for all of us."

"Well, no one asked you to," Maggie says.

"You have a point," I admit.

"But so do you, Liz," Maggie says. "You have a point too. I secretly admired you for confronting things head-on. I was glad someone was standing up to him. I didn't know where you got the courage to say what you thought, to ask for what you wanted. It impressed me, and it frightened me. Both."

"I should have toned it down," I say. "I should have talked to you! We could have been a team. We could have been Maggie-Liz back then. I'm sorry I barged forward without including you."

"I'm sorry I was such a chicken," Maggie says. "I'm not a fighter. You are. One's not right or wrong. It was just you being you. Me being me. I see that now."

I see it too. I close my eyes and see everyone in the family—all the girls and our parents, all of us just trying to be ourselves in a sea of selves. Bumping up against each other, without the wherewithal to talk things over, to meld and mend, to work things out as a whole.

"And what about high school?" I hear Maggie asking me.

I peel back the cobwebs of my memory and go back to a time that I have tried to forget—those awkward, lonely high school years. But I can't place Maggie in any of the tableaus, even though we were at the same school, even though we waited together for the same school bus, knew the same kids, did the same crazy things at the same parties. "I don't really remember you in high school," I say.

"Exactly," Maggie snorts. "You basically ignored me."

I know she's right. High school had felt like a struggle for survival. Besides the usual angst of being a teenager, it seemed the whole world was in free fall. Every year another national figure was assassinated, another boy I knew shipped off to Vietnam, and racial tensions were high. There were marches and strikes, riots and lockdowns in the school. And at home, the year I graduated, a crazed neighborhood man broke into our house on Long Island through the window of our youngest sister's bedroom. She awoke to find a man with a stocking on his head leaning over her bed. My father heard her screams and frightened the intruder out of the house, but my parents were so shaken that within a couple of months they had packed up and moved full-time to Vermont.

I try to place Maggie in the halls of our high school, at events, on the bus, anywhere. "I'm sorry," I say to her. "It's as if you weren't even there."

"Your loss." She laughs. "But it was always like that. I always wasn't there. You were the big sister, the one Marsh favored, the smarter one, the one going places. I never measured up."

"Really? That's how you saw me? That's not how I see it. That's your story of how it was, but—"

The therapist interrupts me. "Just listen to what Maggie says. Take her word for it. She's telling you how she felt."

I look at Maggie and she looks back at me, her big brown eyes shining with a strong and steady light.

"I didn't know," I say. "I never bothered to know. I'm sorry."

"I'm sorry too," Maggie says. "I spent the next years paying you back." Which is also true. All during the years when we were in college, and first getting married, and raising our children, we spent time together—some of it wonderful time—but when I tried to get close, Maggie rebuffed me. Now I tell her how much I had wanted to be in her life, how confused I was every time I visited and she kept herself shielded, unwilling to share herself with me.

"I so much wanted to be your friend, Maggie," I cry, telling her for the first time a deep hurt I have carried around with me. "I always wanted more of you than you wanted to give."

My tears shock her. She says she knew she had kept me at arm's length, but she had no idea I even cared. "You were so strong, Liz," she says to me. "You were living this big life out in the world. I thought you were looking down on me, and my funky log house at the end of a dirt road, and my little job, and my little family. I was just a fake artist and a fake doctor, and you were the real thing. I never in a million years imagined anything I did would have an effect on you."

I shake my head. "That's crazy," I say. "You made that whole story up!" I suddenly feel the great loss of those years. And the great irony of our relationship. "Maggie, I never thought of your life as little, or you as a fake anything. Quite the opposite! Your house, your family, your job, your art: to me all of that was the real deal. I was the one living the counterfeit life. Your rejection of me just confirmed something I feared was true. That I had messed up my life; that I was too intense; that I was unlovable because I was just too damn much. And I should be more like you—unassuming, restrained, down-to-earth."

"That's pretty crazy too," Maggie says. "The very things I secretly admired in you—your courage and strength and self-confidence—you were ashamed of around me. And meanwhile, back at the ranch, I was ashamed of the things you admired in me. How sad is that?"

"Very sad," I concur. "Because all I ever wanted from you was you. Not what you did or where you lived or anything like that. Just you. Because you're my sister, because I love you, because who you are is enough." I take Maggie's hand. "Do you believe that?"

"I'm trying to. I want to." She looks at me. "Do you believe that you are enough? Do you believe that you are who you are, and that's all I want from you?"

"I'm trying to," I answer.

"Is there a moral to this story?" the therapist asks.

Maggie says, "Yeah. We're all a mess, but we're all enough. That's the moral to this story."

We sit quietly. For several minutes no one says a thing. All we can hear is a slight hum of the little refrigerator and the random thumping of the dog's tail. The room begins to fill with a feeling, almost a presence.

Maggie says, "Do you feel that? I think we're in the field. The field beyond wrongdoing and rightdoing." She turns to me: "Liz, all these years I had no idea you were hurt. In my mind, you were the strong one. I was struggling with things I thought you had already figured out. I was ashamed of what was going on in my life."

"Like what? I never knew anything except what I saw. And

what I saw looked pretty perfect. An intact family living the good life. I was divorced. I was a single mother. For a few years I dragged the kids from place to place. But you were doing everything right. You never talked to me about any problems. What were you ashamed of?"

Maggie just shrugs.

"Do you want to talk about that, Maggie?" the therapist asks.

"Not really. It's not worth going into now. It's the past. Let's just say my life was far from perfect, and I wanted it to look perfect, and if I let you in too close back then, I knew you'd want to talk to me about my marriage. And he knew that too," she says, referring to her ex-husband. "He thought you were a bad influence. So it was uncomfortable when you visited me, Liz. I tried to smooth it all over, but I guess you felt it anyway—that push-pull. I wanted to be your friend, but I had to keep you away. And I can't just blame him. I made you wrong so my life would be right. I made you the bad one—you were living out in the world, you had money, you were running a business, you had bought into the system. All of those things were 'wrongdoings' in our rule book. Then you got divorced and became a single parent. Now I really was the good one. The perfect one! I had to see it that way. Black-and-white. If I let any gray in, my whole world would crumble. I didn't know that's what I was doing then. But now I do. And I'm sorry. And I'm glad to be in the field now. Here, with you."

As promised, the therapist gets up to make himself a snack. The dog waddles over to see what's going on. The therapist stirs a small pot of soup on the hot plate and gives the dog a treat. Maggie and I sit close to each other on the couch, but really, we're in a field that is filling with light.

"I wonder what would have happened if we had talked to each

other like this back in the day. Back when we were young mothers, or even before that?" I say to Maggie. "What if we had talked like this sitting on the school bus?"

"We would have been best friends, that's what," Maggie says. "We would have seen each other for who we are. We would have helped each other. We would have had much more fun. And do you know what else we would have been?"

"No, what?" I ask.

"The perfect match! We wasted a lot of time figuring that out—that you don't have to be perfect to be a perfect match. It's kind of laughable."

"You don't have to be perfect to be a perfect match," I repeat. "I like that. And you're right. We wasted a lot of time figuring this out. It's like we were acting from a script we were given when we were kids, and then we kept saying the lines for fifty years without ever checking if they made sense."

The therapist returns to his seat. He looks out the window at the darkening sky and then at his watch. "Liz, if you put down that script and speak from your heart, who do you think Maggie is? Who is she to you? Who was sitting on that school bus? What have you always loved about her? Look at her and tell her what you see."

I look at Maggie and say what I see: "Maggie is a hummingbird. Dancing with life. Full of color and energy and mischief. She's life itself," I tell the therapist.

"Turn to Maggie and tell her that. Tell her what you love about her."

I say to Maggie, "Girl, you might be the most lovable person in the whole wide world. You're like the flowers you pick and press—everyone wants to take you home, to make you theirs. You're bright and beautiful and wild. You're funny and capable and curious about everything. You take care of your patients, your kids, your friends. You cook and bake and garden and make incredible art. You never stop moving, giving, caring for people, children, animals, the earth . . . you take care of everyone except yourself! If you saw yourself the way everyone else sees you—the way I see you—you would bow down to yourself, you would be so kind and gentle to yourself, you would—"

Maggie hits me in the arm. "OK, I get it. That's all I can take. Can I say who I think Liz is? What I love about her?"

"Sure," says the therapist. "Tell her."

"Liz! You *are* the Big Shit. But that's a compliment. Don't you see? All my life I have operated with a timid nature, but you haven't. And it's inspiring to me, and it always has been, contrary to what you think. You're not too much. You're yourself! You're not perfect—nobody is perfect. Certainly not me. But if you could see yourself like I see you, wow. I see you walk tall, stride into a room, be gracious and loving yet firm. You don't apologize for just being your big-ass self. It doesn't matter where you are—talking to my doctors at the hospital, or talking on national TV, for God's sake. I would love to muster that kind of inner strength. I'm just a tiny runt of the litter who at this late stage in life is finally trying to walk upright."

"So you think I have a big ass?" I say. We both laugh. We need to laugh. The field is getting pretty gooey. And it's getting late. I am beginning to feel the flu-like effects of the Neupogen shot; Maggie looks as if she might keel over at any moment. It's almost six p.m. We have been in the field for three hours.

The therapist tells us to close our eyes and bring our attention to our bodies, to our cells, and to the harvest and the transplant.

"Based on what you and Maggie have discovered today," he says, "what do you want to tell your cells, Liz, as you go into the harvest process?"

I keep my eyes closed and let that question penetrate my bones. I put one hand on my hip bone, where I feel the pressure of the stem cell growth. I put my other hand on my heart because I feel movement there too as the old stories release and the truth rises to the top. Deep in the marrow of the bones the stem cells quiver with pure and generous intentions. And touching my chest, I feel the goodness and purity of my heart's intentions; I remember who I am in the marrow of my soul. The waters of forgiveness wash over me—forgiveness toward myself, forgiveness toward Maggie. I vow for the thousandth time in my life to be true to myself and to love others for whom they really are—all of us flawed miracles, each of us straining to follow the trail left in the woods by our Juno, our Genius.

"Tell Maggie what you are seeing," the therapist says, as if reading my thoughts.

"I see who we really are, Maggie. And we're good. And we're strong. And we're enough. And we can do this. We can do this transplant. We've already started."

"What do you see, Maggie?" the therapist asks.

"I see love," Maggie says. "That's all that's left. That's all that matters. I see that we are deeply connected in love and light. What more could I want?"

"Yeah," I say. "All those stories were just covering the truth. And the truth is I love you." Even those words don't express the huge, abiding sense of love that has been filling the room, lubricating our ability to let go of the past and arrive, finally, in the safe harbor of each other's hearts. As if sticks and gunk had been damming a river, and now the water pours into the space between us, around us, within us. And it's love. And it's real. It's the only thing that ever has been real.

Now the therapist asks me to give my stem cells some direction—a prayer, or marching orders, or whatever I want to call it. I close my eyes again, and I see millions of cells waiting to fulfill their purpose. I sit up tall. I feel like one of those maple trees Maggie loves so much. A prayer appears fully formed, simple and true. I say it out loud: *"May my cells flow like maple sap on a warm spring morning. May they give you sweet life, Maggie. May they keep you with us for many years to come."*

"Maggie?" the therapist asks. "Do you have a prayer for the transplant?"

"It's not a prayer. I don't do prayers," Maggie says. "It's more like a wedding vow. The wedding of Maggie-Liz. *I vow to make my body the field beyond wrongdoing and rightdoing so that your cells know they are home.*"

The therapist rereads the questions I had given him at the start of the session.

"So, let's see if there's anything left for us to do here." He reads the paper aloud:

Here are things I have done that may have hurt you. Will you
  forgive me?
Here are ways I have felt hurt by you. Can I safely tell you my
  truth?
Can I be myself with you?
Will you accept me?

Will you love me?

Will you make a place for me, all the way down to your marrow?

"Check, check, check," Maggie says.

"Amen, sisters of the revolution," I add.

---

field notes • may 31

liz is 2 years older than i am. we of the 4 sisters are the closest in age, but my memories are of constant fighting as children, unfairly favorable treatment of her by my mother, and even though we shared similar experiences in highschool and college (we were sisters of the revolution: sex, drugs and rock n roll) and then both got married and had babies around the same time, she went a spiritual route and i went back to the land. we grew farther apart than we were as kids. i lived in rural poverty and she didn't. i felt judged for not being spiritual, even though i smirked at her lifestyle. little did i know that she felt judged by me and wanted desperately to be my friend. and then she did the absolute worst thing my mother's daughter could do; she got divorced. now her badness was confirmed. and i could still be the good girl. that was the story. but today we changed it. liz asked me pre transplant if i would go with her to a therapist to clear away any obstacles that could impede the acceptance of her stem cells. i liked that idea. i loved it. and so today we went to a therapist and met with him for several hours. what went on in that room will get covered in chemobrain cobwebs soon, so i want to write it down and remember it forever. it showed me things about myself, and things about liz, and rearranged the furniture of our relationship. it cemented our deepest love for each other, and strengthened our commitment to move forward with mutual love and support.

TRUTH-ACHES

THAT NIGHT, I LIE IN bed in Maggie and Oliver's guest room. They have gone to sleep. I toss around in the dark, thinking about the therapy session, feeling an ache in my bones as the stem cell production accelerates. I don't know if I'm restless because I'm thinking about the stories we unearthed in the session or because my cells are pushing their way out of my bones. The processes seem similar: stimulating growth even if it's painful, mining the deep and hidden places for healing, offering ourselves to each other as gifts of love.

The therapy session today was unlike any I've experienced before. We dug up the past, kept what we loved, and dropped what we didn't. Just like that. It was more like what people who have had near-death experiences report—where, in the process of dying, one's past is vividly reexperienced from a higher perspective, and suddenly the whole meaning and purpose of a lifetime is revealed.

For years after the publication of my second book, *Broken Open*, I led workshops for people who were going through difficult times of change and loss. One of the exercises I concocted was a simulated experience of dying. I led this exercise many times—for small and large groups—sometimes ten people, sometimes three hundred. All sorts of people took the workshop: those suffering from trauma or illness and those dealing with the mundane concerns of daily life, including the terminal condition of being human. I'd have everyone spread out around the room and lie down. I'd turn the lights down and the music on, and lead the group in an hour-long death meditation.

First we'd imagine the reason and time and place of death, then we'd relax our hold on the body and personality, and then we'd look back over the events and people and lessons gleaned over a lifetime. And finally, we would move into whatever concept we have of an afterlife (including no concept at all). At the end of the experience I'd guide people back into the body, back into life. We'd sit up, return to our chairs, and write a letter to ourselves, with instructions on how to live from now on.

Before entering into the death meditation, I would always ask if anyone in the room had had a clinical near-death experience where, due to an accident or heart attack or other trauma, they were pronounced dead but were later revived. And almost always a few people in the group would raise their hands and describe the experience. The stories were eerily similar—not only in the classic details of the tunnel, and the bright light, and the sense of swimming in a sea of unconditional love, but also in the way their perspectives changed afterwards. They came back from the other world wanting to release past grudges and wounds because they had seen the reason behind events in their lives. They understood now that everything could be used as grist for the mill of growth and gratitude, and that the only purpose of life is to shine the light you were given.

All sorts of people reported this—the people you'd imagine, like the woman wearing a purple dress and a crystal necklace, or the minister who described seeing Jesus on the other side. But more often than not, I would be surprised by the sorts of people who recounted near-death experiences: a New York City cop; a corporate lawyer; a cynical hipster who had never believed in anything until he had a brain aneurysm, was pronounced dead, but came back to life changed forever. All those who had a near-death experience reported the same change: the commitment not to waste their lives in complaint or regret, but rather to approach each day, every endeavor, and all their relationships with a fearless and faithful attitude. On the other side, these people had encountered their own soul, had seen its goodness and its purpose, and returned wanting to speak its truth.

At the end of the death meditation in my classes, many people also reported a change of perspective and a desire to live with less fear and more gratitude. An oft-repeated insight was how unnecessary and harmful it was to hold on to grudges. Many people left the class planning to clean up their relationships, to tell some unexpressed truths, to sow the seeds of forgiveness and peace.

Back when I first had the idea to clean up my relationship with Maggie for the sake of the transplant, I began noticing how other relationships of mine could also use some dusting off. I'd be with someone at work or home, and just below the surface I'd sense truths clamoring for attention. And rising to meet the clamoring were some questions: Do I have to clear up everything with everyone? That could become a full-time job. What issues are better left unexpressed? Is it always worth it to risk going deeper?

Tonight, lying in bed, feeling the ache in my bones, I think about other people in my life—my husband, my kids, my other two sisters. As the night goes on, the aching pressure in my bones intensifies. The hospital has given me prescription painkillers, but I don't reach for them. I want to feel what is happening. I want to pay attention to the bone aches, as if they are messages from the stem cells as they mobilize and prepare for action. I don't want my fear of pain to shut down the cells' productivity.

And I want to pay attention to other feelings too—to what the Canadian author Jeff Brown calls "truth-aches." Not toothaches, although a truth-ache sometimes feels like a toothache—deep and insistent and problematic if not dealt with. Maggie and I told our truth-aches today. I want to feel them and remember them and consecrate them to real change within myself. I want to feel and listen to other truth-aches so I can get down to what matters most with the people in my life.

William James wrote, "We are like islands in the sea, separate on the surface but connected in the deep." This is the change I most want to activate—to relate less to the surface of the people in my life and more to the depth of our connection. When that connection is hidden under layers of petty annoyances and knee-jerk reactivity, or when my sense of unworthiness and shame makes me an island unto myself, I want to dive deeper. I want to take a risk and break the spell of separation. And if I am met with rejection—if the other is unwilling to meet me in the deep—still, I will emerge having tried. Maggie and I left our separate islands today. The life-and-death necessity of our situation gave us the courage to do what we could have done all along: to hold hands, take the plunge, and swim through deep water to the other shore.

On the other shore we discovered a few things worth remembering. The first is that our stories are outdated—rote and partial versions of the complex humans we have become, and always were. In the society of our sisterhood, in the roles we fulfilled in the family system, we never got to enjoy the fullness of each other's beings, the roundness of our natures, the depth of our souls. We diminished each other, not deliberately, not even consciously, but because we had never turned and faced each other as we had done today; we had never interrupted the storytelling; we had upheld the one-dimensional roles we had assumed on the family stage. And then, when we joined the larger human stage, we dragged those roles with us and adapted them at school, and at work, and with friends and intimates. And like most other people, raised in other human families, we felt the diminishment as a vague pain, the loss of something we barely remembered—the phantom limbs of our soul.

On the other shore we also discovered that we had taken things personally that weren't even about us; that we had judged ourselves more harshly than the other judged us. We discovered that just because we're imperfect doesn't mean we are unlovable. In fact, by admitting to each other our human imperfections, lo and behold, we became the perfect match. We became Maggie-Liz.

And the biggest discovery of all was this: There is a field; it is made of love; it is our home. *I'll meet you there.*

THE HARVEST

OVER THE NEXT FOUR DAYS Maggie and I make a daily trip to the hospital for my injections. And then we return to her house where we lounge around—Maggie nauseated and tired from chemo, me achy and tired from the Neupogen shots. We rest in the window seat overlooking the field. We watch the bluebirds scratch at the ground and carry bits of straw and twigs to the nesting boxes that Maggie and Oliver have placed where the field meets the forest. The birds are busy; we're not. I know this drives Maggie crazy. I know this because we were raised in the same boot camp, where lying around in the middle of the day was heretical. Maggie is itching to get out into the garden; it's hard for her to witness the industriousness of the birds and not join them in their spring ritual. But the doctors have forbidden her from digging in the dirt. We'll see how long she obeys their orders.

With each Neupogen shot, the ache in my bones travels deeper, until I experience it not so much as pain but more like an echo from an unexplored cave where the body and emotions are one. Sometimes I have to go into the guest room and close the door and cry, unable to determine if it's heartbreak or bone ache that is causing the tears. The amount of love and protection I am feeling for my sister is overwhelming. My mind knows that the bone marrow transplant may not work, that the cancer may come back, that Maggie may die sooner rather than later, but my heart and bones have other ideas. They are attached to the outcome with a fierceness I have only felt before as a mother.

On the last night before the harvest, I can't sleep at all. I turn on the light and read until dawn. I watch the sun rise over the Green Mountains. The light settles in the valley and illuminates the fields outside the window. In a few hours I'll drive to the hospital and begin the harvest. Thinking about it, I'm reminded of a verse by the ancient Japanese poet Fujiwara no Teika:

> *From the beginning*
> *I knew meeting could only*
> *End in parting, yet*
> *I ignored the coming dawn*
> *And I gave myself to you.*

Teika wrote those lines about two star-crossed lovers who ignore the inevitable parting for a taste of love. This morning, I recite the poem for my stem cells so they might give themselves fully to Maggie, come what may. And isn't this what all of us must do? Give ourselves to each other, even though we know one day we must part? Give ourselves to this life, even though we know it will end? This is the paradox at the heart of being human. Nothing stays the same; everything will change. And yet the love we long to feel, and the love we were born to give, can only be ours if we abandon ourselves to each moment, each breath, each other. If we wait for the perfect time, the perfect person, the perfected self, we'll stay frozen in an idea of love. But if we fearlessly engage with the life spread out before us, we will be rewarded with a heart that can hold it all—happiness and messiness, clarity and confusion, love and loss.

Now the sun is up. I leave the house before Maggie and Oliver awaken. I back my car out of the driveway and onto the muddy dirt road. I wind around the now familiar back roads that lead to the highway, and then I speed north to the hospital. When I walk into the main entrance of the vast Dartmouth Medical Center, my husband and one of my sons are waiting for me. They've come to sit with me over the many hours and multiple days it may take to collect the millions of stem cells required for the transplant. I can feel the cells spilling into my bloodstream, raring to go; my bones might just explode on their own if I'm not hooked up to the machine soon. My son has flown in from California to be with me; my husband and he have driven up from New York early this morning. Seeing them—two refugees from my everyday life—shocks me out of my typical "I'm brave enough to do this on my own" stance, and I break down and cry in their arms.

Dartmouth Medical Center is a beautiful hospital, with huge windows in every patient's room, gardens and terraces, and an airy inner solarium where a piano player fills the halls with classical music. But for some reason, the cell collection happens in the basement—in a cold, cement-floored room with no windows. Fortunately, my overprepared husband has brought me a sweater, shawl, and even a down vest. He's famous for this. We make fun of him for carting around extra raincoats, boots, water bottles, and warm clothing regardless of the season. We also make shameless use of his forethought, "borrowing" extra hats or gloves or whatever else we secretly rely on him for packing.

The transplant team greets us in the apheresis room with the kind of cheerful enthusiasm rarely experienced in a hospital. Maybe it's like this up in the maternity ward, but after spending the year with Maggie in the cancer wing, I'm used to distraught

the first time since we arrived at the hospital—maybe for the first time since I started the Neupogen shots; maybe for the first time since receiving the phone call from the transplant coordinator in the Miami airport. It's finally happening—my perfectly matched cells are being collected. I'm glad there's been enough time and enough talk between that phone call and this harvest—time for Maggie and me to revise what "perfectly matched" means to us. I close my eyes and encourage the stem cells to come on out. *"May my cells flow like maple sap on a warm spring morning,"* I say out loud, remembering the prayer from the therapy session. My son joins in. Soon my husband does too, and then Nurse Brian: *"May these cells flow like maple sap on a warm spring morning,"* we all repeat.

It's critical that the patient does not move her hands and arms during apheresis. And so, for however long it takes, Nurse Brian will flank my side—scratching an itch on my face, holding the bedpan when I pee, giving me water to drink, checking the flow of blood in the tubes, and interpreting the beeps and lights of the machine. My husband and son talk to me, talk to each other, talk to Brian, but soon I lie back and close my eyes, and visualize the activity in my bone marrow as the stem cells reproduce and push their way into the bloodstream. I think of how we go about our daily life, unaware of the dazzling feats occurring right beneath the skin. Will I remember this when the drama of the transplant is over? Will I remember to be awestruck by the human body, by the beautifully choreographed dance of the stem cells in the marrow of the bones? I inhale, and my lungs fill with air. The lungs filter out oxygen and send it to my heart. My heart pumps oxygenated blood to every part of my body. I exhale, and what my body cannot use is sent back into the atmosphere. Who thought this miracle up?

I awake from my reverie when a team of residents enters the

apheresis room to observe. They stand around me, paying more attention to the other actor in the drama: the machine. It has begun separating the stem cells from the blood. I listen to the doctor explain to the residents how to "read" the blood as the centrifuge spins off the salmon-colored stem cells and collects them in what looks like a common plastic baggie. After the stem cells are isolated and collected, the bulk of the blood is pumped back into my body through the tube in my other arm. The doctor tells the residents that stem cell apheresis is usually performed over several days until enough cells—at least two million, but preferably five million—have been collected.

"Most donors," the doctor says, pointing at me, "provide sufficient stem cells within two to four days of apheresis."

I smile. "I'm exhibit A," I say. But the residents don't seem to get the joke. They file out of the room. I raise my hand to wave goodbye, but Nurse Brian puts his hand on mine.

"No movement," he reminds me. Then he shakes his head and says, "Sorry about those numbskulls. I don't know where they find these people."

At hour four, Maggie and Oliver arrive. They've brought lunch and we all sit together, having a little party. Maggie feeds me grapes. I ask her to peel them. She does get the joke. As we're eating, the doctor comes back to check on things. After reading the printout, he motions for Brian. They study the pages together, and then Brian pushes some buttons that elicit more beeps. After a while, the doctor turns to me with a puzzled look.

"Uh-oh," I say. "What's wrong?"

"Nothing is wrong," the doctor says.

"Au contraire," says Brian. "It seems you've produced a shit-load of cells, if you'll excuse my French. We have to recheck the numbers, but if they're correct, we can close up shop here. We've collected eleven million cells in under five hours. I guess that maple-sap prayer worked."

And just like that, we're done. Nurse Brian pronounces me the Stem Cell Queen. Several nurses swarm into the room. Two of them begin to work on me, unhooking me from the machine and removing the catheters. Another nurse arrives with a minifreezer on wheels. Before she can abscond with the stem cells, Maggie stops her.

"Can I have that for a minute?" she asks, reaching for the bright orange bag of stem-cell-laden blood. It looks like pulverized lox. The nurse shakes her head no. But Nurse Brian takes the bag from her and hands it to Maggie.

"Gorgeous," Maggie says. She holds the little sealed baggie in her palm and kisses it. "I'm a vampire," she says to the nurse.

She hands the bag to me, and I kiss it too.

"You're gonna label this, right?" I ask the nurse.

Maggie laughs. "Label it 'Maggie-Liz.'"

The nurse snatches the bag from me, puts it in the freezer, and wheels out of the room in a hurry.

"See you soon, girls!" Maggie yells to the stem cells.

BE CAREFUL WHEN A NAKED
PERSON OFFERS YOU A SHIRT

HOME FROM THE HARVEST. STILL foggy-brained and tired from the procedure, but I am told I will feel entirely better within a couple of weeks as my cells replenish themselves. Eleven million healthy cells are now in their well-labeled baggie, in a subzero freezer. They will stay there until Maggie is ready to receive them.

I am frozen too—unable to enter back into normal life. Maybe I feel frozen in solidarity with my cells, or maybe it's hard to feel lively as Maggie is preparing for transplant, receiving just enough chemo to kill off her bone marrow but not too much to kill her outright. For these reasons, I am suspended in time, waiting for the green light, for the moment when Maggie's tests come back clear of cancer and the transplant can happen.

I try to describe the stem cell harvest to a couple of friends, but the vampire nature of the procedure makes them queasy. And describing the therapy session is even harder. When I talk about it, people hear it as a challenge. "So you're saying I should confront my father, right?" one friend says after I explain what happened in that room with Maggie and the therapist. A colleague at work shakes his head. "That may have been appropriate for your situation," he says, "but if we have to go deep all the time at work, meetings will last *forever*. Shoot me first!" And another friend says, "I could never do that with my sister. She would bite my head off. Aren't some people just too nasty to tangle with?"

So I stop talking about the therapy session until I can figure out how to do so without kindling defensiveness. I don't want to guilt-trip people into doing what Maggie and I did. Nor am I suggesting the exact methodology for everyone. Something else might work better for you: a walk in the woods, a chat over coffee, a spontaneous phone call. And I don't want to insinuate that it's safe or smart to jump into the deep end with all people. Some folks are, in fact, too nasty to tangle with. And others are just not ready, or they don't have the patience, or the interest, or the courage. Or maybe you don't. Sometimes we have to do our own healing before mixing it up with another person. Sometimes we have to wait for the ripening—the right time, the right place, the right chemistry. This is on my mind now because ever since Maggie and I aired our truth-aches, I sense truth-aches everywhere, waving their hands like impatient kids in a classroom. I especially feel this when I am with my other sisters. Maybe I'm oversensitive at the moment. Or maybe I'm taking things too personally. This wouldn't be the first time. Even though I know that, nine times out of ten, I should take nothing personally—with my sisters or with anyone else for that matter—still, there are things rising up between the sisters that need to be dealt with. We should probably get in a boat and go down the truth-ache rapids, aiming for the wide-open, calm waters that Maggie and I reached.

I ponder this as I wait for my brain to unfog and my energy to unfreeze. I am interested in the truth-ache questions not only as they apply to me and my sisters, but also for all of us humans in all our relationships. What issues should be addressed, and what is better left unsaid? Who is safe to invite on a river ride? Are some relationships just too wounded to heal? When is the right time to have conversations about hurts and forgiveness, about what we need from each other and what we mean to each other? I don't want to wait for a life-or-death situation with my other sisters to reveal and heal what is in our hearts. But I also don't want to be a drama queen or an oversharer. I don't want to force depth on anyone, I don't want to pick at a scab that would heal on its own, and I don't want to set myself up to be hurt.

But I do want to have what the poet Adrienne Rich calls "honorable human relationships." She writes:

> *An honorable human relationship—that is, one in which two people have the right to use the word "love"—is a process, delicate, violent, often terrifying to both persons involved, a process of refining the truths they can tell each other.*
>
> *It is important to do this because it breaks down human self-delusion and isolation.*
>
> *It is important to do this because in doing so we do justice to our own complexity.*
>
> *It is important to do this because we can count on so few people to go that hard way with us.*

My whole body relaxes when I read that last line: "It is important to do this because we can count on so few people to go that hard way with us." This tells me to carefully choose the people I invite into the field, to practice with those closest and dearest to me: those with whom I feel safe, those to whom I can reveal my complexity, those with whom I can take responsibility for my past transgressions because I trust they will do the same with me. And by doing the deep, hard work with just a few people, I can grow my capacity to bring all different shades and levels of honor to my other connections as well.

Sometimes bringing a little more honor to a relationship is less complicated, time-consuming, or dangerous than you may think. Having a simple and direct conversation in real time, as opposed to years down the road, can prevent a misunderstanding from becoming a wedge between two people. Just asking "Why did you say that? What did you mean by that?" can change the course of a relationship. Sometimes a few words sincerely spoken—*I am sorry, I love you, I see you, I was wrong, you were wrong, we both blew it*, etc.—are all it takes. I think people forgo having difficult conversations because they fear they will get trapped into endless quagmires of psychobabble, or that they will discover dramatic wrongs to be righted, or will be blamed for things they didn't do or didn't mean to do.

But I swear to you, most of the time, you don't need an advanced degree in mediation to make inroads into honorable human relationships. When Maggie was treated for lymphoma the first time, I met Dr. Ira Byock while standing on line buying a muffin at the hospital's coffee shop. I shook his hand and thanked him for helping Maggie deal with her pain and anxiety during her monthlong stay in isolation in the cancer wing. Dr. Byock was a professor at Dartmouth Medical School at the time, and the director of palliative medicine at the hospital. I recognized him from the photograph on the jacket of his book, *The Four Things That Matter Most*—a book that had helped me tremendously when Maggie first became ill. After years of helping family members deal with terminal illness, Dr. Byock believed there were only four things people need to say to each other to heal and restore relationships: (1) "Thank you." (2) "I love you." (3) "Forgive me." (4) "I forgive you." Without trying to implement Dr. Byock's plan, Maggie and I had ended up doing just that in the therapy session: we thanked each other and expressed our love; we asked for and granted forgiveness. And that was enough to transform years of missteps and misunderstandings.

I believe in daring to err in the direction of connection—expressing love, naming the elephant in the room, and asking for and giving forgiveness. Someone has to start the ball rolling because we are all so shy when it comes to emotional intimacy—afraid of being rejected or blamed or exposed. And yet we crave connection; we stand around waiting for it—like awkward teenagers at a dance. It can take the most modest invitation to make magic. In most cases, it's worth a try.

But not always. Sometimes, the process of becoming closer and more truthful is as hard and dangerous as Adrienne Rich says it is. Sometimes it takes courage, as much, if not more, than what we normally consider brave behavior: rushing into a burning building, marching for justice, going to war. I've met many courageous people—activists, elected officials, first responders—who have risked their lives, or stood for justice, or spoken truth to power in war-torn corners of the world, but in their personal relationships, they have run from seemingly smaller confrontations with their mates or kids or colleagues. Big strong guys afraid of marital conflict; powerful women who don't say no to anyone out of fear of not being liked; leaders who have no problem standing up in front of thousands but who are scared to bare their hearts one-on-one.

For many reasons, being vulnerable with our fellow humans—telling the truth about the messy lives we have cocreated—is profoundly challenging and difficult. And therefore, we should not undertake the kind of soul river ride I took with Maggie with everyone. I have learned this the hard way. And I mean the hard way, because I have a very hard head, and it was clonked over and over until I realized that some people are not going to take that ride with me, and in fact should not be brought into my boat unless I want someone to drown (and that someone could be me). Some people aren't safe to air your truth-aches with because they aren't strong enough in their own sense of self. An invitation to travel deep, to meet in the paradoxical middle of a shared human experience, will feel intimidating, confusing, foreign. With these people it is best to go slowly and lightly—to meet them where they are as opposed to overwhelming them with your need for profundity. It won't ring true. Or it will feel like a judgment or a threat. Meeting another person at his own level of readiness is a form of kindness and respect.

Some people are not safe to invite on a soul river ride because they will push you overboard. They will not take care of your soul because they will meet you with their ego, with their defenses, with their fighter's gloves. They may say they want to meet soul to soul, but what they really want is to go at it mano a mano. When you bare your soul self to someone who is locked in the ego self, you are asking for trouble; you are being naïve; you will create more ache, not more truth. Some people are just too shut down, or angry, or wounded to be trustworthy. Not everyone in life wants to try to go beyond ego for the soul. You cannot force loving, responsible, honest connection on anyone, but you can determine whose heart is trustworthy, and whose isn't.

In determining whose heart is trustworthy, you can use Maya Angelou's naked-person metaphor. "I do not trust people who don't love themselves and yet tell me, 'I love you,'" Maya Angelou said. "There is an African saying which is: Be careful when a naked person offers you a shirt." You can ask yourself, does this person have enough love of himself to know how to love me? Does he suffer from excessively low self-esteem or narcissistic self-regard (two sides of the same coin) to be able to really see me for who I am beyond the roles, the wounds, the past? Will this person be patient enough to hear me out, brave enough to confront me, and game enough to travel with me to the field beyond wrongdoing and rightdoing? Has she demonstrated that kind of self-awareness in other relationships and situations? If the answer is no, then be careful. He or she may be a naked person offering you a shirt. A person cannot give you what he doesn't have.

Another heart you must investigate is your very own; you must test your own trustworthiness. Sometimes we think we're more genuine in our motivation than we really are. Sometimes we're manipulating others as opposed to truly wanting to grow a new kind of relationship. I am taking a vow after my experience with Maggie in the therapy session: I vow to apply Maya Angelou's metaphor to myself first and foremost before venturing into the field with another person. Am I ready to do this? Do I really plan to take responsibility for my side of the story? Or am I pushing an agenda? Am I too hurt, too impatient, too needy, too reactive, too confused to listen well and speak the truth? If so, then it's better to say nothing, to wait, to do my own inner work before inviting this kind of exchange with someone else.

And at the same time, I remember what Maggie said in the therapy session: "You don't have to be perfect to be a perfect match." None of us does. We don't have to achieve sainthood before meeting in the field. We don't have to wait for someone else to magically transform before inviting him on the journey. Even if the invitation is met with a big fat "no," it will have been better to err in the direction of connection. Then you can make an informed decision about the relationship. You know how far you can go, what you can give and receive.

Bottom line: Err in the direction of connection, but be careful when a naked person offers you a shirt.

THE WORD

I DON'T MEAN TO SAY that every conversation we have must be deep and meaningful. God forbid. I'm all for harmless gossip and funny repartee, debate and argument. I engage in my fair share of unrehearsed confrontations, rants, jokes, and off-the-cuff running of the mouth. These kinds of communication are part of the repertoire; they make us human. But if they are the only ways we reach out to each other, we betray the power of language, which has the capacity to connect us soul to soul. We would be wise to remember the deeper language, because without it, we make such a mess of our shared lives, telling old, worn-out stories or using words as weapons or as ways to hide. How you use your words matters.

Human beings began talking to each other fifty thousand years ago. I like to imagine those early conversations—a small band of people motioning and grunting around a fire, or pointing at the stars, or laughing at an early attempt at a joke. Giving names to things, alerting each other to danger, expressing pleasure, teaching, complaining, arguing, and evolving the species into Planet Earth's great communicators—masters of poetry and polemics, oratory and talk shows.

But still, we barely know how to say what we really mean. I sit across the table from my husband, this man I have lived with for almost thirty years. Inside my head a cauldron of thoughts bubble and brew. My heart is alive with changing feelings, at one moment loving, at the next petty. I try to find words to carry the thoughts and feelings out of myself on a boat of language, and sail them into my husband's harbor, where we can commune and experience our differences and our oneness. The words form, they come out of me, they float across the dinner table, and they land at my husband's port of call. Sometimes they come close to expressing what I want to say, sometimes he hears them as I meant them, but quite often the words I wrap around my innards might as well be the grunts of the first humans.

How is it that fifty thousand years later humans are still learning to talk to each other? The problem isn't just our clunky way with words or our lack of listening. The bigger problem is that we are speaking from the surface of our self to the surface of the other person's self. From one reptile brain to another. From one ego to another ego. Reptiles and egos defend or attack. When language is sourced from the surface, our words add to the general confusion of the world. How could they not? Our shallow thoughts and feelings are a jumble of desire and love and need, mixed with fear and defense and reactivity. No wonder monks and nuns of all wisdom traditions take vows of silence. One of the first Indian gurus I met was an old man who had not spoken a word since he was twenty. He used a small chalkboard to communicate in blunt, pithy sentences. Someone asked him once why he didn't speak, and he printed carefully on the little board, "To stay out of trouble."

But humans long to communicate. It's as strong a pull as gravity, this need to find each other through words. As the neurologist Oliver Sacks writes in his foreword to Susan Schaller's book, *A Man Without Words*, "language is an extraordinary coming-together of two people on either side of a great divide." Prisoners in solitary confinement create their own form of Morse code on

the walls of their cells, sending out an SOS to anyone who will
listen and connect. In *A Man Without Words*, Susan Schaller writes
about her experience working as a sign language interpreter in
Mexico. In a rural town she encountered a twenty-seven-year-old
Mexican-Indian man who was born profoundly deaf and had never
been taught even the most basic language. Schaller felt compelled
to teach him what Oliver Sacks calls "the essentially human birthright of language." In an interview Schaller described the moment
the deaf man suddenly grasped the meaning of his first sign: "He
just went crazy for a few seconds, pointing to everything in the
room and signing whatever I signed," Schaller recounted. "Then
he collapsed and started crying, and I don't mean just a few tears.
He cradled his head in his arms on the table . . . sobbing." She
writes about that moment in the book: "He had entered the universe of humanity, discovered the communion of minds . . . He
could see the prison where he had existed alone, shut out of the
human race for twenty-seven years."

Given how much we crave communication, you'd think we'd
put a premium on studying, practicing, and teaching ever more
soulful ways of talking and listening to each other. Talking about
love and hate, about fears and needs, about thorny and tricky and
touchy things. Giving words to both the darkness and the light in
our hearts; hearing the other's point of view; telling each other our
deeper feelings before they turn into intractable divisions; praising
and pleading and asking and explaining so that we can make our
way together through the labyrinth of our lives. It always amazes
me that there are colleges for war and not colleges for the opposite
of war, which I believe isn't a kumbaya kind of peace but rather a
mature and studied capacity to talk wisely and listen openly to each

other, to use the human birthright of language to reach across the divide. It seems like such a lapse in rationality that society would study how to fight with weapons but not how to put them down and pick up "the word."

"In the beginning was the Word." Biblical scholars interpret that line in a variety of ways. I understand it to mean that there is a deeper word within all of us. A deeper language, the soul's language, the language of love and clarity. "In the beginning was the Word": discerning, fearless, luminous, kind, wise. The light of consciousness dawned in human life with the language of the soul. Without that kind of language we are in darkness; we are trapped in our egos, unable to truly know ourselves and each other.

SPECIAL

I HAVE NOT USED THE word "ego" much in this book. I have left it out deliberately because that one little word—"ego"—contains a complex concept that is often misunderstood and misused in popular culture. And to confuse matters more, different traditions use the same word to describe different ideas. In certain psychological schools of thought, there's a healthy ego and an unhealthy ego. The healthy ego gives one a strong, authentic selfhood that can play well with others, while the unhealthy ego is wounded and weak. It's the part of you that views life through an obsessively competitive, comparative lens. Some spiritual traditions describe ego as the mistaken notion of a separate self. The true self feels connected, while the ego feels threatened.

Here's how I tried to explain the ego to my four-year-old grandson, Will. Two of my grandchildren live in my town. Their parents live here too—but it's those grandchildren I'm after. On Thursdays I pick Will up at preschool. When I go into Will's classroom, I feel more privileged than if I were walking the red carpet. To be part of his childhood is a rare gift in this fractured age of family diaspora. I don't take being a hands-on grandparent for granted. Holding those little animal bodies close to mine is a form of medicine for me. And because I'm a professional voyeur of human development, daily exposure to grandchildren makes me as lucky as the astronomer with top secret clearance at the Hubble Space Telescope. Grandchildren are the ultimate laboratories for witnessing little human beings navigate the art of becoming themselves. Parents don't get to watch that. They're too close, too invested, too exhausted.

Thursdays are my Sundays in the church of grandparenting. I get to be with Will all afternoon, beginning with the car ride home. If you've raised kids and you also drive, you know that your car is the best place to find out what is going on in a child's mind. There's something about the intimate yet private quarters of an automobile—you in the front seat driving, the kid behind you, staring at the back of your head—that makes children open up and say something other than "nothing" when asked that most offensive question, "What happened in school today?"

Today, as I drive Will home, I am listening to a radio interview about the ego, between Oprah Winfrey and the spiritual author Eckhart Tolle. Tolle is a soft-spoken, elf-like man from Germany whose books have sold millions of copies around the world. I have the volume turned down low, just in case Will decides to actually talk to me. Like most little kids, Will has a remarkable ability to practice selective hearing. Whether it's a radio talk show in a car or a conversation around the dinner table, one never knows if he's paying rapt attention or completely ignoring the grown-up world. One would assume that a preschooler would tune out Eckhart Tolle, what with his hypnotic voice, German accent, and esoteric subject matter.

So there we are, me driving, pondering Tolle's words about the ego, with Will in the back, slouched in his car seat. I look in the rearview mirror. Will is gazing out the window, his eyes on the treetops. I turn my attention back to Oprah, who is asking Tolle about the patterns of the unhealthy ego—patterns that keep us isolated from each other, or in conflict, or unable to be in loving, constructive relationships:

> TOLLE: Every ego wants to be special. If it can't be special by being superior to others, it's also quite happy with being especially miserable. Someone will say, "I have a headache," and another says, "I've had a headache for weeks." People actually compete to see who is more miserable! The ego doing that is just as big as the one that thinks it's superior to someone else. If you see in yourself that unconscious need to be special, then you are already free, because when you recognize all the patterns of the ego—
>
> OPRAH: What are the other patterns?
>
> TOLLE: The ego wants to be right all the time. And it loves conflict with others. It needs enemies because it defines itself through emphasizing others as different. Nations do it, religions do it, people do it.

Suddenly I hear Will talking to me from the backseat.

"Granda?" That's Will's name for me.

I turn off the radio. "Yes?"

"But Granda," he says with grave concern, "I *want* to be special."

I try not to laugh. I know this is the age a child builds his healthy ego—his sense of being an autonomous and valid person. I know that Will is only four. But it sounds so funny coming from a child, this obvious ploy of the emerging ego. I try to explain what Eckhart Tolle means anyway.

"Well, Will, you are special. But so are all the other kids. You see—"

"No, Granda," Will says, with great authority. "Only one person can be special. That's what 'special' means."

I laugh out loud. "You're right. It does mean that. But everyone wants to be special. So either everyone is special, or no one is."

In true four-year-old fashion, Will pretends he hasn't heard me. That's OK. Like all human beings, if we are lucky, we spend our formative years building up a healthy ego that can go forth into the world, establish boundaries, and express the soul's purpose. And if we are even luckier, we spend the rest of our life learning how to tame that ego when it gets puffed up or deflated. If we want to know love and experience community, if we want to be part of creating a more peaceful world, we will work to understand this: Either everyone is special, or no one is. Putting yourself or another human being on a pedestal—making yourself or someone else right all the time—is a sure recipe for disappointment or conflict or loneliness.

As I unstrap Will from his car seat and help him out of the car, Will says to me, "And also, Granda, I want to be right ALL the time."

I think of asking him this question: "So, Will, do you want to be right or do you want to be happy?" But I decide not to. He'll have to learn this himself. He'll have to go on the same damn journey we all do—first the strengthening and then the softening of the ego. For now, at four, he's taking his first steps: being special and being right. An appropriate phase for a kid. But if you are older than four and are struggling with the people in your life, you may want to consider moving beyond those steps. Spiritual maturity is the territory beyond being special and being right. It's also the territory beyond thinking other people are inherently better than you. Both are afflictions—symptoms on either side of the authenticity deficit disorder spectrum.

I actually remember when I first met my own ego. It is a vivid, visceral memory. I must have been six or seven. I was with my family—my mother and father and my three sisters. We had left our car in a parking lot by the beach, and were heading out to spend a day at the ocean. I ran ahead of the family down a path lined with dune grass and sea roses, feeling a rush of independence, as if the need to be me, and not part of a group, had dropped suddenly from the sky and lodged in my psyche. When I was far enough away from the others, I stopped and dug my toes into the soft sand. I felt the sun on my body and heard the muffled sound of the waves crashing on the shore. I was alone in the dunes. I was me—just me. It was a big, new feeling, one that needed to be marked. I picked a sea rose and put it behind my ear. Then I turned toward my advancing family. I wanted to say, "See me? See how unique I am? How special?" But I didn't say it, because along with the rush of exhilaration at my sovereignty came an equally strong feeling of shame and self-consciousness, as if a reproaching inner judge had also dropped from the sky.

And so, there it was—my new friend, my ego—in all of its authentic finery and all of its delusions of grandeur and all of its lonely confusion. Thus began a lifelong spiritual journey—the journey toward knowing and loving my uniqueness, even as I understand my unity with all, my nothing-specialness because we all are special. Both are true, and until we make peace with our uniqueness AND our oneness, life here on earth is hard. Here's the truth: It's not either/or. It's both . . . and more. Ego is not the enemy. But it's not the whole story either.

We come into the world a potent little acorn, a distillation of the oak we were put here to become. The ego fears it is less than others, or it strives to be better than everyone else. But the acorn only yearns to be the oak. That's the better urge; that's the original urge—to be the oak. To be the oak we do not have to keep others from growing into their full selves. We can stand side by side and still reach for the sun. We all belong here. There is room for all of us.

Humanity sure doesn't act as if there is room for all of us. How did we get to this place of trying so hard to elbow each other out of town that the end result may be a planet that can't sustain any of us? And how can we work on making things better? My answer always comes back to the most basic human pairing. You don't have to join a United Nations peacekeeping unit to make a difference in the world. You can start small—with your husband, your kid, your friend, your sister.

Sigmund Freud famously said in 1929, "The great question that has never been answered and which I have not yet been able to answer, despite my thirty years of research into the feminine soul, is 'What does a woman want?'" Seventy-five years later, another smart dude, the Nobel Prize winner Stephen Hawking, was asked by a science journal what he thinks about most often. "Women," he answered. "Women are a complete mystery." This from a man who has unraveled some of the most complex mysteries in cosmology and quantum physics.

I have an easy three-step suggestion for Freud and Hawking: (1) Ask a woman what she wants. (2) Respect her answer even if it differs from your worldview. (3) Tell her what you want. Then, together, the two of you might be able to meet halfway and get on with whatever it is you are finding so mysteriously out of your reach. This same line of thinking applies to all sorts of distinctions between humans. Instead of bemoaning that you don't understand how a Republican could think the way he thinks, go have lunch with one and find out. Ditto with your gay cousin. Or born-again friend. Instead of building a case in your head against someone who looks different, talks different, or whose way of life differs from yours, get to know people, find the acorn in the heart of the other, and share stories about becoming the oak.

There will always be distinctions between people; at least I hope there will be. Diversity is a hallmark of our life on earth. Biodiversity (which includes human diversity) is necessary for healthy ecosystems. It's not the diversity that's the problem; it's our own ego's fear of not being the most special one—the special one in our family, at school, at work. A member of the most special tribe, race, religion, nation, species. The Zen teacher D. T. Suzuki said, "The ego-shell in which we live is the hardest thing to outgrow." Outgrowing the ego-shell is the ultimate freedom.

There is a land beyond the ego's striving to be "better than," or its fears of being "less than." That land is where we know ourselves to be both sovereign and connected—"part of" as opposed to "better or less than." When you come home to the truth of who you are in the marrow of your soul, you begin to break the ego-shell.

SWIMMING UPSTREAM

SEPTEMBER. HERE WE ARE AGAIN, in the hospital, ready for transplant. It's taken Maggie longer to arrive here than we thought it would. Two weeks after my cells were harvested in May, and just a day before she was scheduled for transplant, the cancer broke through the chemotherapy and began spreading again. Maggie's summer was a haze of full-body radiation and more and stronger chemo—strong enough to assault and destroy all of her bone marrow. Every few weeks she landed back in the hospital with infections and close encounters with the terrifying nearness of death. But eventually, the cancer was beaten back, and Maggie was free of infection and ready for transplant.

After all the complex treatments she has received, the setup for the transplant seems low-tech, even anticlimactic. Just Maggie, in a bed, hooked up to some fluids. The administering doctor explains the procedure. "In a few minutes," the doctor tells Maggie, "your sister's frozen stem cells will be wheeled into the room. We'll thaw them here, in a warm water bath. Once thawed, I'll extract five million of the cells with this." She holds up a large hypodermic needle. "And then I will push them into your vein," she says, examining the central catheter in Maggie's chest.

We wait for more information, but the doctor has finished her explanation.

"That's it?" I ask.

"That's the transplant," she says. "The whole process will take about fifteen minutes."

"Then what happens?" Maggie asks.

"Well, it's really quite miraculous," says the doctor. "Once your sister's stem cells enter your bloodstream, they know where to go. They have a chemical homing signal that directs them to the bones. And then, over time, they engraft in your marrow and start to replenish your blood. You can think of them like salmon that instinctually swim upstream to spawn. Salmon swim for the headwaters. Stem cells swim for the bones. It's as if they remember where they came from and are looking to return home," she says, sounding like a narrator in a National Geographic film.

The doctor leaves to oversee the transport. The band of sisters (including Oliver, whom we have inducted into the sisterhood) circles around Maggie in the bed. A nurse who has cared for Maggie during many harrowing stays in the hospital is also with us.

"So what really happens?" Maggie asks the nurse. "It's not really as simple as that, is it?"

"Well, that is actually what happens," the nurse says. "We'll transfuse you with millions of new stem cells. You may feel a little woozy, maybe a little nauseous. But that will last just for a few minutes. That's it. It takes about twelve to fourteen days for the cells to engraft and start producing new blood cells. It's afterwards—over the next months—that you'll have some hurdles to get over."

"I don't want to hear about them right now," Maggie says. "Right now I want to dance. Who has music?"

"You want to dance?" the nurse asks, regarding the tiny, emaciated bald woman in the bed.

"It's something we do," I explain. "When the going gets tough, we like to dance."

I take out my iPhone. The only danceable music I have is Michael Jackson's "Billie Jean." I don't recall why I have it on my phone, but it will do. And so for the next ten minutes as we wait for the stem cell delivery, we dance around the room to "Billie Jean." Several nurses watch from the doorway. This is probably the first time a patient and her family, all wearing masks and protective clothing, have danced to Michael Jackson while waiting for a bone marrow transplant. Maggie dances like a funky little dervish, somehow managing to look sexy at ninety pounds.

There's a passage in Toni Morrison's book *Beloved* where Baby Suggs preaches to freed slaves going out into a dangerous world. We have to love ourselves first, she tells her people. You can't count on anyone else if you don't love yourself first. "In this here place, we flesh," she preaches. "Flesh that weeps, laughs; flesh that dances on bare feet in grass. Love it. Love it hard." She lists all the bodily things they must love: their guts and blood and bones. "The dark, dark liver—love it, love it and the beat and beating heart, love that too. More than eyes or feet. More than lungs that have yet to draw free air. More than your life-holding womb and your life-giving private parts, hear me now, love your heart. For this is the prize."

I watch Maggie dancing, dragging the IV pole around the hospital room. What courage she has shown as she's learned to love herself—body and heart—even in the midst of cancer's assault. She's loved her flesh. Even as it has drooped and burned and ached and aged, she has loved her flesh hard. Now my flesh will become part of her flesh. Now our physical hearts will beat the same blood through our bodies. Our spiritual hearts—our souls, our true selves, *the prize*—have already merged. This has been the real miracle: As Maggie has learned to believe in herself, as she has loved her heart *hard*, she has received the prize of love from the whole world. As her frightened ego has released its grip, she has joined the flawed human race; she has danced more freely with the people in her life. She's given herself a soul marrow transplant. And now it's time for the bone marrow transplant.

The doctor wheels a cart into the room. I turn off "Billie Jean." And sure enough, there are my salmon-colored stem cells, in that same little baggie (well marked). A technician thaws and prepares the liquid gold for the transplant, and then hands the bag to the doctor, who draws up the cells into the big syringe. We take our positions around the bed. I close my eyes and remember something a friend of mine said, right before I was to undergo my bone marrow harvest. She said, "Give from your strength, and give to your sister's strength. Don't be the big sister helping the little sister. Don't be the strong one helping the weak one. Don't be the fortunate one helping the victim. Give from your strength to her strength. *Strength to strength*."

Now the doctor pushes the cells from the syringe into the central line. I hold Maggie's hand, silently repeating "*Strength to strength*" as millions of my cells rush into her. For a minute Maggie is nauseated and dizzy, but the storm passes, and there she is—lying in bed, part me but still Maggie.

---

field notes • september 10

i was as ready for transplant as any patient; i had waited so long; 6 months from relapse to transplant. just DO IT. just put me in there and torture me however you please, but get ON with it. i was admitted 1 week before the transplant to begin the last round of chemo. on the first day, i began the descent into hell. on the last day, sister katy and liz videoed me dancing wildly just moments before the transplant began. the team of doctors arrived, a wonderful nurse took her position at the central line installed in my chest. my wrist bands and verbal self identification matched the WELL LABELED bag of stem cells. and then it was time. because liz had produced a tremendous amount of stem cells, they only used half of the bag, and froze the remainder. the nurse drew up the cells into a 20 cc syringe and over the course of 5 minutes gently pushed the cells into the central line. i felt hot, nauseated, ready to vomit, dizzy, and then, i was fine.

we celebrated and i settled in for the fallout.

CHIMERA

FOR THE FIRST COUPLE OF weeks post-transplant, Maggie's recovery is swift. By week two, my stem cells have almost fully engrafted in her bones and are beginning to spawn fresh, healthy blood cells. After only three weeks, she is released from the hospital and sent home with instructions to eat well, rest well, and stay away from crowds and people with contagious illness. Everyone is thrilled and hopeful. She's still taking a pharmacy's worth of pills—eleven different medications a day, and when I look them up online, five of them note nausea, diarrhea, and headaches as side effects. The other six have side effects that include mouth sores and immune suppression and life-threatening infection. She will be on these pills for up to a year. She spends the winter resting as well as a hummingbird can rest, managing side effects, trying to stay positive on this long, painful ascent to health.

On one website, I read that bone marrow transplant recipients are called chimeras. I have a vague recollection of my mother reading us a Greek myth about a creature called the Chimera, but like so much of what she taught us, the story is now gathering dust in a disregarded region of the brain. When my mother died, I took some of her books—not many, because there were just too many. I took the ones that were part of her canon, like the classicist Edith Hamilton's *Mythology*. We were raised on Edith Hamilton. As a child I thought she was a friend of the family—that's how often my mother quoted her. (I also thought Eleanor Roosevelt was my mother's best friend.)

I find my copy of *Mythology* and brush up on the myth of the Chimera. I learn that the Chimera breathed fire, was female, vicious, and powerful. She was one single creature with the strength of three separate animals. "The Chimera was held to be unconquerable," Edith Hamilton wrote. "She was a most singular portent, a lion in front, a serpent behind, a goat in between." Now the term is used to describe any fictional animal with parts taken from other animals, or it can also mean an idea or a thing that is "wildly inventive and implausible."

Well, this whole transplant thing strikes me as wildly inventive and implausible. Maggie is now part me and part herself. All of her blood is "mine," and the rest of her is . . . well, Maggie. Even the medical people think it's wildly inventive and implausible—otherwise why would they call transplant recipients chimeras?

I tell Maggie that she is now the Chimera. "You're part lion, part snake, part goat. And you're vicious and powerful. Edith Hamilton herself says you are unconquerable. OK?"

"OK, Mom," Maggie replies.

But as the weeks, and then months, go by, Maggie feels anything but unconquerable. Rather she feels beaten up and held down, conquered by exhaustion, skin rashes, and diarrhea. Several times she spikes a fever and is rushed to the hospital. And then she begins to experience symptoms of graft-versus-host disease, meaning my cells are attacking her body. The doctors tell her not to worry; that GVHD is common; and that an upside of the disease is that the newly transplanted cells are not only attacking Maggie, but also seeking out and destroying cancer cells that may have survived the chemo and radiation.

Besides pointing to GVHD, her symptoms may also indicate that her immune system is rejecting my cells, which can lead to transplant failure. *Rejection* and *attack*. Maggie says her body feels like a battleground where our cells are fighting each other—like those Civil War stories that pit brother against brother. I urgently attempt to make contact with my cells. I close my eyes and imagine them, some resting patiently in the quiet center of Maggie's bones, others swimming around in her bloodstream, diligently doing what they're told, and some on the lookout for cancer cells. And then there are those other ones—the overaggressive troublemakers as well as the reluctant self-doubters. I thank the well-behaved cells and cajole the ne'er-do-well ones into compliance. "Come on, guys!" I say to them (in my most prayerful voice). "Get with the program. Follow directions. Attack the cancer cells but spare the patient." Then I encourage the insecure cells to believe in themselves. Now I'm a coach: "You can do it! Show 'em what you've got!" It all feels reminiscent of when I tried to help my kids with their homework. How much is too much involvement?

I pay close attention to the way I react to the news, to people different from me, to perceived threats. Am I unwittingly sending a message to my cells to be on vigilant alert for strangers who might do them harm? I know I have the tendency (that we all have the tendency) to turn anyone who isn't me into a stranger, into the "other."

Or perhaps it is something quite different. Perhaps, if Maggie's body is rejecting the transplant, it is because my cells are too wimpy to take a stand for their very existence. Are they responding to my all too human fears of unworthiness? Is my impostor syndrome acting up, flooding my cells with insecurity and making them question their ability to fulfill the task of the transplant? I do my best to remember the dignity of my soul as I go about my daily life. I brush the dust off my meditation practice and dedicate it to my cells. Throughout the day I sit up tall, close my eyes, and come home to my soul. I ask it to take charge of this wildly inventive and implausible situation.

I wonder if my cells think I abandoned them—do they need something from me? Did I prepare them adequately? Did I even ask their permission to be extracted, frozen, thawed, and then pumped into a foreign body? I can't remember if we had that conversation before they were wrested from my bones. I wonder if it would have made a difference. I wonder if I'm crazy. I'm beginning to feel a little crazy. Am I assigning way too much importance to this notion that my thoughts can influence my sister's survival? Am I on some sort of power trip? Maybe I should stop thinking of them as MY cells and let Maggie take over. I bring this up, four months after the transplant, when I visit her in the dead of winter. She sits huddled in the window seat, wrapped in a down comforter, as scrawny and bald as a baby bird.

"Your cells are behaving poorly, Liz." She wags a finger at me.

"Maybe we should stop thinking of them as mine," I suggest. "Maybe they need me to get out of the way. Maybe they want you to take over."

Maggie looks at me like I am deserting the ship and leaving it in the hands of the emaciated, lost-at-sea crew. I immediately retract the idea.

"Good," Maggie says. "You have to stay connected to those cells, Liz. I need you to."

i haven't written in a while. i am so tired, so distraught, that the idea
of writing makes me want to scream. instead, i will scream into these
words. i awoke in the deepest sink hole of grief, unable to tolerate myself. i had 3 hours to kill today before the drive north to the hospital for
a checkup and blood work. i was internally raging, feeling that whatever
anyone said, it had no value to me. places in my lungs hurt the way
they hurt when the cancer first came back—is it the graft vs host disease or are the tumors back? i climbed the stone steps to my art studio
and tried to do some work to distract me from me. i stand in the studio
that oliver built me for this art business that became something i never
imagined it could. a success! i still don't think i'm a real artist, but as liz
says, the proof is in the fact that my work hangs in people's homes all
over the country. so i stood there in my church. curved ceilings, multiple tall windows, french doors leading to a porch with its own curves
and designs. it was all lost on me today. i only saw the piles of my life
that would need to be dealt with if i die. and i felt too tired to consider
how i was going to dig through it all.

i walked back outside and stood in the winter sun. it was then that i
realized i had completely lost touch with my breath, with stilling my
heart, with grounding my feet on the earth. i did what i forgot to do; i
held my left wrist with my right hand, and breathed from my pelvis to
my heart and lungs, slowing my pulse. and then, it was time to go to the
hospital. olly and i got in the car, me driving, heading north. we meet
with the docs. the labs were stable. no reason to worry they say. live
your life they say. so we headed to norah's farm, and she and i spent
2 glorious hours in her greenhouse, winter sun warm under the glass,
music playing, planting the first of the season's endless trays of shallots,
onions and scallions. wheel barrows of soil gave up their aromas as we
poured warm water over them, stirred and then filled the starter trays.

to be working, to be planting, to be with my amazing daughter, i could feel my true self emerge from the gutter. there i was, intact. completely unscathed underneath psyche-crushing cancer.

note to self: remember to breathe. remember that i can return to my joyful self, remember to hold left wrist in right hand.

---

field notes • march 2

someone asked me how i am doing. i say, i don't know and i don't want to know. so instead i read novel after novel, losing myself for days in other lives. i cook, bake, walk endlessly, watch movies, sleep. any conversation about my health, my disease, makes my heart race. i try to breathe, to clear my head, to think of other things. a tiny cough, the recurrent discomfort in my chest, fatigue all remind me of what i am facing. i simply am uncomfortable in my own skin. i feel like a time bomb. i am in limbo between life and death, health and illness, joy and devastating sadness. as always, no one can say the right thing. if they agree with me when i talk about the poor prognosis, then i am sure i am going to die. if they tell me i will come through this, i am sure they are clueless idiots. no one can win. i have intolerance for anyone without a death sentence. and just so you know what NOT to say to your sick or dying friends, "no one gets out of here alive" and "we are all dying" are phrases that make me want to strangle the bearer.

STRENGTH TO STRENGTH

IT'S HARD TO KNOW HOW to help the people we love, whether they have a serious illness, or a headache, or a heartache. I've become clear about some ways NOT to help, at least how not to help Maggie. I've observed how she retreats into a shell when a well-meaning friend offers unsolicited advice about the curative power of juice fasts, or rambles on about the amazing clinic in Germany where her friend's hairdresser was successfully treated. I've watched Maggie's face twist into a look of wrathful disbelief when someone suggests that negative thinking, or grilled meat, or early exposure to pesticides might have caused the cancer. How could any of this help Maggie at this point in the progression of her disease?

Here is a good rule of thumb to follow if you are confused about how to help: Do not offer unsolicited advice to people who are sick. If you must, go ahead and ask them if they want to hear about promising new treatments or stories of those who beat the odds. Ask in such a way that the very vulnerable, very tired patient, or the equally weary caretaker, can easily say "No, thank you" to articles, books, and links to treatment plans and meditative YouTube videos.

One day, months after the transplant, I get a phone call from my father's old friend Pete and his wife, Jane. Pete and my father served in World War II together, and Jane became my mother's friend. Pete and Jane and their kids are like family to us. Now Pete is ninety-one years old and almost deaf. Jane is in her eighties and forgetful about what she or the person she's talking to said several minutes previously. In other words, fast-forward a few years and we all will be Jane and Pete. Well, we would be lucky to be them. At a recent family gathering, they pulled up to the party in a little sports car. Pete was driving. Jane was sitting next to him. As one of their sons said, "She's the only one crazy enough to drive with him."

My parents' old friends are calling with what they say is exciting news.

"What's so exciting?" I ask.

And then Jane begins to read aloud from a magazine she found at the dentist's office, about ten ways to beat cancer, starting with the "exciting news" that if Maggie refrains from using refined sugar and ingests large quantities of Japanese green tea she can totally heal from her disease. I try to interrupt, to tell Jane that Maggie is not attracted to these kinds of remedies, but due to Pete's poor hearing and Jane's indomitable spirit, she continues. " 'Lisa P. from Jacksonville, Florida,' " she reads into the phone, " 'was told to go home and put her affairs in order. Six months later, after working with Dr. M's regimen of eating only superfoods rich in antioxidants, her tests revealed the cancer was completely gone.' "

"Jane!" I yell, hoping that if I raise my voice loud enough perhaps Pete will hear and intervene. "Jane!" But she continues with the article. Every now and then Pete asks her to repeat what she has just read.

"You mean about the green tea?" Jane asks him.

"What?" Pete shouts.

"About the green tea?" Jane yells back.

"Yes! The green tea."

" 'Green tea,' " she repeats, " 'has been shown to reduce tumors in many cancers. Craig S. from Bensenville, Illinois . . .' "

This goes on for a long time—Jane reading and Pete asking her to repeat what she had just read—until I finally get their attention. In a loud voice, I explain to them that I know about many of those treatments, have seen them work for some people, and if I ever got cancer would try them myself. Jane responds by saying, "Call me a cockeyed optimist, but let me just read you one more part of the article," and she launches into a long description of coffee enemas.

I begin to feel as if I am in a *Saturday Night Live* skit about how not to help someone. I know my parents' friends are motivated by love. They can hardly bear to think of my sister being ill. They just want to help. We all want to help when someone we love is sick, or suffering a loss, or struggling in any of the ways we human beings struggle. But sometimes we go overboard and fill the awkward spaces with too much advice, too much talking. And sometimes, in our confusion about what helps and what doesn't, we pull back completely. We don't make the phone call, we don't visit, we don't bring a meal, because we don't want to say the wrong thing or intrude on someone's privacy. But avoiding the one who is hurting also goes into the how-not-to-help category.

So how do you best help? It's a lot simpler than you think. Not easy, but simple. First, get in touch with your own marrow—the deepest, truest part of yourself. Sit in the still dignity of your authentic self. Fill your whole being with the light of who you are. Then, just show up with nothing but the gift of your most authentic, unadorned, unafraid self. Because when one person is at home in his own skin, he can help the other person be less anxious too. Reach from the inside of you to the inside of the other. Remember what my friend told me before the transplant: "Don't be the

strong one helping the weak one. Don't be the fortunate one helping the victim. Give from your strength to her strength. *Strength
to strength.*"

And listen to the person who is suffering. If he says he is scared,
don't tell him to be brave. Instead, ask him to tell you about it.
Listen with empathy. Just listen. Just be there. If she says she is
dying, don't change the subject. Go there with her. Find out what
she's feeling, what she needs. Be a vessel for her dreams and fears
and plans. Don't preach and don't shrink back. Be real. Be open.
Be strong, and find that kernel of strength in the other. *Strength to
strength.*

Before we hang up the phone, Jane asks me if I think Maggie is
giving up.

"Why won't she try alternative therapies?" Pete asks. "What
about meditation and prayer? Will Maggie consider that?"

"She's a lot like your mother," Jane says. "Your mother gave up."

I start to tell them that multiple chemotherapies, and full-body
radiation, and a bone marrow transplant aren't exactly giving up,
but Pete doesn't hear me, and so I stop talking. For a while we stay
on the phone in silence. I want to tell them that indeed Maggie is
so much like my mother. I want to ask Jane what my mom had
been like as a young woman, what had made her so afraid of life,
so afraid of her own magnificent self. I want to tell Jane and Pete
how Maggie has used this awful disease to step boldly into her life,
and how I believe, in taking the reins, she is honoring our mother,
living out her dreams of liberation. I want to tell our old friends
this, but it's not the kind of conversation that can be shouted to a
ninety-one-year-old man and a cockeyed optimist over the phone.

DEAR DEEPAK

AS THE WEEKS TURN INTO months, and the winter turns to spring, Maggie continues to experience big swings in her health. One week she feels strong and hopeful; then she spikes a fever, returns to the hospital, and goes back downhill. She comes home again, bolstered by steroids and antibiotics. She throws herself back into life, but then symptoms of graft-versus-host disease reappear. My cells are attacking her cells. This may be good if my cells are going after any remaining cancer cells. But this may not be good if my cells are attacking whatever they randomly determine to be "not me."

I sit quietly and put my attention on my far-flung cells, miles away, in a different state, in Maggie's bloodstream. Once again, I try to contact them. I start by imagining the blood cells in my own body responding to my calm breathing and my healing thoughts. And then I picture my cells in Maggie's body; I send them comforting energy; I ask them to stop attacking Maggie haphazardly. I envision them as precise warriors who know a cancer cell from a healthy cell. I ask them to make wise decisions.

There are some healing techniques that may seem like woo-woo voodoo, but they have been scrutinized by science and found to be helpful. Research shows that certain meditative relaxation techniques can affect one's health at a cellular level. There have been studies that prove the efficacy of "nonlocal healing"—the idea that one person, over here, can affect another person, over there, through prayer or visualization. But what about when that person over there actually has cells in her from the person over here? Would that increase the likelihood of nonlocal healing? I search for studies but find nothing.

There must be someone who knows about these things.

I e-mail one of Maggie's doctors—the one who told me way back before the harvest that my stem cells would keep Maggie alive for the rest of her life. I ask her to explain the science of engraftment, the mechanisms of graft-versus-host disease, and the role my cells are now playing in Maggie's body. How much control do I have over the destiny of Maggie-Liz? I ask the doctor. Does she believe the mind-body connection can affect my cells even though they are no longer in my body? I don't care if the doctor thinks I'm slightly mad; I've lost all shame when it comes to asking doctors questions.

The doctor kindly admits that her medical training prevents her from "magical thinking," but she's intrigued by the notion of the donor's mental state having an effect on transplanted cells or organs. She suggests I submit a proposal to conduct a study at her hospital. I decline. It feels too clinical—a way to distance myself from the job at hand. But I do appreciate her explanation of the science of engraftment: "Maggie's stem cells that are responsible for making all of her blood cells are now yours," the doctor e-mails. "And inside the nucleus of each of your cells there's an identical copy of your entire genome—a complete set of your DNA. A complete set of what makes you, you. So, yes, you could say that you, Liz, are now swimming around in Maggie. And therefore, to the extent that you can willfully influence your own immune system, I suppose you could influence Maggie's, but this is way out of my wheelhouse!"

And so I ask someone else. Many years ago, I met a young cell biologist and medical doctor who had recently come from India to teach and practice medicine in Boston. He had just published a book about the mind-body connection. I invited him to speak at a conference I was organizing. This young doctor—Deepak Chopra—became a pioneer in the intersection of meditation and medicine, spirituality and science, and a frequent speaker at Omega. I figured he'd be as good as anyone to shed light on my cell obsession.

In my first e-mail to Deepak Chopra I ask him if he thinks my state of mind is affecting my sister, even though the transplant was months ago. "Is there something I should be doing?" I ask. "Is it like when I was pregnant and eating for two? Am I now behaving for two? Or should I not even think of the transplanted cells as mine? Are they now her cells? Or are they just energy in the form of cells, and therefore they belong to neither of us?" I type out these questions and e-mail them to Dr. Chopra, hoping he will respond with a laundry list of proven healing methods.

Instead, he tells me I have done all I can. "You have given your sister your stem cells," he writes, "with a clear intention and with all your heart. Now it is time to release control of the outcome." It isn't up to me anymore, he writes. I will have to trust that something else is in charge now. He quotes Sir Arthur Eddington, the renowned British physicist, who said, "Something unknown is doing we don't know what." Handing over the reins to that unknown something is the best thing I can do, Deepak Chopra writes.

This is an inspiring yet unsatisfactory answer. I write back, and use language from Dr. Chopra's own books about the properties of cells and the double-blind studies done on prayer and healing. Isn't there some research that applies to our situation? The more I push for a definitive answer, the less clinical he becomes. After several more volleys of e-mails, his final answer is: "Just think of it all as God. Your cells, her cells, you, your sister—everything—as God. No separateness. And then surrender to the unknown."

This was not what I had in mind. So I contact a well-known science writer who has authored books on the subject. Her answer is so similar to Dr. Chopra's that I wonder if the entire mind-body community has received a memo warning them about the crazy lady who donated her stem cells to her sister. I go as far as asking a psychic who speaks to dead people who tells me that my parents are trying to get my attention but I keep ignoring them. "They want you to know," the psychic says, "that they will take over now. They are proud of what you did, but they've got it covered." Everyone—doctors, researchers, spiritual teachers, even my dead parents—seems to be saying the same thing: "You've done all you can. Now just let go."

And so I try. I try to let go. I allow myself to feel helpless, powerless, useless. These are uncomfortable feelings for me, but I'd rather be uncomfortable than crazed. I listen to the advice of Deepak Chopra, reminding me that I am not the one in charge here; that there are forces far greater than my own little ego; that the destiny of my sister's life, of my life, of all life is out of my control. And that on some level, everything is OK, just as it is, and my work now is to know that, to trust that, to be at peace with whatever comes next. Yet every time I release my vigilant need to *do* something, I hear Maggie saying, "You have to stay connected to those cells, Liz. I need you to." And I'm right back where I started.

One early spring morning, Maggie sends me an e-mail after an emergency visit to the hospital:

> whoaaaaaa. our cells are in battle. i have gone from
> 95% engrafted to 75%. diarrhea. nausea. they put me on
> steroids. saw both my kids on the way home and that
> helped tremendously. then grabbed my garden clippers
> and just walked about hacking away at things. i think
> it's time to see the therapist again. i think it's time
> for me to take over. i think those cells need me to
> lead the way now. love you m

A wave of relief rushes over me. I can almost feel a weight lift from my shoulders as I think of releasing the impossible, erroneous task of saving my sister's life. That line Deepak Chopra quoted, the one from Sir Arthur Eddington, comes back to me: "Something unknown is doing we don't know what." At this point, something unknown sounds far better equipped to handle the situation than I am.

I call the therapist and we pick a date to see him again. He wants to know what we have in mind this time. I tell him my intention is to hand off the transplanted cells to Maggie and, even more than that, to "something unknown [that] is doing we don't know what."

"Good idea," he says.

"And Maggie's intention is to take her health, her life, whatever comes next, back from me or from the doctors. To gather her courage and follow her own instincts."

"An even better idea," the therapist says.

AMOR FATI

MAGGIE AND I CLIMB THE stairs to the therapist's office and arrive on the landing. The door opens right away, and the first thing the therapist says is "Do you realize that this day—May thirtieth—at this very hour—three p.m.—is exactly one year since we saw each other last? One year to the day, to the hour!"

We follow him into the room, say hello to the dog, take our perch on the couch, and jump into the session as if no time has passed at all. Except time has passed. Apparently one full year. You can read the passage of time in Maggie's postchemo hairdo. Instead of wearing a hat to cover her baldness, she now proudly displays bristly tufts sticking up all over her head, as if she had gone to a salon in a Dr. Seuss book. But for someone who has been through so many medical procedures and on so many drugs, her face looks the same. She still looks inexplicably, adorably, like a girl.

Once again, the therapist asks why we are here. Maggie gets right to it. "I don't really know why we're here," she says. "At first I thought it was because our cells are battling it out in my body. Liz's cells are attacking me. And I'm rejecting her cells. And maybe by being here we could stop that cycle. But I don't think that's really why I'm here. I don't think that's the problem at all."

"What's the problem, then?" the therapist asks Maggie.

Maggie exhales sharply with pursed lips. "I'm just so tired of riding the roller coaster," she says. She coughs and sighs. "I wake up every morning fighting pain and nausea, and thinking it's all hopeless, because the cancer's going to come back anyway, and I should just give up and let whatever happens happen. I go to the hospital for tests and they say everything is OK, but I don't believe them. And then sometimes I do believe them and I get optimistic, which fills me with fear. I have to fight that fear, that panic, all day long. Sometimes I feel so much love for everyone, and then sometimes I'm so angry because no one has the foggiest idea of what this is like for me. And it makes me want to curl up into a little ball and die. Because it's just all too much—how much I love everyone, everything, and how terrified I am, and how exhausted I am, not just by the physical symptoms, but also . . . I don't know. Sometimes death looks comforting. Like the only way out."

"Out of what?" the therapist asks.

"Everything. People. Me. I just can't do things the way I used to. And I think it freaks people out."

"How did you used to do things?" the therapist asks.

"However anyone wanted me to. I tried to know what they wanted even before they knew what they wanted." She shakes her head. She has tears in her eyes. "I lived like that for most of my life."

"What was that like for you?"

Maggie puts both of her hands on her belly. She looks straight at the therapist. "It made me sick," she says. "It made me anxious, and then it made me sick."

"And the only way out of that is to die?" the therapist asks.

"Yes. On some days, that's what I think. But I also know there's another way out. And I've been doing it a lot this year, I really have. And it's been amazing. But it's hard to teach an old dog new tricks. Apologies to you," Maggie says, looking over at the therapist's dog. He wags his tail.

"Tell me about some of those new tricks," the therapist says.

Maggie pauses. "It's embarrassing to admit it."

"Admit what?"

"That it's taken me this long to learn the big trick."

"That is . . ."

"Being who I am. Just being who I am. That's the big trick. I spent so many years trying to be someone else; trying to be what I thought I was supposed to be, or what someone wanted me to be. And then trying to get what I wanted for me from the scraps, or by sneaking around and doing things behind other people's backs. Exhausting. Let me tell you, it's an exhausting way to live. But the cancer stripped me down. Nothing left to lose, as they say. So this year I said to myself, fuck it, no apologies, I'll just be who I am. I'll see how that works."

"And what happened?" the therapist asks.

"It *worked*." Maggie says. "It surprised me. The more I stopped trying to be a perfect little human for everybody else, the more I stopped expecting other people to be perfect. The more I trusted myself, the more I trusted other people. It's the darnedest thing. I thought the opposite would happen. I thought it was either me being me all alone, or me being what people wanted me to be. But instead, the more I let myself be me, the better things got between me and other people. Like with you, Liz."

Maggie looks at me, as if she'd forgotten I was there. "I wanna tell my kids this. I wanna tell them not to care so much about what other people think. Not to be afraid of saying what they want, what they need. I wanna say, don't dim your light; don't live small. You're not damaged goods; you don't need to be fixed. Just be who you are—'cause that's what the people who really matter want anyway. The truth of who you are."

"Preach it, sister," I say.

The therapist comes over to Maggie and sits by her on the couch. He takes her hands. "Maggie," he says, "this is good. This is true. This is how to live. You don't have to die to live like this. Do you understand?"

"Yeah," Maggie says. "But I backslide all the time. And then it just gets the better of me and I want out. Out of all of it."

"That's OK," the therapist says. "We all backslide, all of us, all the time. It's hard to attain what you are talking about, and it's even harder to stay there. It's the ongoing work of a lifetime. The hardest work, and the best work. All you have to remember is this is the way to live. It's a way of life—becoming yourself, being yourself." He returns to his seat. "Now, what do you want to say to Liz's cells? Speak from the voice of the Maggie who knows who she is."

Maggie sits still for a few minutes. When she speaks she keeps her eyes closed: "I see your cells, Liz, and they are kind of dancing around and waving good-bye to you. They want you to know they are very, very happy in their new home." She smiles to herself. "Some of them even like it better in here, better than they did over there." She reaches over and pats my leg. She opens her eyes. "Really, that's what I see. A lot of happy, healthy cells waving good-bye to you, having a good time, loving their new home. I guess they love it because I love it. It's a very good place, you know. It's fun in here. It's a good place to live—my body, myself."

The therapist interrupts her. "Say that again, Maggie."

"It's a good place to live. Me." She smirks at the therapist, suddenly hip to his tricks. "You made me say that! But you're right. It *is* a good place to live." She turns to me again. "Your cells want you to know that there is nothing more for you to do, Liz. Just love me, love yourself, and they will do the rest."

I look at her. I look into her eyes and she looks into mine. I don't think I have ever felt as uninhibited locking eyes with another person. I see her; she sees me. We are ourselves, and we are each other. I pick up my hand and wave good-bye to my cells. "Have fun in there," I say.

"And what about you, Liz?" The therapist turns to me. "Why exactly did you come here today?"

"To hear that. To let go. To stop being hypervigilant about my cells, about Maggie's health, about my work and my kids and you name it—somehow I have it hooked up in my head that it's my job to stay on top of *everything*. If I do, then maybe I can control the outcome. Like I have to be smart about everything all the time. That's the job description of me."

"So you think being smart and being in control are the same thing?" the therapist asks. "That hypervigilance is the same as intelligence?" He doesn't wait for me to answer. "I don't think they're the same. I think it's pretty stupid sometimes to try to control life. And pretty smart to let things go. To surrender. And the smartest people, the wisest people, know when to hold on, and when to let go. So maybe you weren't as smart as you thought you were," he says with a twinkle in his eye.

"Mm-hmm," I say. "This is what I seem to have to learn over and over. This is the ongoing work of *my* lifetime—to let go, to let the world take care of itself. I mean I know it's good to help, to try to make things better, but people can help themselves. They want to help themselves. And they even want to help me! I stay so hypervigilant that people rarely see I need help too. That's not very smart, is it?"

"And what would happen, Liz," the therapist asks me, "if every now and then you let the world take care of itself? How would that make you feel?"

"Useless. And anxious." The words just pop out of my mouth. "I'd feel anxious that I was falling down on the job, that things wouldn't get done, or they wouldn't get done right."

"Well, things are falling apart in the Middle East, Liz," the therapist says gravely. "I think you better go over there right now and make yourself useful."

I laugh. "You know, I actually feel guilty that I'm not over there right now. And every other place in the world where there's a problem. Maybe I could help."

"Oh dear," the therapist says. "You have a huge job on your hands, don't you?" He smiles at me. "There's no way you can help everyone and everything," he says. "This world will always be falling apart and coming together and falling apart. *You* will always be falling apart and coming together and falling apart. So will your friends and family. You cannot control this unruly life of ours. Can you be OK with that? Can you be better than OK? Can you celebrate the unruliness?"

"I can try," I say with all sincerity. "I am trying."

Maggie pats my hand. The dog thumps his tail. The therapist just sits there. After a long silence he says, "You know, I think we covered everything. I think both of you know what you have to do. You sisters work fast! Let's not complicate the beautiful work done here today. Go get an ice cream cone down the street."

We leave the therapist's office. It's only four o'clock. It feels like we're cutting out of school. We walk down the street holding hands, get ice cream cones, and then Maggie decides we should visit her daughter, who lives nearby. We take the scenic route, following the Connecticut River, which flows between New Hampshire and Vermont. It's a beautiful, bright, windy day. The late-afternoon sun falls on the trees, turning them a color that has no name. Shamrock?

Green apple? Chartreuse? Nothing quite describes the electric color coursing through the leaves, suffusing the atmosphere with an emerald light. The river is glacier green, swift with snowmelt from the mountains. Everything is moving, changing, alive.

The road turns sharp where the big Connecticut River meets the smaller Ompompanoosuc River. As we take the turn, Maggie says, "There's something I forgot to say in the therapy session."

"What?" I ask. I look over at her. She's crying.

"I forgot to say that this has been the best year of my life."

My breath catches in my throat and my eyes fill with tears. I pull the car to the side because I don't want to drive off the road and into a tree. Maggie's put way too much into staying alive for me to kill her in a car crash.

"I know I mostly complain about my aches and pains to you, Liz," Maggie says. "And I don't thank you enough. I know it's your cells that are keeping me alive."

"You don't have to say that," I interrupt.

But she keeps talking, as if the same force that is moving the wind in the trees and the water in the rivers is moving through her. Her words come fast and strong. They tumble over each other like a waterfall. "I need to tell you what a privilege it is to live the life I have lived," she says. "Sometimes I feel like the wealthiest person in the world. Wealthy with our childhood, our parents, our values, our education. Wealthy with my amazing kids and Oliver and the best sisters in the world. Wealthy with a warm home, and good food, and friends, and just being alive here on the amazing earth. I am greedy for more. I want thirty more good years. But I want you to know I'm also at peace with dying. I will embrace it because we all must! And for the record, I have had fifty-eight great years. Even the bad years are OK now because of how good the past years have been. I know it must sound weird that the years of my life with cancer have been the best years. And especially this year—this terrible year has been the best year of my life. So thanks for that, Liz. And I don't want you to worry about me, OK? Promise me that. I want you to trust that I can handle whatever happens. No matter what the end of this looks like, I want everyone to know that it's been for something. Something good. Will you remember that, even if I forget? Because I probably will forget."

"Yes, I will remember—for both of us. For all of us. I promise."

We sit at the side of the road watching the green leaves flutter in the sky and the wild river rush below. I think about the awful miracle of this year, this best year of Maggie's life, and how she turned her crummy fate into something beautiful.

"Amor fati," I say.

"Amor what? Is this some Edith Hamilton thing?"

"No, it's worse. It's from Nietzsche."

"OK, lay it on me," Maggie laughs.

"It's Latin for what you just said. Amor fati: love of fate. Nietzsche said if you could say yes to everything, even if your fate sucks, if you could love it and not just bear it, you would find beauty and meaning everywhere." I leave it at that. We drive on, the beauty of the day speaking for itself.

Back home, I find a passage from Nietzsche—written in the midst of an illness that would eventually take his life.

I want to learn more and more to see as beautiful what is necessary in things; then I shall be one of those who make things beautiful. Amor fati: let that be my love henceforth! I do not want to wage war against what is ugly. I do not want to accuse . . . And all in all and on the whole: some day I wish to be only a Yes-sayer.

SAME-SAME,
BUT DIFFERENT

AFTER THE THERAPY SESSION AND Maggie's rhapsodic rant at the side of the road, I stop wondering whether or not my state of mind affects Maggie; I stop asking doctors and researchers and spiritual teachers their take on the connection I may or may not still have to the cells in Maggie's body; I stop researching the power of prayer and peace of mind to influence recovery from disease. I stop asking the questions and start *being* the answer.

The Vietnamese Zen monk Thich Nhat Hanh was exiled from his homeland during the Vietnam War, and now travels the globe teaching what he calls "being peace." He says, "Being peace is the basis for making peace. Only by establishing peace in yourself can you be helpful in establishing peace for others, for the world." One of the most powerful teachers of meditation in the world, this small monk, dressed in plain brown robes, offers one simple practice wherever he goes: the practice of "interbeing," of developing the awareness of our connection to each other, to the earth, to the stars, and to the universe itself. We are made of the same stuff, the same elements, the same molecules. You don't have to go through a bone marrow transplant for this to be true with all your relations, colleagues, friends, even those you may call enemies.

The air you breathe is the air I breathe. We pass molecules back and forth, in and out, around the world. We feel what each other feels; we face the same hurdles and confusions; we strive for understanding and love. We share the same planet; we need each other; we *are* each other. We are strands in a tapestry we cannot see because we are part of it.

So instead of wondering if love heals, I try to be love. I infuse the atmosphere around me with as much love and kindness as is genuine and real. Whenever my heart sends shriveled little bombs out into the world—when I'm jealous or judgmental or pissed off, like last night when the people renting my neighbor's house were blasting headbanger music from the deck—I stop myself and revert to being love (and *then* call them). If my cells up the road in Maggie's body are still connected to my inner landscape, then radiating love and practicing kindness in all situations is an intelligent way to proceed. And if what I do has no bearing whatsoever on Maggie's health, it's still a better way to live—for me and for all those around me.

Does peace heal? Then be at peace. When reading the newspaper, when confronting suffering and ignorance and brutality, breathe in peace, and breathe out peace. I drop my shoulders, soften my belly, feel the cells in my own body vibrate to a more peaceful rhythm. Actions that emanate from a place of peace tend to be more effective than actions that spring from chaos and rage. I have found this to be true at work and with my kids and as an activist in the world.

Does the truth heal? Yes, because the truth sets my soul free in a world hungry for authentic soulfulness. One person speaking the truth emboldens the souls of others. Therefore, it is an act of healing to speak from my own true voice with love and conviction—to care less about what others think of me and more about what I know is good and right.

What I'm beginning to understand is how much easier it is to think about things like love, peace, and truth, or to read about them, or tell other people about them, than it is to actually do or be them. To actually put into action what Dr. King called "the practical art of living in harmony." It's remarkable the lengths we will go to turn a plain message into a complicated theory. Jesus preached the most pared-down, dirt-simple kind of truth, and then a bunch of theoretical thinkers messed with it and turned his words into a religion with rules and punishments and things to memorize and get dressed up for. Same with other saints and prophets from every religion—their words are basic, but we humans go through all sorts of convoluted maneuvers to metabolize their wisdom.

Even though it may seem that human beings are the most obstinate species ever created; even though it often looks like we'll never learn how to be peace, or love, or truth—we *do* learn, we *can* change. Thich Nhat Hanh suggests that his students start each day with this prayer:

> *Waking up this morning, I smile.*
> *Twenty-four brand new hours are*
> *before me. I vow to live fully in each*
> *moment and to look at all beings*
> *with the eyes of compassion.*

Today I vow to be love, and though I break the vow over and over, I keep coming back to it. When I awake, I vow to be love with my husband. I vow to be love even though he hasn't shaved, even though I've heard the story he tells at breakfast many times before. Instead of being impatient, I turn to my husband and offer my whole self to him—no resistance, no irritation, just love. And miracle of miracles, the whole feeling in the room changes. It's as if the sun breaks through a cloud, bathing us in its healing warmth and magnanimous spirit.

I head off to work, and before entering the office, I vow to be love with every colleague I meet with. At first the best I can do is pay attention if I'm antsy or annoyed.

But as the day goes on, being love gets easier and easier, as my acceptance muscles get stronger than my attacking ones. At the end of the workday, I hug the UPS man in the parking lot. I may have taken the exercise a little too far.

Thomas Merton, the Trappist monk and social activist, said that as he grew older he realized it was not ideas that change the world but simple gestures of love given to the people around you, and sometimes to those you feel most at odds with. He wrote that in order to save the world, you must serve the people in your life. "You gradually struggle less and less for an idea," Merton wrote, "and more and more for specific people. In the end, it is the reality of personal relationship that saves everything."

When we know and love ourselves, down to the marrow of our bones, and when we know our oneness with each other, down to the marrow of our souls, then love becomes less of an idea and more of the only sane way to proceed. We are one, we are many, and love is the bridge.

There's a saying I heard a lot when I visited Thailand, especially when buying food from carts on the street. It wouldn't matter what kind of food I was interested in. I could be eyeing a noodle dish and ask the vendor, "Is that chicken?" The man would hand me the food, tilt his head side to side, and say, "Same-same, but different." Or I'd see a pile of sticky rice balls with bits of color and ask, "Are those pieces of mango?" "Same-same, but different," the lady would singsong. What did that mean? If I tried to clarify, like if I said, "Is that mango or papaya?" I'd get the same answer: "Same-same, but different."

Now, several times a day, I find myself using that phrase. I tilt my head side to side and say, "Same-same, but different." We are same-same. And yet we are different. Maggie and I are one, linked forever through ancestry, and blood cells, and love. And yet each of us has our own path and fate. Same-same, but different. This one little line gets to the gist of some of the most esoteric, dense, and secretive spiritual texts ever written. With apologies to Lord Shiva and Buddha, Jesus and Saint Teresa of Avila, Muhammad and Jalaluddin Rumi, and with deference to tomes like the huge and rambling Hindu Upanishads, *The Tibetan Book of the Dead*, and the mystical Jewish and Christian and Islamic holy books, I follow a riddle-like saying I heard at a food stall. Same-same, but different. It brings the wisdom of the ages together for me; it helps me to remember that our life is our own, and yet we belong to each other. We are individual selves, each with a unique purpose to be discovered and expressed. And we are threads in a tapestry beyond our imagining.

Part Five

THE DAYS BETWEEN

And there were days I know
When all we ever wanted
Was to learn and love and grow
Once we grew into our shoes
We told them where to go
Walked halfway around the world
On promise of the glow
Stood upon a mountain top
Walked barefoot in the snow
Gave the best we had to give . . .

—ROBERT HUNTER/JERRY GARCIA

PLUM JAM

IN EARLY SEPTEMBER, ONE YEAR after the transplant, I come up to Maggie's house to drive her to the hospital for tests. We haven't seen each other since our session with the therapist—the longest we have been apart since we signed on for the marrow ride. It's been good for both of us to disentangle from our Maggie-Liz identity. My obsessive sense of responsibility has quieted down. And Maggie has claimed her life again—with all its unknowns and possibilities, its terrors and hopes. She has settled as best she can into living in the unknown. When she talks about this year, I am reminded of the words to the Grateful Dead song "Days Between," when Jerry Garcia sings, "Once we grew into our shoes, we told them where to go." This, of all the years in my sister's life, is the one when she grew into her shoes and told them where to go. The year she dipped down into her marrow and found the freedom to "learn and love and grow."

Now I am sitting in the waiting room of 3Z, the wing of the hospital where people get PET scans that can detect the smallest cancer molecule anywhere in the body. We are here because a mysterious growth is wrapping itself around the medial nerve in Maggie's arm, causing terrible pain and, of course, the fear that the cancer has returned. The growth may just be a side effect of so much chemotherapy, or it could be swelling from graft-versus-host disease. But the rolling cough has also returned, the one that was the first sign of the lymphoma's recurrence eighteen months ago: another reason for the PET scan.

The scan involves injecting a small dose of a radioactive chemical into the vein of the arm, which travels through the body and is absorbed by the organs and tissues. Then the patient lies flat and perfectly still for an hour in the PET scanner—a large, doughnut-shaped machine. The scanner records the energy given off by the radioactive substance and turns it into three-dimensional pictures. Areas of the body that contain the energy of cancer light up like bulbs on a Christmas tree.

The great poet-sage Khalil Gibran said, "Work is love made visible." I think the PET scan is love made visible. The whole hospital is love made visible: doctors, nurses, PET scan operators, cleaners, clergy, cafeteria workers, all making love visible through their daily work. I have no patience for those who berate Western medicine or hate hospitals. Modern medicine has its usefulness, and is as sacred as any other attempt to make love visible. When things get really tough, hospitals are where the love-angels dwell.

As Maggie is in the scanner, I sit in the waiting area with my fellow human beings. Some, like me, are comparatively healthy. Others wear baseball caps covering chemo-head baldness, or are in hospital gowns, or have that scared-animal look in their eyes. We all sit and wait.

At a conference I organized, a man asked the spiritual teacher Eckhart Tolle a question about waiting. "Are there specific meditation practices to do while waiting for someone to arrive or for something to start?" the man asked. Eckhart Tolle sat in silence for quite a while as we waited for his response. "There is no such thing as waiting," he finally answered. "There is only being present to each moment. There is no such thing as the past or the future; there is only the Now. Don't waste this moment. Don't waste all the moments of your life. It is not uncommon for people to spend their whole life waiting to start living."

This has been my practice for years and years—to stop waiting. To quiet the mind from its compulsive rehashing of the past and its restless worrying about the future, and instead to be curious and nonjudgmental about the here and now. And so, instead of waiting in the hospital waiting room, distracted by my own thoughts, I dive into the moment and swim around with the other people. A young woman is being taken away in a wheelchair. Her little boy runs after her, crying. She tries to kiss him good-bye through the mask over her face. A morbidly obese woman walks in, leaning on two canes. An orderly finds her a wheelchair, but it is too small for her enormous behind. She rests against the wall, short of breath. The orderly stands next to her, holding her hand. A few minutes later, a man is wheeled in and parked in the middle of the room. He is draped only in a thin white blanket. He has a big lump growing out of the top of his head, and he shivers and coughs. People avert their eyes, wanting to spare him the indignity of his helplessness.

After a while, merely observing the present moment becomes unbearable. The poor man with the lump on his head is still alone. It's been ten minutes and no one has come for him. Those entering the waiting room must step around his wheelchair. He lowers his eyes each time this happens. Should I do something? Eckhart Tolle also says, "Any action is often better than no action . . . If it is a mistake, at least you learn something, in which case it's no longer a mistake." I get up and ask the man in the wheelchair if he'd like me to wheel him somewhere else. He nods. There's a flash of grace when our eyes meet. I push his wheelchair to the side of the room, where he can sit in relative privacy, and return to my seat.

It's work to stay awake and curious in the midst of everything life throws our way. I don't think its something we can do alone. We're like the big woman leaning against the wall. We need someone to hold our hand, to prop us up. We're like the man in the wheelchair, marooned in the middle of daily life. We need someone to give us a push.

Sometimes I think I will get to my deathbed, look around at my loved ones, and with a sigh of relief say, "Whew, I made it here alive. Because of you. Thanks."

After the PET scan is over, Maggie wants to leave the hospital right away. "Let's get out of here," she says. It's what she always says. We drive in silence through the blazing Indian summer. She is drowsy from a sedative. She closes her eyes. The hour-long stretch of highway between the hospital and Maggie's town is spectacular in all seasons, but today it is achingly lovely. The sugar maples have turned overnight, their leaves scarlet against the bluest sky. And the passing woods are dark and green and piney, speckled with birches, their thin white trunks and gold petals shimmering in the September sunlight. I drive, sailing us through the day, as Maggie goes in and out of sleep.

Right before we turn onto her road, she sits up and decides we should visit the nearby orchard so she can make plum jam. "Fuck living in the present moment," she says. "I want to make jam for the future whether or not I will be in it." And so we park and walk into rows and rows of gnarled trees and berry bushes and grapevines stretching up a long hill. Apple trees bend to the ground, heavy with fruit. Yellow bees loop around, like drunks. The air smells of cider. The plum trees look as if a pointillist had painted hundreds of purple dots on the branches. We pick way too many plums and a bucketful of Honeycrisp apples, and then some late-blooming red raspberries.

We come into the house carrying bags of fruit. We're laughing about something no one else would find funny, or maybe they would for a minute, but they wouldn't repeat it over and over in different accents, cracking each other up every time. The phone is ringing. I answer it. It's the hospital. And in a second, everything changes—again.

The lymphoma is back. It's in Maggie's lungs, in her groin, in her uterus, and in the growth in her arm, the other arm, her bones. The Christmas tree of her body lit with cancer energy everywhere. Mantle cell lymphoma—the alien invader she's been fighting for almost a decade with several rounds of big-gun chemotherapy, full-body radiation, one autologous stem cell transplant, one allogeneic bone marrow transplant, and a host of other treatments to deal with the side effects from the chemo, radiation, and transplants. How much more can her small body take?

The evening is a déjà vu. This is the third time I witness Maggie tell her kids that she is close to the edge of death. The third time she wonders aloud to us about how to die—slowly and painfully, or more deliberately using pills to hasten the process? Once again, her son holds onto her and weeps. He is building a house up the road for a future he so dearly wants to share with his mother. Her daughter calls, and I listen to their conversation as if I'm hearing two actors read their lines. I want to tell the playwright that people don't really talk like this—it's too intense, too raw. Tone it down a little, I want to say. The audience needs some space to breathe.

Later that night, as I am falling asleep, I think about the present moment and I wonder if I've ever fully understood what it means. I have been a diligent student of mindfulness since I was nineteen. I may have said the words "being in the moment" as often as I have said "hello" and "good-bye." But what is a moment? Are moments separate things, strung together one after another like the beads on a rosary? Is each moment like an inch mark on a ruler, or a rung on a ladder that we climb, hand over hand, breath by breath, now, now, now? The wise ones tell us not to get attached to each moment, and not to look behind or ahead either. We're instructed to hold onto the ladder rung with full attention but no attachment—each step up the ladder a brand-new clean moment, free of the past and unclouded by the future. "Beginner's Mind" is what the Buddhists call it. That's how to meditate: begin again with each breath, which is practice for living.

But right now, the classic meditation instructions seem too dry for real life, with its sticky past and its undoubtedly messy future. Perhaps that spanking-clean present moment is not what I have imagined it to be. Perhaps there's no such thing as a bunch of separate moments at all. Instead there's just one unfinished, imperfect, ever-changing, superfascinating, interconnected tapestry of time and space where all things happen simultaneously, undivided, forever. Suddenly, I want spiritual instructions that tell me I *should* look behind and ahead and all around at the whole confusing, scary, embarrassing canvas with great affection—even with attachment. That it's OK to wallow in nostalgia when I hear a song from my youth, or to plot the future with trepidation and hope. To enjoy what comes; to grieve what is lost; to laugh at my clumsy missteps and at the innocent hubris of my plans. To be a wide-open eye in eternity, a heart beating in wonder, an inquisitive mind with an ironic sense of humor.

Perhaps this is what those wise ones have always meant about being in the moment. Because I don't think we can live here on earth as human beings without dragging the past with us into the present. I mean, you wouldn't bring home bags of fruit if you didn't cherish memories of making jam with your mother. And you wouldn't stay up with your sister till almost midnight—two witches cackling over a cauldron of bubbling plums—without an eye toward the future: a future of someone sitting at the kitchen table on a cold winter morning, with a cup of coffee and toast with plum jam. So tonight I revise my mindfulness instructions, for myself only. You can make up your own. Here are mine: We are made from the past, and for the future. Both are embedded in the present moment. Without the pain and sweetness of what came before, and the enticing lure and heart-pounding fear of what comes next, we cannot celebrate the fullness of the living moment.

Everywhere I look in Maggie's house there are emblems of the past and signs pointing to the future. Memories and dreams: the photos of her kids at different ages, and the forced bulbs that will bloom at Christmas. The old oak kitchen table that belonged to my parents, and the can of new paint waiting to cover the chipped kitchen cabinets. The compost bucket full of wrinkled plum skins, and those jars of jam cooling on the counter. Add all of that up, and what you get is Now.

I think of my own memories and dreams. I know the difference between the ones that keep me stuck and the ones that add flavor to my life. I think most of us can tell the difference. The ones that taste of envy or blame—those are the memories and dreams we'd be wise to let go of. But the other ones are ours to keep. They strengthen the soul and feed the imagination. Like the memories of my parents that I hang in my heart like priceless artwork— mysterious, colorful, complex. Or like my dream of running away with Bruce Springsteen and singing backup in the E Street Band. I know I won't do this, but I like keeping that imaginary door open. You never know.

OTHER SUNSETS

I AWAKE IN THE MIDDLE of the night with middle-of-the-nightism. Dreadful scenarios begin to form miles out in the ocean of negativity. They swell into high waves and roll toward the shore, one after the other, dragging with them cunning arguments for why their dark attitude is far superior to hope or faith. I know I should stop their advance. I know they are figments of my fearful mind, and that while they may contain slivers of possibility, most paranoia-crusted nightmares do not come true. Therefore, I should roll over, and go back to sleep. A good rule of thumb: *don't believe anything you think between midnight and dawn.*

But of course, as I lie in my sister's guest room, tossing around on the futon sea, I allow the waves to roll over me: waves of blame, waves of suspicion, waves of dread. I blame my cells for not working hard enough, or maybe they contained some kind of mutant irregularity that caused Maggie's cancer cells to morph into an even more virulent strain of lymphoma. Perhaps we never should have gone through with the transplant. Before I can get battered by that one, a new wave lands: I wonder if living so close to an orchard—the very one where we picked the plums—gave her the cancer in the first place. Did toxic pesticides leach into the soil and flow down the hillside and spread through the air, making this pristine-seeming valley a death trap? And now the jars of wholesome plum jam cooling on the counter contain little poison bombs that will detonate in someone else's body. Even as I sleep under the open window with the cool autumn breeze blowing through the curtains, I am breathing in death. The waves of doubt and doom murmur their frightful opinions; I believe them all.

I'm just about to drown in middle-of-the-nightism when, for some reason, I see in my mind's eye the large woman from earlier in the day. There she is, leaning against the waiting room wall, holding onto the orderly, reminding me that one can ask for help when drowning. So I turn on the light, get out of bed, find my laptop, and fire off an SOS to my husband. I tell him about the day—about the test and the results and also about a walk Maggie and I took at sunset, after the hospital had called. When we passed her vegetable garden she said in a voice laced with sad astonishment, "I thought I would have one more year in the garden." And when we walked across the bridge she said, "I thought I would swim in the river again." And when we came to the barn she said, "I have so much art left to make; I thought I would have more time in my studio."

I tell my husband that I am having trouble staying above water; that I'm in need of a spiritual life raft. "Please help me find hope. Please remind me of the soul's eternal journey," I pound out on the keyboard.

In the morning, this is in my in-box, written by my husband in the light of day:

> Here's the best I can do on short notice. Keep a pure heart, and you and she will indeed see other sunsets and bountiful gardens and swim in flowing rivers and make art from nothing but your own visions. All the best that your heart can feel and imagine will be

realized on the next plane and in the next time you
are alive here. Just stay in love now, and after she
dies. And also, you can still talk to her after she has
passed. I know how much you two like to talk.

---

field notes • september 12

the report shows the cancer is everywhere, from bones to organs, so this is very real. meantime, i feel pretty good. so i made a rustic plum tart, picked beans not damaged by frost, observed what frost damage occurred (minimal), and am heading to the studio because the frames arrived for a new piece and i am excited to frame it up. i may be dead by the winter craft tour, but i shall keep doing the work. i am meeting with my print photographer today who is going super fast knowing my situation, to print the new work. i am uber excited. as liz's friend says "dance the wild dance of no hope". i have never understood depression, even in my sad illness. i am not depressed. i am sad to be leaving all the beauty. i think beauty is the answer to any problem. beauty and love. loving your kids, your partner, your friends and family. loving the growth of gardens and plants and the miracle of seasons. sharpening your awareness of the wind, sun on your face, the feel of dirt when you pull weeds, the beautiful smallness of life. i will miss it so.

ROOTS AND SEEDS

IT'S NOVEMBER AND ONCE AGAIN I am on the road, driving to Maggie and Oliver's house. By now, the three-hour drive is as familiar as my commute to work. As are the feelings that ride along with me. I start out energized. I turn on the radio. I sing along. I listen to the news. I switch to a far-right talk show for some cultural diversity. Then I get restless, bored, or overcome by worry and self-doubt. Am I doing enough for Maggie? Am I doing too much? Should I visit so often? Should I stay longer? As I get closer to Vermont, I want silence. I turn off the radio. I quiet my mind. I feel what I am feeling.

Today, as I near Maggie's house, I talk out loud to my parents, whose presence I often sense on these drives. To my father I say little—it's more of a quick check-in, as if I am confirming he'll indeed be at the dock when Maggie's ferry comes in. With my mother, I enter into the circular conversation I've been having since her fretful death ten years ago. "Why didn't you tell us you wanted to die?" I ask my mother for the thousandth time, clenching the steering wheel. "Why did you make it so hard on yourself and us? We could have helped you." I listen closely for her answer. I hear nothing but the swish of tires on the rain-wet road. But a few minutes later a word appears in my mind's eye: "COURAGE."

Like on a teleprompter, the word "courage" moves slowly across the screen in my head. Maybe my mother wants me to know she did the courageous thing—she spared herself and us years of disability and dependence.

"Yes, I know you were brave," I tell my mother. "But you didn't have to be brave all alone." I think of my mother in her final days, choosing to die instead of weighing down her daughters. It still clutches at my heart—her loneliness. It still makes me mad—the way she handed us an impossible task. We were supposed to help her die even though she denied she was dying. But this was her way in life as it was in death: hidden, nervous, never wanting to call attention to herself or to burden us. "But we wanted to be burdened, Mom!" I say out loud to the ghost in the car. "We loved you. Love means being burdened." Now I am laughing at myself, remembering the line in the Erich Segal romance novel *Love Story*: "Love means never having to say you're sorry."

My older sister Katy and I were hitchhiking in Europe the summer the movie adaptation of *Love Story* came out. I had finished my freshman year in college. Katy had graduated and was living in Europe. We met in London and went wherever our thumbs took us—England, Ireland, Italy, Switzerland. Eventually, we ended up in Paris. One day, tired of working so hard to speak and understand French, we went to the cinema in the middle of the afternoon. We chose the American film *Love Story* because it was in English with French subtitles, and it gave us a language advantage over the Parisians. At the end of the movie, after Ali McGraw's beautiful young character has died, Ryan O'Neal says the famous last line about love meaning you never have to say you're sorry. As the music swelled, Katy and I guffawed over the sniffles of the viewers sitting next to us and then ran out of the theater, laughing hysterically like the snotty, sarcastic girls we were back then. That was before living and loving and losing had knocked the snot out of us.

My mother's death, unlike the one told in *Love Story*, was not a tearjerker. In fact, I didn't cry much at all during the whole confounding mess of her decline. None of us did because the seriousness of her illness took us by surprise. For years, she had not let us in on a carefully guarded secret—that her Crohn's disease was killing her, that she was in pain, that she needed surgery. We didn't cry because we didn't know, and then when we finally did, she wouldn't let us. Even after emergency surgery, even when she was actively dying in her bed at home, going in and out of consciousness, she denied she was sick. She had not eaten for days, and this time we hadn't put her back in the hospital to have nutrition pumped into her stomach.

A week or so previously, a nurse at the hospital had taken me and Maggie and Katy aside as we were collecting our tiny mother for the third time since her colon surgery. "Your mother doesn't want to come back to the hospital again," she said.

"But she doesn't eat," I told the nurse. "She'll die."

"Your mother asked me to tell you not to readmit her," the nurse repeated.

"Did she say she wants to die?" Katy asked. "Because she hasn't told us that. Is that what she wants? To die?"

"She just asked me to tell her daughters not to bring her back to the hospital," the nurse said in an even tone.

"But if we don't bring her back—" Maggie started up the refrain again.

The nurse interrupted. "Sometimes the best a person can do is to speak in code," she said kindly. "So, I'll say it again: Your mother does not want you to bring her back to the hospital."

That was the clearest statement we were to get, indirectly, from our mother about her plans to die. I would say "her plans to commit suicide," but does one call it suicide if the person is eighty-two, has had surgery she didn't want, and now has a permanent ostomy bag? Someone whose definition of life is independence and activity? Someone who was raised in a religion that denies the reality of the body but now has a graphic manifestation of its most private function strapped to her belly in the form of a plastic sack of excrement? Is it called suicide if a person just stops eating and slowly, quietly, furtively slips away, even though her doctors have told her she could live many more productive years once she got the hang of the ostomy bag?

Whatever you call her death, my sisters and I clucked over our mother as she was dying. In her final moments, we gathered around her bed. Maggie—the seeds of cancer asleep in her blood—stood at my mother's feet. My mother, down to eighty pounds, the hue of death already dusting her face, had been breathing irregularly for several minutes, intoning a sharp "ha" on the inhalation and a long "laaaaah" on the exhalation, like the Sufi zikr chant done by the dervishes in their all-night prayer circles. Her last breaths were whispered prayers. On each inhalation she would gasp, "Ha!" She would pause and we would wait, and then she'd exhale: "Laaaaah." "Ha . . . laaaaah. Ha . . . laaaaah. Ha . . ." She held onto her last inhalation for a long, long time and finally exhaled with a whistling sound. When that last breath left my mother's body, Maggie jumped backwards, as if the exhalation had struck her. Later, she told us she had seen a rod of light, the color of molten iron ore, leave the center of my mother's chest and come straight at her. The gold light entered her, she said, at the very center of her body. A bright yellow star, she called it, trailing a warm and soft tail of green light, like a meteor. For days afterwards Maggie said she felt bathed in that green light. She didn't question the vision. She received it, knowingly, and took it into her own body as a parting gift of courage.

At the time, Maggie was the last person I would have imagined having a deathbed vision of molten ore flying out from our mother's heart, depositing a star of strength in Maggie's body. If anyone would have seen such a thing, it would have been me, and then no one would have believed it, writing it off as one more dubious story from the woo-woo member of the family. But coming from the pragmatic and skeptical Maggie, the apparition had clout.

Within a year of that moment, Maggie left her marriage, and in two years she was diagnosed with cancer. Had my mother been alive during Maggie's struggles, she would not have known how to help; she would have judged Maggie's decision to leave her husband, and she would have crumbled with the news of her illness. And then she would have retreated into nervous isolation. But in her final moments, my mother must have gained the grand perspective she lacked as an anxious, self-doubting human. She must have seen what was ahead for her beloved third daughter—the daughter most like her. And with that last breath, she summoned up every bit of energy left in the shell of her body and shot an arrow of courage into Maggie.

This is what I am thinking about when I pull into Maggie's driveway. I get out of the car and shake off the memories. It's now. It's not then. It's Maggie, not my mother. It's been two months since Maggie's cancer returned. No one is giving us a straight answer about what to expect now—not because the doctors are keeping information from us. They just don't know what will happen. Although we'd like them to be gods, doctors are people, and people cannot and do not know everything—especially in moments like these. In our last meeting with the team at the hospital, one of the doctors advised us to call in hospice, while another suggested Maggie join a drug trial for a promising new cancer medicine. She chose the drug trial, although so far it doesn't seem to be changing the course of the disease.

I get my bag from the trunk and head up the path to the house. What will I find? Will she look different? Will she be in pain? Is death near? The last bend of the journey from my house to Maggie's always ends with these kinds of questions. Sometimes I will have had a lively phone call with her the night before, and I'll expect to find her up and about. Instead, when I open the front door, she'll be curled up in the window seat, sleeping in the late morning, her skin pale, her breath shallow. Or the opposite: I'll expect her to be napping, but instead she'll be hauling around a wheelbarrow full of compost.

Today, I imagine she'll be in bed, with several pain pills under her belt. But before I get to the house, I hear her voice. She runs out from the big barn, waving her arms, calling, "I'm up here! Come see what I'm working on." Her studio is a long, bright room—the upper story of a barn that Oliver built for them just a couple of years ago, anticipating a long life with Maggie. He keeps his wood-working tools on the bottom floor. She dries and presses plants, and creates her botanical art on the top floor. I walk up the rough granite steps and there she is—a tiny sprite, looking so much like my mother it's laughable. She shows me a huge five-foot giclée print of her newest botanical creation. It's a photograph of a wood-land plant—false Solomon's seal, *Smilacina racemosa*, Maggie in-forms me—complete with its root tendrils and its dying leaves and its brown seedpods, standing upright against a stark white background. She's taken the autumn berries off the plant, smashed them, and used the brilliant color as paint—a swash of crimson bursting out of the seedpod and seemingly off the top of the print and out of the frame. The print is a departure from the small, careful pressed pieces she has been making for the past twenty years. While they have sold well at fine craft shows around the country, this one should be in the Museum of Modern Art.

She says she's been pushing herself to work on these new pieces—collecting plants in the woods, pressing and drying, smashing and painting, photographing and framing, racing to create enough new work for a show in a renowned gallery. She's calling the exhibition *Gone to Seed*. "I may not be able to do this much longer," she tells me. "And this is what I want to do with the time I have left." She asks me to help her write a few paragraphs to hang along with the pieces. This is what we come up with:

Gone to Seed

I have been tromping through the woods for 25 years, foraging for wild plants and springtime ephemerals for my botanical artwork. I've stayed close to home in the Vermont woods, stopped along roadsides all over New England, and traveled far and wide in the Alaskan forests and tundra.

Now it is fall; not my usual collecting time for wildflowers and green shoots. But I am dying. I may not have time to wait for spring. Here in the autumn woods in Vermont, my heart leaps at the broken, eaten, rotting, golden foliage and the many colored fruits standing straight up, or lying on the ground to plant their seed. Life is so rich, even as it prepares to die.

I am calling this series "Gone to Seed." I never intended it to have such profound importance to me. As it has evolved, it has become a clear metaphor for my life. I see the whole cycle of life in the plants in this season, just as I see the whole cycle of life in me. My roots are my exceptional family that nurtured and grew me, and my children are the brilliantly colored seeds, bursting out of the pod and into the world, as I float out of the frame and into the universe.

MOTHER LOVE

THIS TIME, WHEN I AM about to return home, Maggie clings to me.

"Can you stay longer?" she asks.

I want to say, "Why? Why me? Ask one of the other sisters. Ask Katy. Ask Jo. They live closer; they love you too." But I don't say this because she has already told me she can barely be around anyone anymore besides me and her kids and Oliver. That's her team; that's what she wants. And therefore, that's what I do. I unpack my bags, and I stay. I take a chicken out of the freezer to prepare for dinner. I settle in for another night. I shouldn't. I am letting people down at work; I have neglected my home and my family. But I feel a force pulling at me to stay—it's the same force I felt in Montana eight years ago, the same force I felt in my bones when the marrow cells were proliferating.

How did I get here, to this plateau of devotion to my sister, to this place out of time and out of step with the rest of my life? I have been consistently surprised by Maggie's need of me, and by my response to her. Not because the role of caregiver is a new one for me. Cooking, cleaning, chauffeuring—I actually love these caregiver skills that mothering three kids ground into me. And medical researcher. My favorite part of the Sunday *New York Times* is the section where a misdiagnosed disease is finally deciphered by a diligent doctor who won't stop searching until she knows what's killing the patient. And I've never shied away from guts and gore, bodily fluids, hospitals, or standing up to the medical establishment so as to get the best care, the most honest answers. I'm a big fan of Albert Einstein's guiding principle: "Unthinking respect for authority is the greatest enemy of truth."

It is the other roles I have stepped into over these years—or, rather, that we stepped into together, Maggie and I—that have surprised us both. We have become the best of friends. And biggest surprise of all, I have, in many ways, become Maggie's mother and she has also become mine. We are remothering each other. In my constant (and sometimes obsessive) care of her, I am rewriting how we were raised. I am giving her the kind of attention we rarely, if ever, received. The kind that says through constancy and presence, "You are my precious, cherished, worthy girl. I will put you first. I will do this because you are my girl, because you belong to me, we belong to each other, and you belong here on earth with us. And as long as you are here, you deserve to be seen and tended to." That's not the message—expressed or implied—that we received from our parents. They loved us, but they did so without much fanfare or tenderness. They felt it their duty to give us a moral compass, and then we were on our own to go forth as good citizens of the world. Demonstrations of love, acknowledgment of one's unique character, guidance and solace after falls and traumas—these were for other people. These were Hallmark Card coping strategies for the weak and the silly.

The idea that Maggie and I were reparenting each other came to me early one morning as I sped up the New York State Thruway toward Vermont on one of my increasingly repetitive three-hour drives. I was passing the same forests, the same fields, the same road signs, wondering once again, why I am doing this? Should I be doing this? Is this what Maggie really wants, needs? Am I overstepping my bounds, taking up too much space, filling roles better suited for others? And suddenly, ping! The answer to the riddle of "Why?" dropped fully formed from the sky—like a pebble hitting the windshield. It was such a vivid realization, I had to stop on the shoulder of the highway and sit in my car, letting the traffic whizz by.

The answer started as a physical feeling, as if a strong magnet was pulling me toward Maggie, and Maggie toward me. What was it? A line from a poem came to me: "Let yourself be silently drawn by the stronger pull of what you really love." Rumi wrote that. I said the line out loud, several times, as I sat in the muted calm of the idling car. "Let yourself be silently drawn by the stronger pull of what you really love." I was being pulled by the strength of unconditional love. I knew that pull; it was the force I felt when I first laid eyes on my babies. It was primal. It was the response a mother has to a child's cry. It was the response we each long for as children—to be seen by our parents for who we are; to be loved, just because of who we are; to be cared for not because we have done something right but because we are here, we matter, we belong.

I remembered a conversation I had with a friend during the relentless days and nights of being a young mother. My friend, a childless colleague at work, asked me why in the world anyone would have kids. All she could see from the outside looking in was the thankless tedium of snotty noses, interrupted sleep, and the inability to concentrate at work.

"What is the payback?" my friend asked.

Payback? I had never stopped to think about that. But I knew the answer right away: "It's the only shot I'll ever have at unconditional love," I said.

"But children don't love their parents unconditionally," my friend replied.

"That's not what I mean," I said. "It's the only chance *I* will get to love unconditionally. It doesn't matter if my kids' love for me matches my love for them. There's no math involved in this. It's just an incredible feeling. Almost holy. And that's the payback. It's a steep price, you're right. It sucks a good deal of the time. But to love so fully, day in and day out . . . No expectation of anything in return, no real concern for myself. That's the payback."

My friend looked at me like I was crazy, which, of course, I was. Parents *are* crazy. They have fallen in love with a pint-sized tyrant. They have committed to the relationship for life. And although they will never fully live up to the unconditional-love arrow that has pierced their hearts, they will try and try and try, and in that trying will taste the blessed wine of egoless love. But that kind of love is impossible to practice every moment, every day, in the complexity of family life. Monks leave the imperfect world behind in order to pursue God's perfect love. What is the opposite of being a monk? Being a parent.

The longing for unconditional love is universal, and yet I have noticed that few people feel they received enough of it. Rather, they got imperfect parenting from imperfect people. And even though the experts—from neurologists to wise grandmothers— agree that the developing brains and hearts of children need huge doses of tenderness and acceptance, and even though most parents do the very best they can, we can't seem to interrupt the loop of screwy parents creating screwy kids who turn into screwy parents who return the favor to their kids, etc., ad infinitum. If you are a practitioner of perfect parenting, please leave yourself out of the universal "we," and also, please send us some helpful hints.

I once heard Oprah say that during the long run of her television show thousands of interview guests sat on her couch, and every one of them—man or woman—had the same need to be validated, to be seen down to their souls, to be loved for who they were. It didn't matter how old they were, what country they hailed from, what job they held, how much status or money they had, they would sit there like kids, asking the world, "Do you see me? Do I measure up? Does what I say mean something to you?" That lesson was drilled so deeply into Oprah, she made it her life practice to let others know she saw them in their wholeness and depth. "Just saying hello is a way of validating even a stranger," she says.

These thoughts went through my head as I sat at the side of the New York State Thruway, the pebble-sized realization spreading, filling me with an understanding that would guide me for the rest of the days of Maggie's life. Our mother had done the best she could, and now we were stepping in to finish her job; we were responding to the stronger pull of the kind of giving and receiving we had not received as children. We were closing a gap our mother left in the mother-loop. We are stitching the loop with the thread of unconditional love.

SISTERS

IN THE EARLY YEARS OF Maggie's disease, a village of friends and family stepped in to help her heal. I was only one of a large cadre of willing caregivers, including my older sister, Katy, and youngest sister, Jo. But as Maggie's illness began to outpace her healing, and as her fear and then her resignation moved in like a storm, she closed the windows to the world and opened instead to what lay ahead. And little by little, day by day, she began to deny most people entry into her home and into her heart. First it was the outer ring of her friends, then the inner ring, then family, until the only people welcome were her kids and Oliver and me. Even her well-meaning, loyal old friends rubbed her the wrong way; even the doctors and nurses; even her other sisters. And the more she told people to stay away, the more she asked me to come. I would beg her to let Katy and Jo help. And sometimes she would agree, and I would gratefully hand off the baton, return home, and pick up the reins of my own life.

But a week or so later, I'd get a call again. Could I come back? Could I take her to an appointment? Could I speak with her doctors about a new regimen they were considering? Could I call her friends and Katy and Jo and tell them not to visit? I hated telling my sisters to stay away. It felt wrong. But this was not the time to demand that Maggie change her stripes. It would have been better if she gently yet firmly told others what she needed—except she could hardly do that when she was well. And so I tried to explain the situation to my sisters as best I could. Every time I was the bearer of Maggie's messages, I sensed old childhood resentments waking up and sprouting new tendrils. Were Katy and Jo blaming me for taking over? Were they talking about me behind my back? I didn't stop to ask them, and they weren't forthright with me.

Soon I was spending most weekends at Maggie's house, sometimes the whole week. And although it was always hard to leave my own home and work, when I got to Oliver and Maggie's, it was where I most wanted to be. It was where the stronger pull of what I really loved had led me. The world rushed onward, but I got off the train and stayed in the slow, small backwater of loving one person as best I could for as long as I could.

We fell into a routine. Maggie and I would spend mornings in the window seat, in our chosen spots, reading, talking, dozing. We worried and cried; we watched funny videos and laughed; we revisited our childhood; we speculated about life after death. I taught her meditation. She taught me a million things—about planting fruit trees and tending bees, rolling piecrusts and making jam. Much to her chagrin, in the afternoon she would nap and I would do what she no longer could: shop and cook; clean and tidy; call the doctors, check on results, make appointments. Oliver and I would compare notes on research, new drug trials, different doctors. Sometimes I would drive Maggie up north to the hospital for tests and treatments—on the way up, there'd be more talking, more laughing; on the way back, more dozing (her), more praying (me).

In the evenings, Oliver would choose a movie, and the three of us would gather on the guest-room bed with bowls of ice cream—sometimes the only meal of Maggie's day—and settle in for our secret, sacred ritual. It was as if we were having an affair, a three-some that excluded the whole world but was precious to each of us. There were moments in my visits to Maggie and Oliver's house that felt as if I had finally come home, a feeling of not wanting to be anywhere else on earth but right there, in the little guest room, on the funky futon bed, ice cream bowls balanced on our laps, laughing at a movie on their tiny television. Maggie would fall asleep, her head on my shoulder. We'd finish the movie and then say good night, holding onto each other for dear life, for one last hug before she went upstairs and tried, usually unsuccessfully, to turn off her mind, to get beyond the pain and find restful sleep.

From the first moment of her first diagnosis, Maggie must have known something in her marrow, long before she knew it in her mind. Why else would she have called me in Montana and said the two words that calibrated the magnet and set my course for these past eight years? "I'm sick," she had said. And then she asked me to help her, which was stunning since she was not one to ask for help, and certainly not from me. She was more likely to ask our older sister, Katy, the de facto mommy by virtue of seniority, not to mention that Maggie and Katy shared similar personality traits—something they never failed to mention. They were the no-nonsense, athletic go-getters; I was the introspective, intellectual mystic (and this was not a compliment). They lived in Vermont; I lived in New York (another choice I had made that flew in the face of the family values).

Our youngest sister, Jo—the one most like me, the one who also marched to a more meditative drum—had been estranged from the family until recently. Years previously she had married a man who did not like the way Jo had been treated as a child or an adult by our parents, or by us, the sisters. He and Jo viewed our family through a different lens than I did. Sure, our parents had been somewhat neglectful and self-serving, but they were also adventurous and creative. If I had to describe my upbringing using just one word, I would say it was rousing. But that was not Jo's experience. She was a quiet, shy child—a true introvert who barely got a word out in the competitive, fast-paced noise of the sisterhood. We were raised by the same parents, and with the same siblings, but still, we had different childhoods.

One by one, we grew up, we left home, and we went off to college, leaving Jo behind. But she had practice being alone because within the family system she had always felt forgotten, "the least of the Lessers." In her twenties Jo and her husband broke off contact with us. The break was especially hard on Maggie. She and Jo had been a unit as children, and became intimate friends as young women living near each other in Vermont. Maggie missed Jo. We all missed Jo. Our little sister was lost to us. And although she lived close to Maggie and our parents, it felt as if Jo had moved to a foreign part of the galaxy. We would discuss this as a family and wonder if we should try to save her. Jo insisted it was we who needed saving. She had built a life that worked for her; she was happy, she said. My parents were distraught. But they went to their graves without resolution.

During Maggie's first diagnosis and treatments, Jo made tentative steps back toward Maggie. But it wasn't until Jo's husband's untimely death from cancer that she and Maggie began to rebuild their friendship. There were unresolved issues and unspoken hurts, but there was also a bond stronger than the years of separation.

I always thought Maggie would call on Jo or Katy to come to her rescue when she first got sick, but her cells must have known something that none of us could imagine. And maybe my cells perked up, even that first time, when she called me in Montana, and I got right on a plane and flew to her. Perhaps it was because our mother had recently died and I felt a new responsibility. Or was it as simple as this—that my training as a midwife and a spiritual seeker made me the logical choice as a guide through illness? Whatever the reasons, I didn't think twice when she asked for help. And then, when she went into remission, our friendship blossomed. When the cancer came back, and when Maggie was told she would not live without a transplant, and the tests revealed I was a match and Katy and Jo were not, and when the mysterious mother magnet drew me and Maggie together, up out of the ground came buried sibling dramas, competition, jealousy, misunderstandings—as if they'd been waiting not only for eight years but for all the decades we had been sisters.

DON'T MAKE ASSUMPTIONS

GROWING UP IN A LARGE family—and maybe in any family, but certainly in ours—meant living in an atmosphere of competition, a sense that there was not enough to go around. Each of us tried to get more of our parents' (and each other's) love and attention in ways befitting our personalities. In old family movies I can see a preview to the whole story: Katy jumping around, acting out, placating my father, angering my mother. Me noting what did and didn't work with Katy, strategically trying to be what I thought would please my mother—a serious girl, a smart girl. Maggie and Jo waiting like nice little mice in the background, sharing the thin air, their big sisters having already taken up most of the oxygen.

Only now do I understand how much we have competed with each other over a lifetime of being sisters. While our childhood brand of competition might not have taken the form of a football game, we had our own ways—overtly or covertly—of pushing our weight around in order to get the validation and love we longed for. For much of my adult life, I thought of myself as a noncompetitive person, not understanding how I had dragged the same unconscious tactics I used with my sisters into adult relationships, how I had blindly re-created the rules and roles of our sisterhood wherever I went. If there were a twelve-step program for covert competitors, now would be the time for me to ask for forgiveness from people like my ex-husband, my current husband, my friends and colleagues. Now would be the time to say I am sorry for trying every which way to feel loved and valued, respected and taken seriously, instead of the one way that works the best: telling my truth and asking for what I need.

One evening, after an unhappy phone call with Katy, where neither of us seemed to be telling the truth and asking for what we needed, I hear a noise in the living room. It's my husband, hammering in the storm windows, using an old favorite book of mine he's taken down from the shelf.

"Hey! Don't use a book as a hammer," I say.

He looks at the book's cover and hands it to me. "Here," he says, "maybe it's a sign from the universe." It's a book by the Mexican author Don Miguel Ruiz, *The Four Agreements*. I haven't read it in years. As I recall, it's about the power of simple, honest, and bold communication. I decide to read it again, because I need it again, because there is nothing simple about putting simple wisdom into practice. This is true with so many of the "self-help" books I have loved over the years. I don't know what else to call the genre. I'm not referring to superficial books that give pat answers to life's unsolvable mysteries. I'm talking about an ancient genre—the literature of wisdom, the philosophy of living, the books that bear reading over and over. I'm talking about books that place an arm around your shoulder and in a comforting voice say, "Look, I've walked a few steps ahead of you, and I see what's around the bend, and even though you are going to stumble into the same wilderness that I have just scratched my way through, if you take a few minutes, my words may help you avoid some of those same traps and thickets."

Just like religious texts are for some people, or Tolstoy was for my father, or Walt Whitman for my mother, some of the books in my home are my scripture. Sometimes I reread them. Sometimes all I have to do is pass the shelves in my living room and a book catches my eye, and I have a Pavlovian response to its title: *Strength to Love*, *A Room of One's Own*, *Being Peace*. I stand up straighter, I breathe more deeply, I remember my inner dignity, and I vow to spread love and do good work.

This time, the book was being used as hammer. The irony isn't lost on me. I am in need of a clonk upside the head, of an infusion of soul, of courage, of direction. I reread *The Four Agreements*. Don Miguel Ruiz asserts that if you slowly metabolize and practice each of the agreements, over time your relationships will become more truthful, peaceful, graceful. And this will bring joy to you and everyone in your life. Good timing.

The four agreements are:

1. Be Impeccable With Your Word
2. Don't Take Anything Personally
3. Don't Make Assumptions
4. Always Do Your Best

Don Miguel Ruiz explains in more detail the nuances of each of the agreements, and how to live by them. I've been trying to live by the four agreements for years, and when I actually practice them, they help me immeasurably with my husband, my kids, and my colleagues. But there is one arena where I most often forget to apply them, and that is with my sisters. I know I'm not alone in this oddest of human conditions—where the family members we love the most are the ones with whom we behave the worst. Be impeccable with your word at Thanksgiving dinner? I don't think so. Don't take anything personally with your siblings? Don't make assumptions even though you are pretty damn sure you're being unfairly judged? Do your best even when you're worn out from trying to do just that? Years ago, at family gatherings, my most fervent prayer was "Oh, please, dear God, help me hew to these agreements and not revert once again to a paranoid meltdown over something one of my sisters has just said or done."

If I could only practice one of the agreements, I would choose the third: "Don't Make Assumptions." In describing that agreement, Don Miguel Ruiz writes, "Find the courage to ask questions and to express what you really want. Communicate with others as clearly as you can to avoid misunderstandings, sadness, and drama. With just this one agreement you can completely transform your life." This promise may sound like hyperbole, but try it. And try it not only with your family but also with people at work, with people you don't even know, and with the world itself. Stop assuming things—especially the worst things—and you will be surprised how even your most meager attempts will bring welcome changes. Instead of assuming, ask questions; instead of reacting or judging or shutting down, first find out what is really going on in the heart and the life of the other person. Invariably, it is not exactly as you have imagined. First of all, there's a good chance it's not personal to you (see the second Agreement). And if it is, you can approach any problem with the heart of an explorer, with the faith that if you bring enough patience and love to the conversation, both people will benefit in the end.

It can take a long time and some painful reckonings to move through assumptions and into the bigger, blessed truth. But this is the path. You can't go around the hard parts if you want to get beyond "misunderstandings, sadness, and drama" with the people who matter to you.

I began to make all sorts of assumptions soon after I tested positive as Maggie's marrow match. I couldn't tell if I was being paranoid or if the resentment I felt coming from Katy and Jo was real. Was I imagining a hostile tone in a phone call, a snide remark, a lack of warmth? Was I taking things too personally? I had a tendency to do this with my sisters, and especially with Katy, whose love and acceptance I had craved as a little girl, finally gained in adulthood, yet in some deep, childhood place still feared I could lose. Could Katy and Jo possibly be jealous that I was a marrow match and they were not? Did they think I was purposefully leaving them out of caring for Maggie? Is it time now to bring all this up or just let it pass?

"Use the power of your word in the direction of truth and love," Don Miguel Ruiz writes when describing the first Agreement: "Be Impeccable With Your Word." Maggie and I had kept that agreement when we met with the therapist. We had used the power of our words in the direction of truth and love. We had busted up assumptions. And as promised, it had transformed our relationship. But I have resisted doing this with my other sisters. I don't want to create a fuss that will only backfire on Maggie. On top of that, I am exhausted and afraid—afraid to tell the truth to my sisters about their hurtful behavior, and afraid to discover things about myself I don't want to see. Am I indeed leaving them out? Are we reenacting the ancient sisterhood competition? I don't know if I have the bandwidth now to take on one more emotional challenge. But as scared as I am, I am more tired of the tension between us. If there has ever been a time when the sisters of the revolution needed each other, it's now, here at the edge of heartbreak, here at the edge of losing one of us. What the heck, I think. I'm already up to my neck in the ocean of emotions; I might as well go all the way under.

THE PERFECT MATCH

MY GOAL IN CHILDHOOD WAS to win Katy's favor. She was the big sister, the It sister, the cool sister. I desperately wanted to prove my cool—but my bookish nature and the four years between us guaranteed I would never catch up. Katy loves to remind me of an event, one late afternoon in March, when I was a pudgy sixth grader and she was a stylish freshman in high school. It was the end of the day, the end of the weekend, and once again the family was packing up the car to head home from Vermont to Long Island. We were in the muddy parking lot of a ski resort that my father's ad agency represented, where he dragged the whole family each weekend.

As the other sisters loaded skis onto the car's roof rack, I leaned against a tree near the car, by the side of a river, kicking clods of snow into the raging waters. It had been a sunny day, and the cold air rippled with currents of warmth. The foggy moisture rising from the river smelled like spring. I kicked clump after clump of snow into the water, marveling at the way everything changed: snow into water, winter into spring.

Quite suddenly, my loosened ski boot flew off my foot and into the river. "Oh no!" I cried, standing still, watching the boot float downstream. Katy raced to the bank, slid down into the freezing-cold and churning water, and retrieved the ski boot. "And that," she said, tossing the boot at me, "is the difference between you and me."

Even though our differences have shrunk as we have grown—even though I have become less dreamy and more practical, and Katy has, in her own words, become more "pink"—we are who we are. It will always be Katy's nature—her Juno, her soul's fingerprint—to dive into swift-running rivers to save a drowning ski boot, or a drowning person, which I once watched her do. Just knowing that Katy is in this world makes me, and everyone who knows her, feel safer. She's a powerful businesswoman and the matriarch of her family. She's my reference point, my North Star. But Katy can also be impatient and annoyed when something can't readily be fixed, and this makes her less suited for the long and be-wildering process of caring for an ill and dying person.

My contemplative nature served me in the slow, dark nights of midwifery, and it is serving me now as I care for Maggie. But the same trait that makes me a good midwife in birth and death has also made me a serious person, one who can't stop herself from going deep, even when it would be more appropriate (and fun) to splash around at the shore with the other happy kids. I know this about myself. I know that being insistently introspective—*deep*—both inspires and irritates other people. Sometimes they just want to chat or joke around or play a card game, for God's sake. Thank goodness for growing older and wiser—I have actually become younger as I've aged.

Sometimes, when my lofty pontificating irks Katy, she will snap her fingers and bark, "Ski boot!" and I'll shut up and get busy. And when Katy races down riverbanks even when the boot is still on the other person's foot, I'll say, "Katy! Pink!" and she'll soften and slow down. We have earned the right to do this with each other, because over many years, we have cultivated a different kind of love than the one we experienced as children. We have come to rest in "human love," as Anaïs Nin calls it. "Where the myth fails," she writes, "human love begins. Then we love a human being, not our dream, but a human being with flaws."

We didn't start out this way. I came into the world bearing the handicap of being the second-born. Katy took on the role of the eternally pissed-off older sister who resented my very existence, and I responded by being the needy little sister, clamoring for contact and approval. It went on like this until we hitchhiked our way through Europe and survived some harrowing experiences on the road, gaining each other's respect and trust. And although we still misread each other's behavior and hurt each other's feelings, we have learned how to return to love over and over. We are saved by our stubborn devotion and a sense of humor (sometimes).

I know it won't take much for Katy and me to get through the feelings that have hardened around the stress of Maggie's illness. We know how to do this; we have done it before. But still, we break the first three agreements all the time. We take things personally. We make assumptions. And no matter how close two people are it's hard to be impeccable with your word—graceful and truthful at the same time. That's why I've been afraid to have an honest conversation her. But that's why the fourth Agreement is "Always Do Your Best." It's never too late to try to do your best again.

On a cold afternoon in late November I call Katy. I am home. It is four p.m., but it's already dark. Just like me. I am dark and at my wits' end. I call Katy to ask her advice and to commiserate. An oncologist—a friend of a friend—at a renowned cancer hospital in Los Angeles is suggesting a new and promising regimen that

Maggie may try even though it seems we're at the eleventh hour of her life. This remarkably generous doctor is willing to consult with the team at Dartmouth. I have been chasing down Maggie's doctors all afternoon to see what they think, and whether insurance will cover the treatment. Time is of the essence. But everyone I talk to puts me on hold or suggests I talk to someone else. Am I pushing too hard? Should I stop trying to find one more way to help Maggie live? I am getting tired of making these decisions, I tell Katy.

"You're a saint, Liz," she says in a tone I cannot read. Does she mean it? Is she mocking me? Is she insinuating that I am knocking myself out in order to prove how good I am (and how bad she is)? Instead of just wondering, this time I take a deep breath, and I ask her.

"What do you mean, 'you're a saint'? Are you making fun of me? Are you questioning my motives?" My voice wavers and I feel perilously close to falling apart.

I am met with a resounding silence.

"Katy? Are you there?"

A long sigh, and then, "It's OK, Liz," she says, as if I'm a jumpy dog she's trying to calm. "Let's not make a big deal out of anything right now. We're all on edge, all right?"

"No, it's not all right," I say, getting louder. "I want to talk about this. It's been bothering me and I don't have the space for anything to bother me except for Maggie. I need you to be in this with me, Katy."

"Huh," Katy grunts.

"What do you mean, 'huh'?"

"I'd like to be more in this with you," Katy says. "But you keep telling me to stay away."

I feel heat rising in my face, and a truth-ache churning in my belly. I want to yell angry, injured things, but in the back of my brain I hear Don Miguel Ruiz saying, "Be impeccable with your word." Oh, rats. It would be so satisfying right now to release a tirade of heartbreak on Katy. I don't do it.

Instead, I say, "Katy, do you really think I want to do this all alone?"

"It sure feels that way sometimes. Like you do it better than anyone else, so why would you need me?"

I start to cry. Forget it, Don Miguel; forget impeccability. I'm too upset. I let loose a long string of tearful, irate words—about how judged and unappreciated I feel by Katy and Jo. And how confusing it is when Maggie asks me to be the gatekeeper. How I second-guess my instincts all the time. Am I doing this right? Am I keeping people away unnecessarily? Am I a control freak? Do I secretly enjoy being the special one, the one in charge? I end my rant with a flurry of feelings I didn't even know I had: that I'd been abandoned by Katy during the marrow harvest; that I had been scared and needed her; that I'd been hurt when she minimized the procedure and didn't check up on me afterwards. I feel like a little girl throwing a tantrum to get my mother's attention.

"Why didn't you come to the hospital to be with me? Were you mad at me?" I cry.

"What in the world would I be mad at you for?" Katy asks.

"For being Maggie's perfect match!" This unexpected statement takes us both by surprise.

"Oh, honey!" Katy says. "Of course I wasn't mad. I was thrilled at least one of us matched. I was relieved. I was glad it was you. I didn't want to have *my* bone marrow harvested. You seemed so brave. You went into your smart-girl research mode and left me in the dust. I guess I felt inadequate. I feel inadequate now. You know how to be with Maggie. The whole thing terrifies me. I want to fix it and I can't."

Now we're both crying.

"And I didn't know you wanted me at the hospital," Katy says. "I thought you just wanted Maggie there. I should have been there for you, Liz. I didn't know you wanted that."

"I didn't know either," I say. "I was too freaked out to know anything. And we're our parents' girls. We don't ask for help."

"God forbid," Katy says, quoting our mother. "God forbid we ask for help. That would mean we need it. Or deserve it, or something like that. That would put a burden on other people, which is something that one just doesn't do."

"You know what's funny?" I say. "All this time, I've been trying to get Maggie to ask for what she needs. To convince her that she deserves our help, our love, our care. And look at me! I couldn't even ask you for help, the one person who would do anything for me."

"You shouldn't have had to ask," Katy says. "I should have known."

"How would you have known I needed you when I didn't even know it myself?" I say.

"Well, I'm sorry, anyway," Katy says. "Tell me what you need now, Liz."

I think for a while. "I guess what I need most is for you to trust that I'm doing the best I can."

"You're doing more than that, Liz. I really meant it when I said you're a saint. I'm grateful every day. I'm sorry I don't tell you that."

"Yeah, but I'm also a control freak. Have I been all control-freakish these days?"

"Yes," Katy admits. "You have been a tad controlling. Just a wee tad."

"I'm sorry. I just don't know how to do it any other way."

"Me too," Katy says. "It turns out saving a sister is harder than saving a ski boot."

We laugh. The field of love opens. We walk in. I tell her about the doctor in Los Angeles and the new protocol, how the FDA just approved it and only one lab makes it and it will take some effort to get it in time. Katy helps me make the decision to encourage Maggie to try one more time, with one more drug, to live.

"I want to say one more thing, Liz," Katy says. "And don't take it the wrong way."

"What?"

"What I want to say is that we're all Maggie's perfect match. In our own ways. You are, I am, and Jo is too. Do you know that?"

I let those words settle in my heart. I remember what I said to four-year-old Will when I was driving him home from school, and he was struggling with his little ego's need to be the special one. "Everyone wants to be special, Will," I told him. "So either everyone is special, or no one is." Ah! There's some truth here for me. It stings, but I let myself feel it. I give my own four-year-old ego a nod; I recognize that she's still hanging around, still trying to feel special in a family of four special girls. I pat her head. I tell her she is indeed special, and so are Katy and Jo and our beloved Maggie.

"Thanks. I needed that," I say. "We're a perfect match. All of us. We're KaLiMaJo."

As we get off the phone I feel the thread of unconditional love making another stitch in the mother-loop. Why Katy and I waited to talk things out is as mystifying to me as why any two people or groups or nations forgo communication and instead allow assumptions to morph into hard feelings, loss of love, or, worse, hatred and violence. How many wounded relationships in our wounded world could be healed if people would only risk being vulnerable and honest? And hurt and angry too, but angry in a way that leads to positive resolution. This is possible. It's difficult, it's risky, but it's possible. And the opposite has a terrible track record. I like the way the Nobel Peace Prize laureate Leymah Gbowee puts it: "Anger is like liquid, like water—it's very fluid. Pour it in a nonviolent container, or pour it in a violent container."

The opposite of violence is not a world without anger, not a world without conflict. In fact the fear of conflict often leads to violence. It leads to unexplored assumptions, dishonesty, and backstabbing. Nonviolence is the ability to be in honest, patient conflict with another person, to hold each other's flaws up to the light, to talk it all the way through and to discover that, although none of us is perfect, still we can be each other's perfect match. This is the "human love" that Anaïs Nin speaks of. This is what happens when we stop taking things personally, when we stop making assumptions, and when we are impeccable with our word.

And never forget the fourth Agreement: "Always Do Your Best." You will need the fourth Agreement. My phone call with Katy was the result of years and years of trying and failing, trying and failing, doing our best even though it sometimes looked like our worst. I used to think I would never get to Rumi's field—the one beyond wrongdoing and rightdoing—with Katy. I used to think we would always make assumptions and take things personally and withhold our truths and be stingy with our love. But we worked hard for that phone call on the dark November afternoon, in the eleventh hour of Maggie's life. And afterwards, things change between us. We become more courageous with our words—more honest and, at the same time, more kindhearted. We don't want to leave the field again. This is Maggie's gift to us.

It will not be as easy to mend the hurt with Jo, and to pour our assumptions out of the cup and fill it instead with love and forgiveness. She is angry at being excluded. She blames it on me. She's tells me this one day after I tell her not to visit Maggie. She accuses me, and I say all the wrong, defensive things as I try to make her see it my way. We are unpracticed at being each other's perfect match. Perhaps this is what doing our best looks like now. But I make a promise to myself that in Maggie's name I will follow Rumi's directions for as long as it takes and hope that Jo and I will meet in the field.

PRAYER

THE BEST EXPLANATION FOR WHY Maggie's cancer returned is that the treatments given before the transplant did not eliminate all the malignant cells. Even if only one cancer cell remained, hiding out in a dark little corner of the body from the poison arrows of chemo and the killer rays of radiation, that one cell could reproduce and spread. Even if the graft-versus-host process had been routing out remaining cancer cells, a patient with relapsed or advanced disease at the time of transplant is not always protected from recurrence.

Late at night I open my computer and one last time I research the heck out of Maggie's illness, searching for third opinions, radical cures, signs of hope on the horizon. At our last visit to the hospital, there was talk of more rounds of chemotherapy and radiation and even another transplant, but those plans were nixed. There were discussions about other drug trials, but none may be right for her type or stage of lymphoma. For now, she is taking the experimental drug suggested by the doctor in Los Angeles.

This doctor carefully and respectfully explains the new drug to me. One feature of cancer cells, she says, is that they divide rapidly. Chemotherapy goes after and kills rapidly dividing cells. Sounds like a great plan, but since many normal cells also divide rapidly, chemotherapy goes after them as well, setting in motion a take-no-prisoners type of medical warfare. "Ever wonder why cancer patients are bald?" the doctor asks me. Hair cells grow rapidly, she explains. Bang-bang goes the chemotherapy, and soon hair cells and many other normal cells are dead too. After the chemotherapy is over, the hope is that the good cells will repair and renew, and the hair will grow back, but the cancer won't.

The new medicine Maggie is taking is not called chemotherapy. It's "targeted therapy," which is a whole different approach. Years of research by molecular biologists have uncovered therapies that attack cancer cells without damaging normal cells. And even more promising, some targeted therapies trigger an immune response that crowds out the cancer cells, causing even less harm to normal cells. The doctor in Los Angeles uses the metaphor of a key and a locked door to describe the drug Maggie is now taking. Until recently, the doctor says, the best tools they had to unlock the door were explosives like chemotherapy and radiation. The targeted therapies work more like a key.

And now Maggie is using that key. The thing is, the key opens a door to the big unknown. No one can say if it will work or, if it works, what working even looks like. Will it prolong her life for a few months? A few years? Will it stall the growth of cancer until the next key is discovered, tested, and approved? We don't know. Welcome to uncertainty.

A dear friend of mine, a man who has been living with recurring cancer for many years, says it's not death he fears. Even though he can't say exactly what will happen after he leaves this life, he trusts in "something else" on the other side of death. It's being able to "live while leaving" that keeps him up at night. "I want to be able to hold life dear and to live it fully for however long I have left—to live while leaving."

And that is what Maggie says she will do until she no longer can. If there's one thing you can say about her, she knows how to live. This is what she is teaching me. I am in school and she is the teacher and I am taking notes. Because we are all living while leaving. Our seats are reserved on the ferry. We may not be sure of the crossing time, but we will all cross over. My husband says we'll all meet again on the other shore. He's sure of it. He knows it in his bones. Sometimes, when my own faith wavers, I hold on to his. Now is such a time.

I tell him I no longer know what to pray for. That Maggie sets sail quickly for the other side, without too much pain or fear? That the new drug kicks in and unlocks the door, giving her enough time to be at her daughter's wedding in the summer? That she is miraculously cured? My husband suggests this simple prayer: "Thy will be done."

Ahhh, yes. That's a good prayer. "Thy will be done." My own will serves me well in the things I can create and control. But those other things? The bigger things, the mysterious things, the unanswerable things? Those are out of my control; they will not bend to the force of my will. There's a bigger, more mysterious will at work in the world, one we may never fully understand, but that doesn't mean we can't trust it or surrender to it.

"Thy will be done." Maybe those words carry too much biblical baggage for you. If so, you can replace them with a phrase the folks in AA say: "Let go, let God." Or leave off the word "God," and make your prayer be this: "Let go, let go, let go." Sometimes, lying in bed, before I fall into sleep, I hear those words on the wind through the open window—as if the angels are shaking their heads and sighing, "There's only one prayer, dear. We'll tell you again, in whatever words you can hear, and as many times as you need to hear them: *Thy will be done. Let go, let God. Let go, let go, let go.*"

Prayer feels unnatural to some people—encrusted with super-
stition, or connected to a religion one has left behind. If you're
one of those people, and if willfulness or worry gets the better of
you, try this: Sit yourself down at a table and rest your head on
your folded arms. Roll your head back and forth on your arms and
exhale with a loud sigh. You can imagine a few nondenominational
angels standing over you, with rueful, patient smiles, clucking
their tongues and saying, "There's only one prayer, dear . . ." Nod
your head, rest, and for a few seconds, just give up. Surrender. Feel
the grace of what was, what is, and what will be. You can do this
wherever you are—on a train, at school, at a desk before a meeting
at work. You can pull the car into a parking lot and lean your arms
on the steering wheel. You can rest your head, shake it back and
forth, breathe, and whisper, "Let go, let go, let go." No one will
know that you're schmoozing with angels.

Too much talk of angels and God for you? Here's some tough
love from one of my favorite philosophers, Terence McKenna.
"Don't worry," McKenna writes. "You don't know enough to
worry. Who do you think you are that you should worry, for cryin'
out loud? Worry presupposes a knowledge of the situation that is
too vast for the brain's puny imagining. Worry is, in fact, a form
of hubris."

I would never promise you that I know how to put an end to
worry. There's an inherent vulnerability to the condition of being
human, and that vulnerability breeds anxiety for most of us. But I
can tell you that worry and anxiety do not have to dominate your
experience of being alive. Impossible, you say. There's so much to
worry about every day. About our own lives and the lives of the
people we love. It's a crazy world out there; anything can happen,
and across a lifetime, it usually does.

But anxiety and worry do not protect us from the world. In fact, they make things worse—not only for ourselves but also for the people we love. No one likes to be worried about. The cessation of worry is actually a gift you can give to others; it's a vote of confidence in their capacity to find their own strength in the storm.

So how to do it? How to let go of control and ease up on the worry and anxiety? My suggestion may sound counterintuitive. I suggest becoming even more vulnerable. I suggest this to you, because it is what I am finally learning as I confront the limits of my own will and my compulsive urge to fix, and solve, and do. When there is nothing left to be done, and the road ahead has no markers, there is always a choice: I can worry about what's happening, or I can surrender to the road. I can go out into the world like an explorer. I can partake of life just as it is. I can roll around and get dirty with it. I can risk it, enjoy it, suffer with it, feel it, and allow those I love to do the same. Because as Terence McKenna says, worry about the world is a form of hubris. Who really knows what is best for us and for our beloveds?

And so I offer you this one last prayer. It is my favorite prayer—a plea for clarity, for vision. I address it to the angels, to the gods, to God, to whoever is listening to us vulnerable human beings. I say it with humility and a dash of urgency: "Please, remove the veils so I might see what is really happening here, and not be intoxicated by my will and my worries. Remove the veils that I might see beyond my fantasies and fears. Remove the veils that I might see."

Part Six

✣

GONE TO SEED

All goes onward and outward, nothing collapses,
And to die is different from what any
one supposed, and luckier.

—WALT WHITMAN

DEATH WITH DIGNITY

field notes • december 1

i am beginning to think about taking pills to end my life. vermont has just made it legal. i called a friend who worked on that bill. she told me who to talk to, how to learn more. i have lost so much control over my own destiny. i need some of it back. oddly enough, having a way to end my life will give me back my life. no one wants to live more than i do. i don't want to die, but i don't want to be kept alive as a test case either. i know my doctors are trying as hard as they can to help me. but i'm on the inside of this medical world. i know that doctors hate to fail. they think death is a failure. well, its my life and my death and i want them back.

Christmas has come and gone. Maggie spent it in the hospital, which allowed me to spend it with my family. The new drug does not seem to be halting the spread of the cancer, and no other treatments have been suggested. But even as Maggie gets closer to death, a part of me continues to dwell in the delusion that she will get better, that she will be here on earth forever, with us—the four sisters, her kids, her vibrant life. It's a childish fantasy, I know. But like all fantasies, my dream of Maggie's recovery flouts the rules of reality. And it flies in the face of what Maggie herself is choosing now. She has surrendered to the virulence of the disease, to where it is taking her. She wants to go. She's not happy about going. She has so much to live for, she says, most especially her kids. She wants to stay with them, to be here for them, to know their children, to help them, to guide them. She feels guilty to be leaving them.

But she is reading the tea leaves in the bottom of her cup. They are telling her things only she can decipher. More and more, when she talks about life here on earth, her voice is heavy. But when she mentions dying, her tone lightens, becomes wistful. Sometimes she talks about colors and light—a break in the clouds she noticed from her hospital window, a feeling of freedom and movement.

She lies alone in that hospital room, where she has spent so many days and nights, and she scans the story of her life. She tells me she is coming to the last pages. I have to believe her. Maybe, if I were the sick one, I would travel to another state or country where the cutting edge of cancer care is offering this drug trial or that natural remedy. But for whatever reasons—probably wise ones—Maggie has decided not to pursue any more treatment. She has waved the white flag.

Now New Year's is on the horizon. It's the no-man's-land between the holidays. I rattle around in the void. This strange feeling of being on the outside of life looking in is familiar to me; I know it from my years of midwifery—stumbling home after forty-eight hours of attending a long birth, finding the rest of the world brewing coffee, making school lunches, rushing off to work. Leaving me on the couch, trying to sleep, but still hearing the sounds of the laboring mother, still seeing the baby's head crowning and then the new little person wriggling into this world, trailing news from the other one.

When I'm on the phone with Maggie, I close my eyes, and I see her heading in the other direction. I hear the strenuous breathing, the water in her lungs. As if death is filling her up before taking her away. As if death is not the absence of life, but instead, it is something shimmering and oceanic and tidal, bigger and stronger than anything we can imagine, anything we can name. I feel the rope that ties Maggie's boat to the land, to us, slackening. She lies in bed, but already she is making plans, charting her course, preparing for the journey.

Meanwhile, back on this side, I can't make plans. Plans are being made all around me, but I can't make my own. I go to work, where we are planning next year's programs. I come back home and my friends are planning a New Year's party. Old friends call; they are planning to visit and stay at our house. I get tired of my answers to everyone's plans: "I don't know if I can come to a meeting next week"; "I don't know if I will be at the party"; "I don't know if you can stay at our house." I have been saying these words for weeks and months. I have become unreliable to most in order to be completely reliable to Maggie. It's taking a toll on my daily relationships and my work. But *this* is my work now: to help usher my sister out of the world. If I feel overwhelmed, or doubtful, or scared, I just sit still, and I say the prayer: "Remove the veils that I might see." The veils part, and the path is clear, and it leads to Maggie.

This last week of December is cold and snowy. A fitting season, says Maggie, to die. From her hospital bed she tells me that there's only one more thing she wants to do, and that is to put the finishing touches on her art show, *Gone to Seed*, and to see it hung at the gallery. I tell her we will all pitch in and help her fulfill that last dream. But is this possible? No one can tell us. Will she rally or fall off the cliff? Will her candle slowly burn out, or will she take matters into her own hands and snuff out the flame with the help of death-with-dignity drugs? She has been talking about securing the pills since her first diagnosis. What used to be called "euthanasia" (ancient Greek for "good death") and then "physician-assisted suicide" (think Dr. Kevorkian) is now referred to as "death with dignity," and it has recently been legalized in the state of Vermont. Some people, including some health professionals, refuse to use the phrase "death with dignity," and have strong moral opposition to making it available. Others, around the country, are fighting for the legal rights of a terminally ill person to relieve suffering and intentionally end his or her life.

I don't know how I feel about it. But Maggie has always been adamant that a person who only has weeks left to live should be able to decide when to die. Perhaps she feels this way because she's a nurse and has seen up close what happens to real people when the power to choose has been taken away by pain, or dementia, or a drug-induced stupor. Now she is in the same bind. If she doesn't take pain medication, the tumors in her organs and bones wrack her little body, but when she takes the pain pills, she goes in and out of her rational mind, has frightening and confusing thoughts, and babbles incoherently. If she doesn't have her lungs drained regularly, she feels as if she drowning in her own fluid, but the procedures are becoming more and more uncomfortable and ineffective.

She is facing all of this alone in the hospital. Oliver and the kids visit, but not every day because she has told us to allow her to rest, to give her space. Should we believe her? She has spent her life telling people what she thinks they want to hear. Is that what she's doing now? Talking to her on the phone gives me no clarity. In the morning she's angry and dark, and then on the next call she is confused—sometimes giddy, sometimes weepy. Is it the pain medication that makes her say strange things and slur her words? Or has the cancer spread to her brain? Is it the unfairness of an early death that makes her angry or the mess she says she's leaving behind? During one of our calls when she's angry and dark, she tells me she'd rather die right now than have to deal with the mess for one more minute.

"What mess?" I ask. She's been concerned for months that her sisters and kids will have to deal with the tangle of old clothes in her closets and stuff in her studio.

"Are you still stressing over your underpants drawer?" I ask.

"No," she snaps. "Not that kind of mess. I don't care what you all think about my ratty old underpants."

"Then what?" I ask.

"It's just a mess, believe me," she snarls. "All the things I never said. All the things I can't say now."

"About what? To whom?"

"To everyone. The kids, Oliver, the sisters. My friends. I just never said what I really wanted and it's too late now."

"That's not true. It's not too late. What do you want to say?"

"Ha!" she spits at me over the phone. "What do you know about it? You still have a lot of years left. I don't. I can't change anything now. I'm going to die in a few days. You obviously have no idea what you're talking about." She begins to cry. "I'm sorry. I'm sorry, Liz. It's just a mess and there's no going back."

She hangs up the phone. I am heartsick. Should I rush to her? Comfort her? Or does she need to sit in the storm of her life's story, to work it out, to make her own peace? I decide to leave her be for now.

She calls the next day in an entirely different mood. She has just heard from a local doctor, one of the few in her state who prescribes the death-with-dignity drugs. This was her third talk with him; previously, she had gone to his office for the requisite two visits. Now he tells her she can pick up a prescription for the legal and lethal cocktail. Vermont's law is only a few months old, and to date only two people have used it. Will Maggie be the third? Today she thinks she will, and this seems to ease her anger and clear her head. Again she mentions that she's been watching the winter sky from her hospital bed and focusing on the jabs of light that pierce the gray New Hampshire clouds. She surprises me by saying, "That's where I'm going, Liz. It's all about the light." Her voice is both tired and animated.

The next day she calls and says she wants to explain her anger. "Remember what we talked about at the therapist's?" she asks.

"We talked about a lot of things," I say.

"Yeah, well, there's only one thing I'm still chewing on. I've got it down to only one thing. I think that's progress!"

"What is it?"

"How I wasted so much time in my life not saying what I really meant. Twisting myself into knots, trying to make everyone happy. I've been mad about that forever. But you would never know it, would you? I acted like everything was OK, better than OK. Great! Chipper! Happy little Maggie. Blah, blah, blah." She's getting angry again.

"It's OK, Maggie," I say.

She ignores me and keeps talking. "I never wanted to hurt people," she says, slurring her words, rushing to get everything out. "I never told anyone what I really thought. I'd tell one person one thing, what I thought he wanted to hear, and another person something entirely different. I did it in my marriage. I did it with my friends. And with you sisters. I did it at work with the doctors and the nurses. I knew eventually everything would bump up against each other and . . . and, well, here we are. At the end of the line and things are bumping all over the place. It makes me mad!

I'm mad at everyone all the time. All day long. Except I'm the one who created the mess."

None of this is news to me, and none of it seems all that unique to Maggie. Who hasn't created some kind of mess over the course of a life? What does she think we will discover after she dies? If I didn't know her so well, I'd think she was talking about something shocking—like a pile of stolen bills in that ratty underpants drawer. Or a love child being raised by its grandparents in a distant state.

"Oh, maybe I'm just being dramatic," Maggie says, backing away from the subject. "Don't make me talk about it, OK?"

But I do make her talk about it. Because if I don't now, there's a chance we'll never have the opportunity again, and I want her to be able to say what she means in such a way that she finally puts it to rest. I want her to put a stake of selfhood in the ground before she sheds her body and travels into that light she is talking about more and more. I want her to claim her dignity as the glorious person she has been during her time as Maggie.

To me, this is death with dignity.

I remind Maggie that our mother went to her death close-lipped. She was ashamed of something she would never reveal, and so it became a heavy weight in a bag that she dragged behind her for her entire life right up to her last breath. For years my imagination conjured up novelistic secrets in my mother's bag: maybe she had been abused as a little girl; maybe she left her heart in college, perhaps with a secret boyfriend, or maybe even another woman; maybe she had a torrid affair during her marriage, on Long Island, with the handsome man who waxed our linoleum floors, or in Vermont with the choir director at the church. This is where my overimaginative mind goes.

But something must have happened to our mother that made her so ashamed of her body, so unable to speak her mind, so tightly wound around a pit of anxiety. My sisters and I would wonder aloud about what made her so nervous and afraid and at times harshly judgmental, and at other times high-spirited and childish. Now I think her secret was something simpler than my imaginings. Something that we all drag behind us in a cinched bag: The shame of being a flawed, bumbling human. The shame of not being smart enough, or beautiful enough, or rich or thin or sexy or strong enough, or whatever it is we stuff into the bag of our not-enoughness. The shame of having big feelings, big dreams, big "who the hell does she think she is" ambitions. The shame of being aggressive and jealous and mean. Or lazy and dull and small-minded. Of having made mistakes and missteps and *meshuggaas* of all kinds. The shame of being complex and inconsistent and paradoxical. The embarrassment of being human.

Why are we embarrassed? What in heaven's name are we so ashamed of? Why do we hide our whole selves from each other when what we are hiding is merely the commonness of being human? Once shared, my mother's shame would have shrunk. Once expressed, especially to us, her daughters, her anxious insecurities would have melted in the heat of our love, in the humor of our humanness. But she kept her bag tightly tied, and she died ashamed.

"Don't do that," I tell Maggie. "Don't die like Marsh did."

So Maggie revisits her past with me. I've heard it before, but never like this—never strung together as a narrative she is trying to understand and bring to completion. She talks about when she was sexually molested in college by a professor and she told our mother, who forbade her to go to the authorities. She talks about when she married her husband—her high school sweetheart. She put him and the life he led on a pedestal, but she was also afraid to disappoint him and the small Vermont town where her parents and his parents were next-door neighbors. She grew to resent and fear the way he controlled her. But for years, she never confronted their problems head-on, and instead she did what she was told, she swallowed her sense of self, and she put on a happy face for the world. And how all the while, she took remarkable care of everyone—her children, our parents, his parents, her patients, her friends—in a frenzied attempt to prove to the world that she was good and worthy of love.

She kept all the people in her life—husband and friends and kids and sisters and colleagues and customers—juggling in the air. If she dropped a ball, she'd recoil from the conflict, and run from the relationships, and confound the people she loved. And when she finally summoned the courage to tell her husband what had been brewing in her heart for years—the fear, the anger, the plans to leave—he was stunned and incensed. When the marriage ended, there was a whole family of shell-shocked people. And the truths she had repressed felt like a toxic substance in her body.

And with us, her sisters, she felt those same toxins eating at her. For years, she says, she would tell me one thing, and then something altogether different to another sister, throwing us both under the bus so as not to hurt anyone in the moment, so as not to be the bad guy, but now, as the bus neared the terminal, she saw how her terror of telling the truth was about to run everyone over.

"I've created a monster," she says.

"Could you get more specific?" I ask.

"Oh, for instance, I was afraid to tell Jo not to visit me because I am sick of her trying to be my therapist, so I made you tell her for me, and then I told Jo you were bossy."

I laugh. "I am bossy! And Jo's a therapist in real life and doesn't know when to stop. None of us knows when to stop overdoing what we do! We can't see ourselves. We need help. It takes guts to point someone in a better direction, but it's one of the kindest things you can do."

"I know," Maggie says. "I know. I understand. I get it. But what do I do now? There is so much left to say. No time to say it. No energy either."

"Like what? Say it to me."

"Like clearly telling the kids and Oliver who I want to get what, who I want to take over my business. I'm afraid to do this. So I've said all sorts of different things. And like explaining myself to all the people I've told to stay away. I don't have the energy now. I don't want to care anymore. I'm too tired."

"That's OK, Maggie," I say. "You don't have to say anything to anyone. That's not the point."

"Then what's the point?"

"The point is to let yourself off the hook. For once. To know you did your best, and it was pretty damn great. Can you forgive yourself for being a normal, screwed-up person? Just like the rest of us? We all have screwed up in our own special ways. But you have a lot more fantastic things to pay attention to now. Just look at your life! Your wild and beautiful life. Your generous life. Not a perfect life. Remember? Remember how you told me I didn't have to be a perfect person to be your perfect match? You don't have to be a perfect person to be our perfect Maggie."

"Do you really believe that, Liz? Or are you just saying it to make me feel better?" Maggie asks.

"I really believe it. It may be the only thing I know for sure."

Maggie stops talking. I hear her fluid-filled lungs working hard.

Then she says, in a gurgled whisper, "Tell me what else you know for sure, Liz."

"OK," I say, "but can you send me a sign from the other side and let me know if I was right?"

"No promises," Maggie says. "Just talk. Just tell me what you know."

"Well, I know your life may look like a mess to you, but it actually all adds up to exactly what it was supposed to be. To what you needed to learn this time, and what the people around you needed to learn. I know that. I know we're all in this together, for a reason, for a purpose. That we are all each other's perfect match. And that you will take your lessons with you as you head out into the light. And you will leave us with so many gifts, Maggie, even the ones you call the mess."

"I want to believe that," Maggie says. "But I don't know. And I don't know how to be with everyone in the meantime. I just want them to stay away. When it comes time for me to die, I want to be alone."

"No, you don't," I say. "That's another thing I know for sure." She coughs and I hear a nurse talking to her. I wait.

"I feel like I'm drowning," she says to me.

"Do you want me to come?" I ask.

"No," Maggie says. "I need to be by myself now. But keep talking to me, Liz. Tell me what else you know. Tell me what to do. Teach me how to meditate again."

I say what first comes to my mind. I talk about the four Lesser girls—her perfect matches, her sisters who love her unconditionally. "When you feel like you're drowning," I say, "imagine us at the beach. Four little girls at the ocean's edge. Remember?"

"Mm-hmmm."

"Sit there with us, with your toes in the water. Then, see if you can just let the waves drag all your anger and fear and regrets out to sea, and then let the new waters flow in. Let the bright next world come and get you. You don't have to know anything for sure, Maggie. Because, in the end, we can't really be sure about anything. But you can trust. You can relax. Just rest on the shore, with us. OK? Maggie?"

She doesn't answer. I hear the nurse talking to her, taking the phone, gently hanging it up.

I light a fire in the fireplace and I rest in my own not knowing. I think back to when I was a midwife and my laboring mothers would look at me with great expectation, grab my arm, and ask with an intense need to know: "WHEN WILL THIS BE OVER??" And I would assure them that indeed the labor would be over at some point, that there would be a baby at the end of the tunnel, but until then, the best way to speed the process would be to relax into the pain, to surrender to the fear, and to embrace the mystery of not knowing. In return, the laboring women would snarl at me until another contraction rolled in like a tsunami. Days later, the new mother would tell me that she had hung onto my advice to surrender to the unknown, that it was the only thing that helped.

"You sure didn't act like it helped," I'd say. "You almost bit my head off!"

But the women assured me that the reminder to surrender—to the pain, to the fear, to the unknown—got them through. So I will continue to tell Maggie what I told my laboring mothers. Even when she loses the energy to snarl, even when she can no longer speak, I will tell her these few things I know for sure, and I will pray I am doing right by her—that when she wakes up on the other side, my words will have given her solace and strength.

TEACHING MEDITATION AT THE
BRAIN TRAUMA CENTER

IN ALL MY YEARS OF spiritual study, I've come across a lot of practices: breathing practices, chanting practices, prayer practices, healing practices. But the practice I've benefitted from the most, and the one that consistently reminds me to surrender to the unknown, is the practice of meditation. A student asked the Buddha why he should meditate, and the Buddha answered, "Come and see." That's the best advice, because meditation is an experience. But if you are like me, you need more than that; you like to know why; you enjoy some science with your spirituality.

Here's one "why." It's a why that resonated with Maggie. Researchers at the National Science Foundation report that the human brain processes twelve thousand to sixty thousand thoughts per day and that a large percentage of those thoughts are negative and repetitive. We obsess about mistakes we've made in the past and worry about future worst-case scenarios. We run those thoughts through grooves in our brains all day long, and then again the next day, until they're so well-worn that we live in a negative story about the past or an anxious scenario of the future.

The brain studies into repetitive thinking are being done by psychoneuroimmunologists, medical researchers looking to help people strengthen their immune systems. They are finding that if you can interrupt the stream of repetitious thoughts in your head, you are less likely to contract illness—from a cold to cancer—and more likely to increase levels of concentration, calmness, and happiness. This is why they are spending millions of research dollars looking into the very common and very boring content of our brains. And this is one of the reasons I cherish the practice of meditation. But there's another reason to meditate—another "why"—and it's not as easy to describe. Besides bringing peace to the mind and health to the body, meditation also opens a window to a whole other reality, one that our busy minds obscure.

Many philosophers and scientists believe that the brain does not generate consciousness; rather, it functions as a filter. Aldous Huxley called the brain a "reducing valve" for infinite consciousness. The contemporary British physicist and astronomer David Darling writes, "The major organs of the body are regulators. The lungs don't manufacture the air our bodies need; the stomach and intestines are not food-producers. So, if we manufacture neither the air we breathe nor the food we eat, why assume that we make, rather than regulate, what we think?"

In the stillness of meditation, we touch the realm of unregulated, unfiltered, infinite consciousness. And what a realm it is! Vast and free. By quieting the brain's repetitive and habitual patterns, we can stop believing and reacting to everything we think, which is really a reduced, compressed, and tense form of something way more enjoyable to experience: infinite consciousness. In meditation, we begin to experience life beyond the reducing valve, life on its own terms. We become an open-minded witness, as opposed to someone who is always scrambling for a sense of security.

The Buddhist meditation teacher Pema Chödrön says, "Scrambling for security has never brought anything but momentary joy." She describes meditation as a way of stopping the scrambling, of getting unstuck from the need for security. "The process of be-coming unstuck requires tremendous bravery," she says, "because basically we are completely changing our way of perceiving real-ity, like changing our DNA. We are undoing a pattern that is not just our pattern. It's the human pattern: we project onto the world a zillion possibilities of attaining resolution. We can have whiter teeth, a weed-free lawn, a strife-free life, a world without embar-rassment. We can live happily ever after."

But of course, we don't live happily after, because just as one problem resolves, another evolves, and there we are again, seeking resolution, thinking we deserve resolution. "We don't deserve res-olution," Pema Chödrön says. "We deserve something better than that. We deserve our birthright—an open state of mind that can relax with paradox and ambiguity." So this is the other "why" of meditation: to relax into the paradoxical, ambiguous, wide-open, unregulated, infinite consciousness that some call God and others do not name at all.

When Maggie asked me to teach her again how to meditate, I did the best I could to rid my instructions of cumbersome words like "paradoxical, ambiguous, wide-open, unregulated, infinite consciousness," which betray the simple act of meditating. A few days later, I have to pare down my language even more.

Near to my town is a hospital-like facility that houses and treats people who have suffered traumatic injuries to the brain. Some are young—a twenty-year-old construction worker who fell head-first from a ladder; an aspiring opera singer who wasn't wearing her seatbelt; a high school kid who flew into the side of a boat in a water-skiing accident. Others are older. They sustained brain damage through a stroke or disease or a simple tumble on the sidewalk. Some still can talk and move about unassisted. Their thinking is foggy and circular, but perhaps they will recover with time and therapy. Others are strapped into chairs and stretchers, wheeled around the center, heads rolling from side to side, unable to communicate.

A friend who works at the center asked me many months ago if I would visit and teach a small group of residents how to meditate. We pick the week between Christmas and New Year's, because it's a slow time for the residents at the Brain Trauma Center, and normally for me too. Except for this year. In the intensity of taking care of Maggie, I neglect to look at my date book, and by the time I remember, it's the very day of my session—too late to cancel.

I have taught meditation hundreds of times to thousands of people—from elected officials in Washington, DC, to inmates in prison, and from rambunctious kindergarteners to AIDS patients close to death. And so I had said yes to the invitation to teach at the Brain Trauma Center without thinking about it too much. The practice of meditation has been a great friend to me—when I am anxious, it calms me; when I am confused, it clarifies; when I am small-minded, it stretches my perspective. I figured that people suffering from brain trauma were probably anxious and confused much of the time. Perhaps meditation could be their friend too. I've sat in retreats with master teachers and been stunned into quietude by their well-chosen words. But more than anything, it's their presence that has coaxed my anxious mind and fearful heart into stillness and peace. And so I would try to do the same for the residents at the center: strip down to my marrow and show up fully and fearlessly as a fellow human.

As I enter the Brain Trauma Center, though, I wonder what I've gotten myself into. Can you teach people to calm the habitual workings of the brain—the incessant thoughts and unregulated impulses—if their brains have been injured? Meditation is a way of dipping into a deeper form of cognition than the mental gymnastics of everyday thinking. But we use the words and concepts of everyday thinking to teach it. What a conundrum!

At the center, I wait for my friend in the staff lounge and notice this quote from Lilla Watson on the bulletin board: "If you have come to help me, you are wasting your time. But if you have come because your liberation is bound up with mine, then let us work together." That's a beautiful way of describing the best kind of teacher or caretaker. The quote reminds me of when I first began speaking and teaching. I was so nervous before each event I could barely think straight. I was in that jittery state of mind one evening, sitting backstage at a conference where I was to give a talk. A well-known psychiatrist was sitting with me; he was slated to present after I spoke.

"Are you OK?" he asked me.

"No," I said. "I'm terribly nervous."

"Oh, I used to be nervous before I spoke. But now I'm not."

"How did that happen?" I asked. "And how can it happen to me? And soon?"

"Well," the man said, "a couple of years ago, I was sitting backstage, just like you, marinating in my own sweat, and there was a priest or a monk there—a little old guy in a brown robe. He must have noticed how panicky I was. He came over to me and said something I never forgot. It changed everything for me. You wanna hear it?"

I nodded.

"This is what he said. I memorized it. 'They don't need you to perform for them so they know how good you are. They need you to love them so they know how good they are.' You want me to write that down?"

I said yes, and I still have that piece of paper. I keep it in my purse and I come across it at the oddest times. Maybe I'll reach for my sunglasses when I'm driving my grandson to school, or I'll fish around for a pen at a meeting at work, and I'll find the scrap of paper and read it. And once again, it will encourage me to step out of my small self and into my big love. *They don't need you to perform for them so they know how good you are. They need you to love them so they know how good they are.*

And that is the way I go into the room to work with the thirty people with brain damage who have shown up for my meditation class. In the front row are some of the more highly functioning folks. They sit in chairs and welcome me with smiles and hellos. Behind them, strapped into wheelchairs, are several other residents, some of whom acknowledge me as I walk around saying hello, while others look at the ground. In the back of the room is a man in a stretcher, his legs and one of his hands tightly bound to the stainless steel rails. He makes guttural noises when I speak to him, his free arm jerking around as I stand by his side.

My friend introduces me to the group. I start into my prepared remarks, and almost immediately, one of the residents in a wheelchair raises his hand. Before I can call on him, he begins speaking in a loud voice, complaining about his roommate, who has stolen his clock radio. With his hand still up in the air, he launches into a long story about his missing clock, and also his slippers, and a list of other items.

A young woman in the front row turns around and says, "Shut

up, Larry." And then she turns back to me and tells me to ignore him. "He tells the same story over and over," she says.

And sure enough, throughout the hour Larry raises his hand and complains bitterly about his belongings being stolen, followed by sharp "shhhhhhs" fired back at Larry from the other residents, and loud moaning from the man in the stretcher. Each time the ruckus calms down, a white-haired woman stands up and announces that she will be leaving the center to go back to her job in the city after lunch. The same person who told me to ignore Larry tells me to ignore the white-haired woman.

Pretty quickly I realize that the same thing going on in the room is going on in the brains of many of the residents: chaos, bewilderment, anger, sadness. I put aside my stated goal of trying to help these people, and instead come back to the quote on the bulletin board: "If you have come to help me, you are wasting your time. But if you have come because your liberation is bound up with mine, then let us work together."

The goal of meditation is liberation. Liberation from the stormy weather occurring between our skull bones. Liberation from the war within. We meditate to become comfortable with whatever is going on in any moment. To engage with reality on its own terms. The best gift I can give the people in the Brain Trauma Center is my own ability to be with them. To be comfortable with them. To be present. All I can do is meet them exactly where they are. And the way to do that is to love them. Which isn't that hard, but it also wasn't my first response. It's never my first response to difficulty. My first response is usually to get things under control. Well, that isn't going to happen here, teaching meditation at the Brain Trauma Center.

I come from behind the teaching podium and stand in front of the group. If my liberation is bound up with the liberation of these people, then the best thing to do is to be one with them, to be a wounded person among other wounded people—in all our splendor and all our brokenness. I stop teaching, and instead I tell the residents about my own life. I get specific. I tell them about Maggie and how I don't know how to help her these days. I don't know what will happen. I ask them for advice, and while some of the answers are unrelated to the questions, others are surprisingly useful and profound. And a couple of times during the conversation, I offer up some tips on calming the inner storm—my storm, their storm, a world of storms—through meditation. A few people in the front row follow the instructions.

At the end of the hour there are hugs and clapping and a few "Happy New Year"s. Then, class is over and everyone shuffles or is wheeled out of the room. On my way out, I stop to connect with the man strapped into the stretcher. I take his free hand and hold it. He stops moaning. We lock eyes.

"Hi," I say. "Thanks for coming today."

His eyes search my face, as if he's saying, "Please see me. Please see who I was before I got sick, before my brain went haywire, before I ended up here. I'm still that person; I just don't have the right words and thoughts to dress him up, to make him presentable. But please see him; please respect him; please love him."

I nod yes to his silent request. I stand at his side, looking into his eyes, nodding my head. The man makes a noise and twists his mouth into what appears to be a smile. I don't know if it's really a smile. I don't know if my presence today has been helpful to him or to any of the residents. But I'll remember what I learned (for the umpteenth time) at the Brain Trauma Center: that we are souls who have met for a purpose on this mysterious journey; that each of us is here for the other, and all that is required is to strip down to the marrow and to be present. To look into each other's eyes and to search beyond the identity of victim and helper, sick one and well one, weak one and strong one—to look deeper and to find the dignified soul of each being, and to stand in solidarity as a fellow human who is striving to be free.

This is how all of us can try to be with each other, every day—wherever we go and whatever disparities may exist between us. This is the lesson I will take from my friends at the Brain Trauma Center, and the gift I will bring back to Maggie. Like the residents at the center, Maggie has never wanted to be a burden, never wanted pity, and has barely wanted my help. She has just wanted my presence—my strength to her strength—and the sense that our being together is a gift for both of us.

MY MOTHER'S DEATH

ALL LIVES ARE DIFFERENT; THEREFORE, all deaths are different—the way we die looks very much like the way we lived. I only know this because I have spent time with a few people as they died. Before doing so, I imagined that the process of dying would magically wipe clean neurotic tendencies and transform the mean people into nice ones, and the miserly ones into those who can finally communicate their love and impart their wisdom. But as it turns out, we are very much ourselves, breath by breath, right up to the last one. This is why spiritual traditions encourage us to work on polishing the lantern as we live, allowing the soul's essence to shine through, and purging our personalities of their less attractive traits, or else we'll drag them with us when we die.

That being said, magical things can happen in the final moments of the dying process, transforming the dying person and changing those who witness it. The first time I sat with a dying person I was in my twenties. One of my best friends had fought off leukemia for as long as she could, and despite the fact that she had a little boy and a great desire to live, the disease had other plans. Her death came quickly. One day she was well enough to have my son at her house for a playdate, and the very next day her body rejected the transfusions that were keeping her alive, and she fell into a light coma.

As fate would have it, I showed up at her house as she was dying. Her husband begged me to stay. For several hours I traveled with my friend up to the threshold of death. During that time I was surprised to find that she acted, well, just like herself. As she went in and out of consciousness, she was plucky and noble, and she was also angry and cutting. But the closer she approached death, the more peaceful she became, and as she took her last breaths, a warm breeze rose up from nowhere and circled the room, even though it was January, even though the cold winter sun was setting and we had neglected to load the woodstove. As the peculiar wind blew about, my friend suddenly sat up and opened her eyes. A thin trail of blood trickled from her mouth, but even so, she looked radiantly beautiful and happier than I had ever seen her. And then she died. Who can say what she washed clean in those moments before stepping off the edge? Who can say what she took with her to the other side?

Although my father was eighty-five, no one anticipated his death. I think we expected him to outlive us all. He was a health nut long before it was fashionable—he didn't drink, smoke, or allow stress to derail his passions. He was adventurous, imperious, and self-centered in life. Ditto in death. In the morning he had gone off cross-country skiing into the snowy hills. He stayed out all day. He often did this. All through my childhood, he'd just disappear and head into the woods without prior notification. We'd all be together, eating a meal or talking, and suddenly he'd be gone. This was how he died too. He came home from the woods, had dinner, and went to bed. In the last hours of night my mother awoke and heard my father speaking to someone. She called out, and told him he was talking in his sleep. He became quiet again. When my mother got up in the morning, she found my father dead. He had snuck out at dawn, into the wilderness beyond.

My friend Peter died in the spring of 1996 from AIDS. Just one month later, the FDA approved the triple drug cocktail that saved many of Peter's friends. This was just like Peter. He was impatient and impulsive, and apparently it was time to move on. He died at the NYU Medical Center, where many other beautiful young men had been carried away by the flash flood of AIDS. A friend and I sat by his hospital bed for hours, trying to soothe him. He could no longer speak, but he would raise his hand and flutter his fingers. Finally we got the message. He was ready, and our worrywart behavior was holding him back. We left. He died shortly afterwards. I don't feel sad when I think of him. He just went first, to show us the way. I get the feeling he's preparing a fabulous party for us, his tribe of friends.

My mother also died how she lived—saying one thing but meaning the other, frowning on excessive displays of emotion, keeping secrets. I had always thought I would have that conversation with her before she died, the one that would reveal the secret held close since childhood, the one that would explain the sadness and anxiety at her core. But we never had that talk. She became more hush-hush about almost everything as she aged.

It should have come as no surprise, then, that my mother would keep the seriousness of an illness secret, even from her daughters. On top of her usual reticence to talk about herself, there was her Christian Science background, which views disease as a mental error rather than a physical disorder. When we were children, our mother told us that religion was the opiate of the masses, but she also quoted scripture about praying away the illusion of illness when we were sick. This made no sense to me as a child, especially since the word "prayer" was synonymous with voodoo in our family's lexicon. It wasn't until years later, when I made a study of the Christian Science faith, that I understood why my mother called me a hypochondriac whether I had a common cold or a broken bone. When I was twenty, I had to drop out of a semester of college because I contracted hepatitis from tainted drinking water in Mexico. For several months, my skin was yellow and I could barely lift my head from the pillow, and still my mother scoffed and called me a hypochondriac.

After my father died, my mother marshaled her mercurial energies, sold the Vermont farm where they had lived for many years, bought a little house in town, and traveled far and wide with her friends. She continued her work as editor of her small town's newspaper; she hosted holidays for the family at her house; she remained a vital part of her community. All the while, we were to discover, her bowels were being eaten away by Crohn's disease, an autoimmune disorder that could have been treated but instead she ignored. She would complain of stomach problems from time to time, and dropped little hints that all was not well, but nothing prepared me for the scene I walked in on one day when I came to visit. I found my mother on the floor of her bedroom, writhing in pain.

"Marsh! What's the matter?" I cried. I had rarely seen my mother exhibit signs of normal human helplessness, and certainly not physical pain.

"It's nothing," she assured me as she rolled around on the floor, tears in her eyes. "It happens most afternoons and then goes away."

"What are you talking about? It's something, not nothing. You're in terrible pain!"

"I'm fine," she moaned.

"I'm getting you help," I said.

At the doctor's office the nurse took one look at my mother, called an ambulance, and sent us to the hospital. My sisters met us there, and we embarked on the journey that led to our mother's death. I know the word "journey" is overused, but this literally was a journey in that we spent the next three months traveling back and forth between our homes and our mother's, between the hospital and her home, never knowing what we might find from day to day, never knowing what direction to take, bushwhacking the route as we went along. I am sure this sounds familiar to anyone who has trekked the twisty path of a parent's demise.

At the hospital, the surgeon who examined my mother informed us that unless he operated immediately she would die from internal bleeding. When they brought the consent forms for my mother to sign, she refused. "You girls decide," she said. "It's your decision." What could we do? Of course we signed the forms; of course we chose for her to live. But now I know she was trying to tell us that she wanted to die. By bringing her to the hospital we had backed her into a corner where the only option was life. She must have known that the outcome of surgery would be an ostomy bag. And she had no intention of learning to live with a bag of excrement strapped to her waist.

After the surgery, our mother was told she was disease-free and could resume a normal life as soon as she learned the proper care of an ostomy bag. But she wouldn't learn. She wouldn't eat. And she wouldn't tell us what she wanted, except in that way of hers that drove us crazy our whole lives. That way of saying one thing but meaning another.

She said, "I don't want to go back to the hospital."

We said, "If you don't, you'll die."

"No, I won't. I'll just rest until I'm better."

"You don't need to rest," we said. "You need to eat. You need to drink."

"No, I need to rest. 'Rest is the great healer,'" she said, quoting one of her literary heroes, whose name I cannot remember now, but I'd like to, for her sake. When we were children, she had us memorize poetry, and parts of psalms, and Shakespeare's soliloquies. I can still remember whole poems I learned by heart when I was seven.

She would say one thing but mean another: She swore she was getting better, but she was winding her way to death. She stopped eating and drinking. She gathered us around her by telling us to stay away. We hovered like mother hens—her daughters who had never been clucked over. We touched her, talked to her, and loved her with a passion we had never before been allowed to express.

She stopped speaking one day before she died, but she continued to raise her eyebrows, the way she would when she said something but meant the other. During her last hour she mouthed words to an invisible presence in the corner of the room, but when we asked her who she was talking to, she looked the other way. And then, even though the life force had burned down to an ember, she changed course one last time and passed a rod of molten fire to Maggie.

For weeks afterwards, my sisters and I called each other every day. We were baffled by her death. "Why did she do it?" one of us would ask. The other would say, "The doctor said she was free of disease now, that she could live for many more years. Why did she want to die?" Every day we had the same discussion: Did she doubt she'd ever be well enough to resume an independent life? Had years of secret pain exacted too much of a toll? Was the ostomy bag a Christian Science game-changer?

And then Maggie would retell her deathbed vision of the golden rod trailing soft green wisps, how it shot out of my mother's rib cage and entered Maggie's gut, and we would marvel at our mother's final gift. It was almost as if her heart ignited with love, and in that one burning moment, she overcame a lifetime of hiding. She dug into her marrow and from that depth threw a thunderbolt of light on the path for Maggie.

I remind Maggie of the thunderbolt the next time we are on the phone. She sends me her last field notes entry, and I read it as a vote of confidence in our recent conversations. She is digging deep; she is finding her way.

---

field notes • december 15

amazing. yellow fire. green kindness. that is what zinged out of our mother and into me. right into the center of myself. that's what it felt like—like a rod of strength. though tears flow right now, i am grateful for the immense strength i have to move along and welcome death when it comes. i wish all people had that. am i sad? yes, but today i studied the break in the clouds, and i had a momentary flash of letting it all go and felt this warm glow for a nanosecond. it felt sweet. it felt like love. perhaps that is what death is. total, complete letting go of control and thus walking into a never before experienced world. today i feel lucky to see how welcoming death will be. this is all a gift, don't you see? some of us are lucky. so thank you marsh for handing that fire stick with the green tail to me. passing to me your hidden strength that you poo-pooed in life. listen marsh, you raised 4 incredible women, you went back to school and taught little highschool brats and were the best teacher they ever had, you bought a house in vt with your money, you moved us all north, dealing with a domineering husband, dealing with wild teenage daughters, you started a newspaper, you were an integral part of your town, arguing at town board meetings, caring for your grandchildren, growing and putting up food, cooking and knitting and reading and tutoring children, marching in peace rallies in nyc, working to help people get elected. you did all of that, but you had the curse of wanting everyone to like you. not knowing how to say no. you could never say no. remember how you would stay on the phone because you didn't want to offend the person on the other end of the line, even if you were tired or late or you had to go to the bathroom? how you shit in your pants once because you couldn't say, oh sorry! i have crohn's disease, i can't control my bowels, i have to go . . . you didn't have to hide, marsh. you could have said what you meant. you deserved it. it's taken me getting cancer to know that. i am sorry you died before you knew that.

MANIPURA

IN EASTERN SPIRITUAL TRADITIONS PEOPLE are said to have two bodies: a physical body and a subtle body. The physical one is made of earthly stuff, while the subtle one is made of energetic stuff. Don't quote me on that. The two bodies interact with each other—the openness of the flow between them affects the state of our physical health and psychological balance and spiritual intuition. That flow can be blocked in the chakras, the Sanskrit word for the seven energy centers of the subtle body.

Let's say you have been stuffing your opinions for years and years, never saying what you know is right, never asking for what you want. If you were presented with a chronic cough, an Eastern healer might tell you that your fifth chakra, your throat chakra, was blocked with choked anger, and by speaking the truth you could hasten the healing process. Each of the seven chakras is associated with different health challenges and opportunities for healing—body and spirit.

After my mother's death, I felt a great emptiness—as if she had gotten out of town as quickly as she could. This was different from my father, who, after death, became my constant companion, my guide. I felt him around me and with me, closer in death than he had ever been in life. It was only in his death that I realized we were perfectly matched in life. That he was the father I needed this time around.

But I could not feel my mother's presence at all after she died. I wanted to. A friend suggested I meet with a psychic, a medium who moves between the worlds of form and spirit—exactly the kind of person my mother would have found appalling. Bearing apologies to my mother, I visited the medium. And in true form, my mother never showed up. But my father did. The medium went into a trance, and within seconds he reported that two men were with us, one named Bob and the other, "Well, he says he's your father," the medium said. "They are laughing and saying there's not enough snow. Does this make any sense to you?"

"Yes," I told the medium. "Bob was my father's best friend. He died recently. They were in the ski troops in WW II together. They loved to ski, and they loved snow! They always wanted more of it." I was astonished. How was this possible? How did the medium know this about my father, about Bob?

"Well, they are quite happy and even festive," the medium continued. "They want you to know that they are taking care of all the girls. They want you to know that. Does this make sense?"

"Yes," I answered, again stunned by how much sense it made. "Between the two of them there are six girls in our families—well, eight if you count our mothers. And speaking of our mothers," I asked, "is my mother there?"

The medium remained silent. I watched his face. His eyes were closed, and he grimaced and cleared his throat several times. "There! I only caught a glimpse," he said. "She came and went like a shooting star. That's all."

During the rest of the session, other people who had passed over came into the room, or into the medium's awareness, or however one describes such a phenomenon. Some of the people were unidentifiable to me; others I knew. And then the doors closed, and the medium opened his eyes, and there we were, two people made of earthly stuff.

"I have a question. Is that OK?" I asked the medium.

"Of course," he said.

"What did that mean when you said my mother showed up like a shooting star?"

"I don't know," the medium said. "I don't know your mother. What do you think it meant?"

So I told him about my mother's illness and her difficult death and Maggie's bedside vision—about the rod of molten ore that she saw leaving our mother's chest, and how it entered her own body.

"Where on her body?" the medium asked.

"Above her belly button and below her rib cage. Right in the middle here." I said, pointing to the spot on my own belly.

"Oh, you mean her solar plexus. Of course. The Manipura chakra," the medium said, as if mine had been the most commonplace description and his answer the only obvious response. "That would make sense," he said, nodding his head.

"What would make sense?"

"That your mother would send a message from her Anahata chakra to your sister's Manipura chakra."

"Why would that make sense?"

"Because I got the feeling from your mother's appearance that she wanted to say something, but she had trouble expressing it. Does that make sense?"

"Yes," I said. "That certainly does make sense."

"You see, your mother's Anahata chakra had probably been blocked her whole life. Anahata is the heart center, the love center," the medium went on. "During the death process, the subtle body takes over, and sometimes you get a last chance to make some changes, to make some amends. Did your sister need something more from her?"

"We all needed something more from her!"

"Well, it seems she sent love to the person in the room who needed it most. She sent your sister a message, subtle body to subtle body."

"What do you think that message was?" I asked.

"Well, she sent the energy from her Anahata chakra to your sister's Manipura chakra," the medium said. He closed his eyes, as if pondering a difficult math problem, and spoke softly and quickly to himself. "Let's see. She sent her most valuable resource— love—to your sister's Manipura chakra, the fire center. She sent love to fire. Love ignites fire. Fire is self-worth. Personal power." He opened his eyes and looked at me. "Does your sister give her power away? Does she know how to protect her core from power vampires?"

"Power vampires?"

"Yes, there are people who will take and take and take unless you put up boundaries. Unless you protect your core self."

"Wow," I said. "You know all this about my sister just from that one story?"

"No," the medium said. "I know it because people are the same all over the world. India, California, Vermont, it doesn't matter. Wherever I go, this is what human beings do. We get stuck. Some of us get stuck in one chakra, some in another. Then we try to get unstuck and to learn our lessons. Or we don't, and then the soul finds other places, other lives, other ways to learn and evolve."

"So, do you think my sister will learn her lessons?" I asked, unaware of what she would be up against within the year. Unaware that her marriage would fall apart and soon afterwards she'd get sick.

"Yes, I think she will," the medium said. "I get the feeling she's had a lack of yellow energy and that can make you overly concerned with what other people think of you. It can cause inertia and confusion. But fire purifies the past and heats up spiritual progress. It pushes you to take risks. Your mother sent her a jolt of yellow energy."

"Yellow energy?"

"Oh, yes, sorry," the medium said. "Each of the chakras has a color. Manipura is yellow. I often speak in colors when I am talking about the chakras."

"What's the color of the other center—the one my mother sent the energy from?"

"Anahata center. Heart center. Green. Green is the color of the heart. The color of love. Does that make sense?" the medium asked one last time.

And one last time I nodded at the medium. Yes, it made sense. It was as if he had been there when my mother died, and when Maggie gasped, and the yellow star whooshed into her solar plexus, like a meteor trailing a tail of green light. And that green light bathed her in the love she would need to make it through her days, all the way until the last one.

NEW YEAR'S EVE

ON NEW YEAR'S EVE DAY, Maggie calls and asks me to come to the hospital and bring her home. All treatments have been stopped and hospice has been ordered. I make the journey north to Dartmouth Medical Center again, glad to escape a New Year's Eve party, glad to be alone in the car and, even though I am afraid of what lies ahead, grateful to be on my way to Maggie once again. I arrive just as she is being taken into surgery, to have a port put into her lungs so the fluid can drain when she's at home. The doctors hope that this will give her some relief for a while longer, although no one will expand on what "a while longer" means. Days? Weeks? No one can—or will—say.

I pack up her meager belongings—a book, a drawing pad, her coat, her boots caked with mud. Then I sit in the uncomfortable chair by the window where I have sat and slept and waited many times before, prepared to wait again. But soon Maggie is wheeled back into the room. The procedure didn't work. They couldn't even start. Her left lung is encased in a layer of tumor cells so dense that the chest tube could not penetrate. She will have to go home without the drainage port. She is crestfallen. This is the last procedure she will receive, the last in a long line of failed attempts to beat the cancer. The last straw. She dissolves into tears. Several of her nurses rush to comfort her, as does the doctor on call, a young resident holding down the fort over the holiday. I leave Maggie in their care and go to the hospital's pharmacy to pick up a boatload of pain medication that home hospice will administer.

When I return, Maggie is bundled up and waiting in a wheelchair. The resident is kneeling by her, talking softly and stroking her head. The nurses—Maggie's champions for so long—cry as we leave. Her favorite nurse, a burly man with a raunchy sense of humor, pushes her through the halls and outside to my car. He leans over and whispers into her ear. Then he makes a little nest for her in the backseat of the car with blankets and pillows he has poached from the hospital. He picks Maggie up in his arms and they weep. He settles her into the backseat, slams shut the door, and stands at the curb as we drive away.

I sense Maggie taking stock of what is happening. This is the last time she will be at the hospital. The last time we will make the beautiful drive south. The sun is setting on this last day of the year, sending rays of pink light through the steely gray sky. As I drive, she sleeps, she coughs, she wakes, she vomits. I pull to the side and clean her up, drive again, stop again. It is dark and frigid when we arrive home. I am worn out, and she is barely alive.

That night, Norah and Hayden and their partners come to be with her. As I make dinner, they gather in the living room, surrounding Maggie. She's just a little heap on the couch, tufts of hair sticking up on her head—her face thin and flushed. She is hooked up to an oxygen tank that makes a continual whishing sound. I bring everyone bowls of soup, and Maggie watches us eat—her big brown eyes bigger than ever and alarmingly bright. Now that she's home, she's not as drugged; she's awake, alert, and in pain. After everyone has eaten, I clear the plates and the kids stand to leave, but Maggie calls us to her.

She wants to tell us a few things, she says. And then she speaks, directing most of her talk to Norah and Hayden. In a torrent of words, in between coughing, she tells her kids how much she will miss them, how sorry she is to be leaving them too soon, how proud she is of them. She tells them how to be good parents, good partners. She unburdens her heart and lists the things she is sorry for. She reminds them of all the people who will be there for them when she is gone.

She tells us how she wants to die, who she wants in the room, where to spread her ashes. She tells us what her favorite nurse whispered to her today as she left the hospital: that he's seen a lot of people die, and the ones who loved the biggest and lived the fullest are the saddest to leave, because they are lovers of life. She tells us that she is a lover, and that we should be lovers.

"Love comes first," she says. "Love each other and love every clod of dirt and every tree on earth." She stops talking to cough and then to catch her breath. She closes her eyes. We wait.

Her eyes open. "Trees," she says. "Do you know how much I love trees? And how proud I am of you, Hayden, to be taking care of forests? And you, Norah, for taking care of the land? I couldn't have better kids." Her eyes grow rounder and brighter as she speaks, until she finally exhausts herself and falls asleep midsentence. The kids leave, and Oliver takes Maggie up to bed. I drag myself into the guest room, into the bed where I have spent so many nights. How many more nights will I spend here?

Be lovers, Maggie told us. Love the earth, and love each other. *Love comes first*, she said. Suddenly I realize that Maggie has solved one of the great riddles of all times: What came first, the chicken or the egg? Neither. Love came first. In the beginning was love, and therefore we should put it first too.

There's something I have to do. I take out my computer. I notice it's a few minutes before midnight and I recall that it's New Year's Eve. I write an e-mail to Jo. I tell her all about what happened today. I tell her that Maggie wants her to be there when she dies. I tell her I have done the best I can, and even though I haven't done a perfect job, somehow it's been what Maggie needed. I ask for her forgiveness in all the ways I have not upheld my end of our sisterhood, and I promise, in Maggie's name, to do better. I write it as a prayer, and send it off as the old year comes to an end.

THE KIND OF BIRD WHO
TELLS YOU HOW

TWO DAYS AGO MAGGIE WAS close to death. Or so we thought. She was under the weight of morphine, going in and out of consciousness, sleeping for long stretches. Her breathing was rapid as her lungs filled with water, squeezing the breath right out of her. The hospice nurse told us to focus on making her as comfortable as possible.

And then, this morning, she sits up in bed, and in a fit of lucid consciousness and hummingbird energy, she says she needs to make sure that the last of the *Gone to Seed* prints are properly framed before we bring them to the gallery.

"We?" Oliver asks.

"Yes," Maggie says. "I want to go to the gallery and see how they hang the show before Thursday. It's Wednesday today, right?"

"Jesus, Maggie," I say. "How do you know what day it is?"

"We don't have much time, so let's get busy." That's her answer. She eats two tiny bites of eggs, and then we trundle through the snow to the studio, and join the friends who have been working around the clock to frame the prints for the opening of *Gone to Seed*, which indeed will happen on Thursday. In a show of super-hummingbird strength, Maggie drags herself around the studio, wheeling the oxygen tank behind her, overseeing the framing.

The next day, after a sleepless night of pain and coughing,

Maggie insists on going to the gallery. Oliver and I bundle her up—all ninety pounds—and carry her into the ten-degrees day, put her in the car, and travel down the highway to the gallery. Her kids meet us there. I have a photo of that day—of Maggie in a wheelchair, with a vomit bucket in her lap, in a down coat that fit her last winter but now seems to have been made for a giant. For an hour, she is full of life, joyful to be viewing her artwork—the botanical plants, with their dried stalks and dying leaves and the swash of smashed berry paint soaring off the edge of the frames.

But soon she tires. In the car driving back she becomes violently ill, retching, over and over, into a bucket, and talking to people who aren't in the car.

When we get home, I go up to the bedroom, change the sheets, puff the pillows, tidy the room, and then Oliver brings Maggie upstairs and we settle her into bed. I sit with her. Outside the sky is silver and streaked with the sun's setting light. A flurry is falling. The snow catches the dying light, and for a moment everything sparkles, and everything feels complete.

Maggie rests for a while and I get up to leave, thinking she has fallen asleep. But she opens her eyes and looks at me.

"Now what should I do, Liz?" she asks. "Just wait?"

"Yeah, now you just wait. That's all you have to do." I sit back down.

She's been fighting the cancer for so long, she doesn't know how to stop. She's been fighting not to leave—her family, her home, her land, her art, all of it. The life she has loved here on earth.

"The gallery show is so beautiful, Maggie," I say. "You should be proud."

"Yeah," she says. "So beautiful."

"How did you figure out how to make those huge prints?" I ask. "They're different from anything else you've ever done. How did you do that?"

"The same way I did other things that scared me." It takes all of her effort to string the words together.

"How?" I ask.

But she's fallen asleep. A few moments later she opens her eyes and says, "A mockingbird told me. That's how I did it."

"A mockingbird?"

"No, not a mockingbird." She closes her eyes again and her breath is quick. "Not a mockingbird," she says again. "I mean the kind of bird who tells you how. That bird," she pants. "The bird who tells you how . . . tells you how to do the things that scare you."

She's been speaking in riddles for several days now. Often she makes little sense. Sometimes I think there is hidden meaning in what comes out, and sometimes I think she's speaking from another world, or maybe it's the morphine. But this evening she has no morphine in her, and she's been present and strong all day.

So I ask her, "Is the bird here now?"

"I have to go find it," she says. She closes her eyes and falls into a fitful sleep.

I sit in the bedroom with her for a long time. In the dimming light, I watch the blood pulsing in her neck. My blood. Her blood. Maggie-Liz. I think back to when millions of stem cells were harvested from my bone marrow and transplanted into Maggie's bloodstream. How they took up residence, duplicated, so that she could live. And live she did—with more Maggieness than she ever had before. I try to make sense of it all—how becoming one with each other made us both more confident in being ourselves, and how when she dies, part of me will die too.

I pick up Maggie's hand and hold it gently. "Take some of me with you, Mags," I whisper. "And leave some of yourself behind." The night covers us. Maggie stops panting and her sleep deepens. I hope she finds "the kind of bird who tells you how" and that it instructs her in the art of flying into the light.

COMPLETING THE CURRICULUM

THE NEXT MORNING, OLIVER TELLS me that Maggie spent most of the night coughing and in pain. The hospice nurse visits, has a long talk with Maggie, and adjusts the dose of the pain medications. I go to town, to fill the prescriptions at the pharmacy and to get away, to clear my head. I run into a friend of Maggie's in the grocery store, a fellow nurse who has cared for many dying people. I tell her that Maggie has been struggling, fighting for life in one moment and wanting to die in the next.

"She doesn't seem to know how to do either," I say.

"Oh, yes, she does," says the friend. "Don't worry. She's doing important work now. She's completing the curriculum."

"The curriculum?"

"The life-review curriculum. She's learning in both directions now—finishing the past and looking into the future. And knowing Maggie, she's getting her PhD."

We chat some more. I leave the store and get into my car. There's a knock at the window. Maggie's friend is standing in the freezing Vermont air, her breath billowing like clouds. I open the window.

"One more thing," she says. "It may take Maggie a long time at the very end. She may lie still for hours, and you may wonder what to do, but just let her take her time. She'll be completing the curriculum. She'll know when to leave."

That night, Maggie suffers the kind of pain that morphine can't touch, and the terror of near drowning in her waterlogged lungs. In the morning she tells Oliver that today is the day she wants to die. That she is going to take the death-with-dignity pills. They stay upstairs for a long time, and when Oliver finally comes down, I take one look at him and I know that Maggie has made her decision.

"Is she sure?" I ask him.

"Yes," he says. "I think she is." He sits at the table, puts his head in his hands, and weeps. I put my arms around him and we cry together.

"She said the most amazing thing," Oliver says. "She said, 'Yesterday would have been too soon, but tomorrow will be too late.'"

I go upstairs. "Today's the day, Liz," Maggie says when I come into the bedroom.

"Why today?" I ask.

"Because yesterday would have been too soon," she says, "but tomorrow will be too late. That's what came to me last night. I just kept saying it over and over to myself. I can't go on like this one more day. Too much pain, too much coughing. And I finished everything I had to do. And it will be too late if I wait much longer. It's time." Her tone is strong. What had felt before like anger now feels like courage. What had felt like frantic energy when she roused herself to finish the prints and visit the gallery now feels like a wind blowing in from another world.

Oliver comes back upstairs. We tell Maggie we understand and we'll help her; we'll stand by her. She asks us to call her kids, their partners, and Katy and Jo. She wants everyone to gather by one o'clock in the afternoon. That's the time she has chosen, and so that's what we do. One by one, her team arrives. The wind from the other world whips around the house. It fills Maggie's sails. She moves through the rooms putting sticky labels on furniture and paintings that she wants people to have. The labels fall off as she leaves each room, blown by the same wind that propels Maggie onward. She sits at the kitchen table and writes letters to friends. And finally she asks her kids to bring her upstairs. "But let me walk by myself," she commands.

They make their way up the stairs, Maggie leading, followed by Hayden and Norah, and they disappear into her room. The rest of us remain downstairs, in the absolute wilderness of this unimaginable journey.

Two o'clock, three. We wonder what to do. Four o'clock. The day is almost done. I decide to go upstairs. And there they are, three beloveds, holding on to each other in the boat of Maggie's bed.

"Liz," Maggie says.

The kids get out of the boat.

"Now what?" she asks.

"Is it time? Are you ready? Do you want to do this?" I ask.

"Yes," she says. "I just don't know how."

I think of that bird Maggie spoke of, "the kind of bird who tells you how." I beg it to come show me the way. I have no idea what to do. I wait. The kids wait. Maggie waits.

"OK, here's the plan," I say. "Why don't you take some time alone with each of us. Just a few minutes with each person. Does that sound good?"

"I'll start with you," Maggie says to me. The kids leave. I sit on the bed. I take her hands.

"Are you scared?" I ask her.

"No," she says. "I'm ready. I'm ready to go. I need to go. Don't make me cry. Help me go."

"I will," I say, forcing back the tears. We look into each other's eyes. There's no need for words. I have said everything there is to say to her: I love you. I respect you. Thank you. I will take care of your kids. She has said everything there is to say to me. We are each other's perfect match, now and forever. I lean down and kiss her lightly.

"OK, now ask Katy to come up," she says. And one by one, the sisters, the kids, their partners, and finally Oliver trek up and down the stairs, saying their good-byes. And at six o'clock, with the sun down and the night coming on, Oliver calls us all to Maggie.

We stand around her bed. She sits up, vibrating with adrenaline and the wind from the other world. Her eyes are huge. She is coughing violently from the water pooling in her lungs. She can barely breathe.

"Help me do this," she whispers to us—to her brilliant and brave children, to her devoted Oliver, and to the three sisters, arms around each other, helpless with love for her. Oliver hands her the first of the pills and liquid, and she takes them. When the coughing subsides, she takes more. And more. Until the full dose is done and she leans back on the pillows and looks around at us one last time. Then she fixes her gaze on the candles burning on the windowsill, and for the first time in weeks, she stops coughing, her breath becomes even, the lines of pain in her face soften, and she relaxes into sleep.

For the next hours we keep vigil by her bed, her boat. Maggie breathes steadily, and although her body never moves, not even a twitch on her face, her eyelids flutter, she is warm to the touch, and there is a concentrated intensity about her. And for the next hours, she becomes the hummingbird again, full of energy and determination, working hard on the curriculum.

We go in and out of the room, reconfiguring the team. Some-one strokes Maggie's head; someone says I love you. We make tea. Sometimes we sit downstairs; sometimes we crowd back around Maggie, sure that the time has come. She inhales sharply, and then a long exhalation, and then a gap of time when nothing more hap-pens. Is this it? Has she gone? But then she gasps. And the steady breathing begins again. The candles flicker in the window.

After another hour and several false alarms—the sharp in-breath, the long out-breath, the gap in time, the gasp, the return of the breathing—Norah suggests that maybe Maggie needs us to leave her alone. "She said she needed space these last few days," Norah says. "She probably needs it now." And so we leave Maggie and Oliver in their room and spread out, looking for places to sleep. We settle in, and a profound silence bears down on the house.

I am just about to drift off when I feel someone standing in the doorway of the guest room. It's Jo.

"Can I get in bed with you?"

"Of course," I say.

She gets under the covers, and we hold onto each other.

"I'm sorry," Jo whispers. "I'm sorry I blamed you. I just wanted to be with her. I just needed someone to blame it all on."

I hold my breath as she is talking. I feel Maggie with us. I feel her completing the curriculum and passing the torch to us.

"We're good, Jo," I say. "We're good now."

And then Oliver is at the door. Maggie is gone, he says.

Epilogue

A FRIEND CALLS ME TWO weeks after Maggie has died. She's one of the most straightforward people I know. She says exactly what she means. Today she tells me, "I'm going to talk and you don't have to say anything in reply." This sounds really good. I have no idea what to say to people these days, how to respond to offers of condolence, how to answer the question "How are you doing?"

My friend starts talking. She tells me that losing a sister is a tragedy. Before I can respond, she says, "I know what you're telling yourself. I know you're thinking everyone loses people, everyone dies, so what's the big deal?" I start to answer, but she talks over me. "Death is a paradox," she says. "Yes, it's a natural part of being alive, but it's still tragic. And this isn't just any death. It's your sister. She died too soon. And she had your marrow in her bloodstream. You were as connected any two people could be. Please let yourself grieve. Let yourself fall into a hole the size of your sister."

As I listen to her, all sorts of reactions rise up within me. Her words bring tears to my eyes—*a hole the size of your sister*. But I also want to interrupt and say, "Oh, it's not really a tragedy, not compared to what's going on in people's lives all over the world." Then I feel compelled to thank her for calling; I want to shift the attention away from me. But instead of saying anything, I do what she has told me to do. I listen. I take in her words.

As she talks, I realize something important. I haven't seen this friend in a long time. In fact, we rarely see each other. She lives in California; I live in New York. We don't even talk on the phone that often. Every now and then we e-mail. But it doesn't matter at all. I am eternally connected to her. It's been this way from the first moment we met. We were introduced by another friend, and immediately recognized each other's souls. That's the best way I can put it. I see who she is, and I feel seen by her down to the marrow. And if we were never together again, if another word never passed between us, I would still experience her as a living and breathing friend.

As I sit still and do nothing but listen, I feel Maggie's presence around me for the first time since she died. If my friend far away in California is eternally connected to me, it's not such a leap to believe that Maggie—wherever she is—is eternally with me as well; that our love for each other didn't die with her body; and if I would spend a little more time listening, I might feel her presence more readily.

Before we get off the phone, I remind my friend of the last time we were together. We were at our mutual friend's birthday party—a weekend event held at the ocean. We had left the group and gone to the beach, just the two of us. We swam out past the waves, and for a long time we treaded water, laughing about our messy lives and mulling over the state of the world.

"Remember when we swam out into the ocean and stayed there for an hour treading water?" I say to my friend on the phone. "I like to imagine that's what we're always doing. Treading water together way out in the deep."

"Always," my friend says. "I am always beside you. And so is Maggie. She's with you always. Remember that."

"I know," I say. "I know she's there, but I sure would like to hear from her."

"You will. And if you need me, call me at any time, day or night. OK?"

When I go to bed that night, I drop the usual prayer for a visit from Maggie. If she's always with me, then praying for her to be with me doesn't make much sense. Instead, as I am allowing sleep to come, I just listen. I open my ears, my heart, even my skin. Prayer is not a demand; it's not a complaint either. "Prayer is a wide-open eye in the dark," the Benedictine monk Brother David says. I had forgotten that. So with every breath, I open myself to the darkness.

Deep into the night I have a dream. I am in a room in a large office building, and quite suddenly Maggie appears. She's young and vibrant and adorable. I run to her and throw my arms around her. I am sobbing. She is smiling.

"But you were cremated!" I cry. "How can you be here?"

Maggie smiles like the Mona Lisa—a mysterious, all-knowing smile. Her eyes sparkle. She doesn't say anything, but her very presence fills me with joy and peace. We stand together, and then, without warning, she leaves through a door that leads to a big room where people are watching a film. I go looking for her. I spot her, in the back row, but when I get to her seat, she is gone. Instead, I find a man there, sitting in Maggie's seat. I sit down next to him. He won't look at me. I tap him on the shoulder a few times. He doesn't turn my way. I desperately want him to see me, but instead he rejects me. And he becomes a mirror for everything that is unlovable in myself, everything I have done wrong, all my mistakes. I tap the man one more time, but he keeps his back to me. I wake up.

At first all I remember from the dream are the feelings of being unlovable and ignored—of my soul being unrecognized, covered by the veils of human mistakes. I lie in bed stewing in those feelings. Who was that man? Was he a composite of all the people I unwittingly stepped on during Maggie's illness and death? Was he my ex-husband and the remorse I trail behind me for the ways I wronged him and he wronged me? Was he my parents? My sisters? My friends and colleagues? I enter a maze of guilt, of self-rejection and self-attack. When I get tired of myself, I get out of bed, go downstairs, and make coffee.

I sit at the kitchen table, drinking the dark magic brew that Maggie loved as much as I do. She once told me that she went to bed each night excited about the first cup of coffee she'd be having the next morning. She drank hers with heavy cream and several slugs of maple syrup. I told her that wasn't real coffee—it was melted ice cream pretending to be a drink. As I sip my coffee, I suddenly see my sister's smile. I see her illuminated face, and the whole dream comes back to me. Maggie! She's OK! She made it to where she was going. Now she's ready to communicate with those she loves on this side of the ocean. Or something like that. I don't really know what I am talking about when it comes to the afterlife; I only know that there *is* one and it's something more than our feeble brains can fathom.

In many cultures, people believe that when the dead cross over they become guides for the ones left behind. If you listen closely, the dead will teach you, they will encourage you, they will help you understand why things happen the way they do, especially the things we can't accept.

As I go through the day, I keep seeing Maggie's smile. It lifts a burden from my heart. I feel a lightness I have not felt in a long time. But why did she leave her seat to a man who would not look at me, who made me feel unseen, unloved? What was she trying to teach me? Who might help me figure this out?

"If you need me, call me at any time, day or night," my friend from California had said. And so I do. I tell her about the dream, and about the man in Maggie's seat.

"Do you think my sister was telling me to work things out with all the people in my life?" I ask my friend. "To have the kinds of conversations with them that I had with her?"

"I most certainly do *not*," my friend says. "Let me ask you something. Who do you think that man was?"

"I don't know. My ex-husband?"

"No."

"Maybe my mother? My father? My sisters? All of the above?"

"Nope."

"Then who?"

"He's you," my friend says. "He's the part of you who still cannot see your own goodness. He's the part of you who keeps turning away—from yourself, from your soul! You don't need the approval of all those other people. Maggie came back to tell you to approve of yourself—of your real self. Your marrow. Remember? Live from your marrow; give from your marrow. You of all people should know this!"

I laugh out loud.

"What's so funny?" my friend asks.

"You're right. About the dream, about the man. You're right. And that's pretty much verbatim what I said to Maggie the last days of her life. It was her issue to the end—knowing her own goodness, not needing anyone else to know it for her. Knowing she's a perfect match for this life even though she's made mistakes. Joining the human club just in time before she left it."

"Sounds like she came back to remind you of your own wisdom," my friend says.

I think of Maggie lying in her bed for all those hours as she was dying, reviewing her life, learning her lessons. How she waited for us to leave the room so that she could leave the world as her own vibrant self. Now she had come back to encourage me to do in life what she could only discover in dying.

"Oh, and one more thing," my friend says as we finish our call. "Can we change that image of us treading water? Working really hard but getting nowhere? Let's stop treading water. Let's do Maggie proud. Swim to shore, walk into the world, and live the heck out of this life. OK?"

"OK."

We end our call and I am flooded with images of Maggie and the way she lived the heck out of her life, the way she sucked the marrow out of her last year on earth. I see her in her gardens; I see her swimming in the stream; I see her working in her studio, baking in her kitchen, walking with her children. And then I see her at the last music concert Katy, Maggie, and I attended together—an Irish fiddle festival in Boston. We went primarily because a friend of mine was producing the concert and he promised us we could go backstage when Maggie's musical idol, Van Morrison, was performing.

As the festival progressed, and the crowd got drunker and drunker, we waited for my friend to escort us backstage to meet Van the Man. Finally, the time came and we filed into the wings of the stage and perched on stools, watching the warm-up act. Alas, we waited and waited, but no sign of Van Morrison. And as the warm-up band—a mix of wild fiddles and screaming guitars— played on, we looked around for Maggie. She had disappeared. Suddenly, Katy pointed to the band. There was Maggie, up front with the head-banging lead singer, his arm around her waist. They leaned together into the microphone, and Maggie sang her heart out to fifty thousand drunken revelers.

Van Morrison never did show up. But now I am happy he didn't. Because I have an image of Maggie I can keep in my heart forever:

my wildflower hummingbird sister, her soul uninhibited, her lively essence flying proud and free. As time goes on, as she becomes less of this earth and more of eternity, this is what I remember most of my sister: her essence.

And what will I remember of my year of living as Maggie-Liz?

Love. Big love. So big that my heart will never shrink back to its original size. Which still astonishes me, because during that year, month by month, day by day, my life shrank—first to the size of a hospital room, then a window seat overlooking a field, then a bed, then a breath and another breath, and then a hole the size of my little sister. But in that shrinking, I became bigger, because I began to use love as the measuring stick. Love makes big from small. Love gives meaning to everything. Love of self, love of others, love of life, come what may. Amor fati, love of fate.

Deep within the heart of the earth and the marrow of the bones is a compass that quivers to the power of love. I doubt the scientific community is going to back me up on this, but that grand unifying force that Einstein went to his grave still searching for? I believe it is love in its many forms: kindness, passion, connection, empathy, generosity, forgiveness, and the guts to tell the truth.

Love is a force—an adhesive force. What keeps buildings and forests, rocks and oceans from flying off the planet and spinning into space? What keeps the elements that make up people and animals from ungluing? A physicist would use mathematical equations to prove to you that gravity and electromagnetism hold the universe in place. But what came before them? What came first?

Love.

Love came first.

Acknowledgments

MANY THANKS ARE IN ORDER for the support I received as I lived and then wrote this story. I offer gratitude . . .

To the team of nurses and doctors at Dartmouth-Hitchcock Medical Center in Lebanon, New Hampshire, including Sue Brighton, Kate Wilcox, Steve Brown, Ken Meehan, Elizabeth Bengston, John Hill, Beth Kimtis, and everyone at DHMC who provided such loving and excellent care for Maggie during her years of treatment. And to the Apheresis/Transplant team who took care of me before, during, and after the procedure. To our unexpected angel, Dr. Alexandra Levine at the City of Hope hospital in Duarte, California: saying "thank you" doesn't fully express the amount of gratitude our family has for the way you took us under your wing.

To Oliver Brody, Maggie's beloved partner, and a friend and support to me. To Richard Orshoff for guiding us into the field. To Maggie's friends—a fan club from childhood, college, nursing school, Vermonters and Alaskans, medical colleagues and patients, fellow artists and art lovers, sugarers, skiers, walkers, bakers, and farmers. She sure loved you, Helen Weld, Raine Kane, Sally and Dick Warren, Margie Levine, Tim Rieser, Lisa Merton, Tim Merton, Peter Miraglia, Peter Veitch, John Labine and family, Sarah Waldo, Maia and Hugh Brody-Field, Julianna Brody-Fialkin, Dinah Pehrson, Libby Silberling, Carol Bilzi, Mary Deering, and her tribe of Putney friends and neighbors.

To my blessed tribe—the friends I leaned on while writing this book: Kali Rosenblum, Kevin Smith, Abbey Semel, Ron Frank, June Jackson, Phil Jackson, Marion Cocose, Ken Bock, Cheryl Qamar, Perry Beekman, Dion Ogust, Jeff Moran, Sally Field, Jennifer and Peter Buffet, Nancy Koppleman, Pat Mitchell, Scott Seydel, Eve Ensler, Amber Rubarth, Srinath Samudrala, Sil Reynolds, Steven and Lila Pague, Sheryl Lamb, Maria Shriver, Eckhart Tolle, Kim Eng, Corny Koehl, Joe Killian, Jenny Lee, Maggie Wheeler, Isabel Allende, Lori Barra, Dani Shapiro, Jeff Brown, Gail Straub, Loung Ung, Mark Nepo, Geneen Roth, Peggy Fitzsimmons, David Wilcox, Nance Pettit, Jim Kullander, Sarah Priestman, Lee Brown, Linda Woznicki, and Ana Leal. And to my Facebook community: thank you for giving me the courage to be a better caretaker and a more honest writer.

A special thank-you to my soul friend, Oprah Winfrey. The conversations we had during a television interview were the seeds for this book.

To Sarah Peter and Carla Goldstein, sisters from another mother.

To my colleagues at Omega Institute, a deep bow of respect and gratitude to all—too many, past and present, to name. But for being so supportive during the writing of this book, I want to mention a few: first, to the one and only Skip Backus—friend and brother— and to Lois Guarino, Joel Levitan, Carla Goldstein, Carol Dona- hoe, Jennifer Bosch, Veronica Domingo, Chris Mitchell, Michael Craft, Kathleen Laucius, Sarah Urech, Terri Hall, Holly VanLeu- van, Chrissa Pullicino, Randi Marshall, Chuck Maccabee, Angela Casey, and to the Omega Women's Leadership Center and Family Week staffs, faculty, and friends. To Omega's Board of Directors, for your friendship and service: David Orlinsky, Patty Goodwin, Sheryl Lamb, Manuela Roosevelt, Jamia Wilson, Bruce Shearer, and Katherine Collins.

To Henry Dunow—my longtime agent, friend, brother, hand- holder, and champion. Thank you for leading me this time to Karen Rinaldi, at HarperCollins. Karen, your superhuman energy, in- telligence, and care kept my voice clear on the page. You knew when to push and when to give space, and you did it all with great humor, skill, and understanding. You're a true ally, as are Hannah Robinson, Lydia Weaver, Brian Perrin, Penny Makras, Victoria Comella, and all the team at HarperWave.

To those who read early drafts of the book, and whose perspective and encouragement made all the difference: Sally Field, Tom Bullard, Henry Dunow, Susan Goldman, Eve Ensler, and Eve Fox. And especially to Kali Rosenblum, who read every word of every version and held my heart through the most difficult times of living and writing this story.

To my teachers, Hazrat Inayat Khan, Pir Vilayat Khan, and Taj Inayat.

And most of all, to my family—my heart, my happiness, my hilarity. My sister Jo once gave me a T-shirt that read, "Careful, or you'll end up in my novel." Well, dear family, you have ended up in this book and I am both grateful and apologetic—you didn't ask to be related to a memoirist. And so I offer my gratitude to: My beloved niece and nephew, Maggie's children and the loves of her life, Norah and Hayden Lake (and to Chris and Hana, too.) To my cherished sisters, Katy "Sorelli" Lesser and Joanne Case, to Ian Roose and Marshal Case, to my nieces and nephews, and to the extended Lesser/Freeman/Bullard/Rechtschaffen families. To Tom Bullard—for the light you shine on our path, for your uncommon blend of pragmatism, clairvoyance, and comedy, and mostly for the love. You teach me to put love first. To my beloved sons who make me proud to be their mother: Rahm Rechtschaffen, Daniel Rechtschaffen, and Michael Bullard; my daughters-in-love, Eve Fox, Taylor Rechtschaffen, and Rebecca Bullard; and my grandkids, Will, James, Ruby, and those to come.

To the memory of my extraordinary parents.

And to Maggie, always . . .

About the Author

ELIZABETH LESSER IS THE AUTHOR of *The Seeker's Guide* and the *New York Times* bestseller *Broken Open*. She is the cofounder of Omega Institute, recognized internationally for its workshops and conferences that focus on holistic health, psychology, spirituality, creativity, and social change. Prior to her work at Omega, she was a midwife and childbirth educator. She lives in the Hudson River Valley with her family. Visit her at www.elizabethlesser.org.

About the book

Read on

Insights,
Interviews
& More...

More Field Notes From Maggie

IT'S BEEN TWO YEARS since Maggie died, and the longer I live without her, the more her essence keeps me company. How wonderful that she left behind her artwork and her writing. I turn to them when I want a shot of that essence: her beauty, her compassion, her hummingbird energy.

When I was writing *Marrow*, I didn't know how much of Maggie's writing to include, what kind of balance to strike between our voices. After the hardcover version came out, I heard from many readers that they loved Maggie's voice in the book and wanted more. Therefore, I am happy for the opportunity to include some more of my favorite "field notes," as Maggie called her journal entries about the varied aspects of her multitalented life. I have divided the entries into three sections. The first section chronicles her early years as a visiting nurse. I chose those entries because they shine a light on Maggie's big heart, her brave spirit, her sense of humor, and her drive to serve others.

The second section with entries that describe Maggie's rapturous love of making maple syrup and reveals another aspect of my sister—a person who revered nature above all else. Being in the woods was her art, her salvation, her devotion. And being in a Vermont sugarhouse on a cold March night was her bliss.

The third section of field notes includes some of Maggie's last writing, from the year after the transplant when she was "living while leaving." It was difficult for me to go back and reread those entries. I felt anew how much she suffered during her "best" last year. And at the same time, I felt comforted that she had slipped through the break in the clouds.

As I wrote in the introduction, Maggie wasn't a stickler for grammar. She never used capital letters, wrote in run-on sentences, made up words, and switched tenses all over the place. I stayed true to her hummingbird ways and made minimal changes to her words and style.

Nursing

when i was a public health nurse, my route took me to a dirt road at the base of a mountain called lower road where one family was living in an old farmhouse. they had 2 teenage daughters, both pregnant. i was called in when the first baby was born because the agency reported the baby wouldn't stop crying. i arrived at the house and the grandfather was in the traditional position men seemed to be in at all the houses i visited on lower road, under a derelict car fixing something. i stepped over tires, tools, toys, and went into the house. the baby was fussing with a weak, thready cry. the young mother had been discharged from the hospital with a case of premixed baby formula in little bottles. for 3 days she had been unable to feed the baby because the family couldn't figure out how to open the tops of the bottles. there was a little trick to those caps; you had to turn them backwards to break the seal. i snapped one open, put on the nipple, and the baby drained the first bottle rapidly. the family gathered around me, gazing at me as though i had extra powers. from then on whenever i would care for them, the whole family regarded me with awe. that was several years ago. recently that same young mother, now a mother of 4, came to see me at the clinic. that very same baby of hers was now 8 or 9 and had witnessed her mother being raped by "a friend," the mother said. she was terrified that her husband would find out and blame her, and that her children had seen it happen. we sat and cried together in my little exam room.

today wendy came with her kids to see me in the clinic. I used to think this family hated me. they had every right to. my job back then was to watch them, to report them to social services, to upset their fragile attempts not to sink into the same shit hole that was sucking at the cement blocks under their trailer. there was something startling about the way wendy's face looked. her big head and thick caked makeup and hairsprayed hair-do jarred me every time i saw her. i wondered if she frightened her children as much as she did me. she was tough, strong, and angry. her current man was either ▶

More Field Notes From Maggie *(continued)*

tinkering under a car in the front yard or drinking on the porch, and wouldn't say anything to me. my visits made them all nervous because i was looking for evidence of abuse and neglect. i had first been sent to their house because one of the children had told her teacher about things her daddy was doing to her peepee. my mother did not like me going to the houses on lower road. and sometimes i could barely muster the courage to go back. as i developed my own pediatric practice and left the road gig, many of my patients followed me. i was surprised when wendy and her kids started showing up at the clinic. it took me a while to realize they loved me. on one visit, wendy was in a foul mood. the kids, filthy, rambunctious, misbehaving, roamed the little office space, opening cupboards, ripping paper off the examining table, until her three-year-old fell forehead-first into an open metal cabinet door. as i sewed up the laceration, there was only silence between us. but it was an understanding silence. i know what it's like to be frustrated at home and at work, but i don't know what it's like to be so desperately poor that you have no buffer left, and you just tune everything out. you let everything fall apart. when I was finished stitching, wendy took the little girl on her lap and kissed her. then she mouthed the words "thank you" to me, and in that moment, we entered into an unspoken sisterhood.

i am paddling my kayak in a beaver pond on lower road. the pond is directly across the road from that same trailer I used to visit, where my patient named wendy lived. I am collecting water plants that only bloom for a short period of time in the late summer. the sky is quickly turning a steel grey as a storm is brewing. i am way out on the pond when i hear voices and loud, muffler-less car noises. i see a group of people trying to push or pull a car out of the mud, relentlessly spinning the wheels. then another car arrives and starts bashing into the first car in an attempt to ram it out of the mud. my car is parked right next to the commotion, and i feel trapped in the kayak, afraid of lightening, but more afraid of the guys in the cars. they are out of control, drinking, mud splattered, yelling. now it is raining. i paddle to the shore. how am i going to get to my car, hoist the boat on top and secure it, and leave here alive? i imagine the headlines: "botanical artist found dead on lower road, beat to death with kayak paddle." as i steer my kayak up onto the pond's edge, a woman comes over. i look up into her face, and before I can place who she is, she screams, "it's doctor maggie! kids, come quick, look, it's doctor maggie!" and there they are, 3 hulking teenagers with piercings, hair the color of gummy bears. she throws her arms around me. "its me! wendy!" she shouts. the kids look down at the mud, shy and awkward. we chat for a while, they help me lift the kayak, and then i drive out of there like a bat out of hell.

it is a late june evening. the air cradles all of my senses. soft pastel colors, soft subtle smells, soft muted sounds; this must be what a larvae feels like in its cocoon. muffled. held. safe. i am driving east on lower road, to my new home and my new life. if the sky was fruit, tonight it was a peach. the inner walls of the cocoon are glowing pink and gold. the breeze is so close, it is on my skin. i don't know why I took this road tonight. maybe to remind myself how far I have come. lower road. so beautiful with its ponds and streams, and with the people in their tumble-down houses, trying so hard. i see an old man sitting on a bench on his porch. his head is bent down, and his hands hang between his knees. he breaks my heart. as i pass the town hall, a teen-age couple is standing by their car as she fixes her prom dress straps. then her shoe straps. i know them. I have known them since they were children. at the end of lower road, i turn in a new direction. i drive home.

Sugaring

i began reading the little house books at age 8. i lived and breathed those books for many years. they became my reality when my parents bought a rundown farm house in vermont. now I could be laura ingalls wilder for real, so i looked for my own almanzo and my own pa all rolled into one, and married the boy next door. it was the early 1970s, and we were intent on being back-to-the-land hippies. we built a cabin with logs we cut and peeled, put in a hand pump in the soapstone sink, and in winter carried the toilet seat between uses to the outhouse and then back to the cabin, running out on icy mornings with a warm seat.

maple syrup was part of the laura ingalls wilder legacy, so after I got married I was determined to learn how. i knew a little already since i had helped people sugar as a teenager. i remember hanging onto the back of a pickup truck with a bunch of smitten vermont boys, drinking beer and bumping over muddy roads, emptying sap buckets into a collecting tank on the back of the truck. one boy was so intent on winning my heart that he did a backflip and broke his arm. ▶

More Field Notes From Maggie *(continued)*

all through my life, no matter how busy i was, no matter how troubled my soul, come early spring, i just had to be out in the woods tapping the maple trees and in the sugarhouse boiling the sap. the sweetness and the heat and the dark night, my refuge. the sugarhouse has been my refuge through so many life changes—marriage, kids, divorce. then came the cancer. i was diagnosed with mantel cell lymphoma on a summer day, in august, on my birthday, and given 3 weeks to live unless i underwent aggressive chemo and a stem cell transplant with my own cleaned stem cells. called an autologous transplant—not the same as a transplant using someone else's matched cells. can only do it once; if it doesn't work, then you use another person's matched cells, which is much more dangerous procedure. by the following february i weighed 85 pounds and was allowed to venture out, after 7 months of isolation into the world. each day i walked a few feet farther up my road, gaining strength and a sense that i might live. by march i was itching to be in the sugarhouse but my oncologist said it was forbidden; too dirty. but what did he know; he was a city boy. sugarhouses are the essence of cleanliness; the syrup is 218 degrees, gloves are worn to prevent burns, the steam is healing, the fire is purifying, the hot syrup is a great source of calories and energy. and the dirt floor and cord wood are CLEAN dirt. and so, against his advice but intent on feeding my aching, grieving heart, i boiled. and i came alive, embraced by people, tradition, love and work. i'm sure i frightened a few visitors, standing at the arch with no hair, a blue mask, skin and bones, with a gleam so intense in my eyes that i probably looked like a mental institution escapee. but what it did for my heart and sense of HOPE saved my life. sugaring said, you're NOT DEAD, you BELONG, you are CONTRIBUTING, you are FULLY ALIVE. sugaring saved my life.

sometimes us sugarers welcome a cold snap. 12 degrees at night, 26 daytime. the sap won't run unless the nights are in the 20s and days in the 40s: that's the biology of tree nutrition, the feeding of the buds with high-nutrient sap, drawn up thru the columnar cells by rising spring temperatures, returning to the roots in the cold nights. the cold snap is a welcome rest for us. we get to come home from work and actually have time to cook dinner, clean up, watch a movie, or catch up on phone calls. in the sugarhouse, it's an opportunity to scrub the pans that are caked with sugar sand, a thick, blond coating like baked on enamel; we crank up the fire and flush the pans with water and cleaner. we walk the sugar bush checking lines for air leaks, coyote-chewed holes, and downed lines from fallen limbs. it is such a short season, maybe 6 weeks or less of actual boiling time, and completely weather dependent. there are years when the weather turns warm too fast and the sap stops flowing altogether.

sometimes i feel like life is just like the sugaring season—like i am living A LIFE COMPRESSED into only a few weeks, trying to cram in as much as i can, worrying about the cancer snuffing me out before i have done it all. there is so much i want to do. i remember one day, back before the transplant, a year ago? two years ago? i awoke with, oliver's arm wrapped around me, his fingers grasping mine; i lay there grateful for this happy phenomenon of love in my life. but the sun pulled me up and out of the nest, and i mentally listed all the things i wanted to do. suddenly i was late for my own life, for all the time I needed. i pulled on clothes with no underthings on, pulled on socks and boots and a coat (it is 22 degrees but the sun will do its work soon) and walked our muddy road checking for spring's progress. the fields are still snow covered, but a tiny piece of my garden is showing up, brown and frozen. somewhere in the snow are stacks of seedling planters. i need to find them! after the sugaring season i need to be ready to plant the seeds. i need to have a garden again. i also need to devise a plan to improve the health of my obese patients. we will meet daily and walk. there will be 50 of them parading through town at 7:30 each morning, rain, shine, or snow, melting away the pounds, lowering the lipid and glucose numbers, bringing down the hypertension, raising the self-esteem numbers. they will stop their lipitor, metformin, and atenolol, their sex drives will return, their marriages improve, their children will thrive in the newfound love and joy in their homes. i design this and a hundred other projects—art shows and dinner parties and trips to italy with oliver and gifts and surprises for my kids.

Living While Leaving

one week post-transplant. i am here in my splendid isolation in the castle on the hill, as i am calling the hospital. here in the room I rarely leave, in the bed I rarely wake from. the days run into each other, but some are better than others. i have a triple lumen port in my chest that delivers 24/7 meds for every possible problem imaginable. sometimes the nurses completely disconnect me and i am weightless, untethered. i can walk the 40 laps that make a mile without tripping over the wide base of the ungainly 8 foot tall ▶

pole laden with 4 pumps, bags of fluids, and plugs, and wires. i can shower without tangling my arms in the tubing—able to wash my body with 2 hands, not one. i can walk to my tiny closet and not suddenly feel the tug on my chest port because i forgot to pull the pole behind me. but most of the time I am connected to the pole. the meds drip drip drip into my veins. just to get up and go to the bathroom is a chore: disconnect the pole unit from the wall, unwrap the pulsoximeter from my finger (beep beep beep goes the alarm), slip on shoes, shuffle to bathroom pushing pole, unload volumes of urine into the front bucket on the toilet while trying to hold back the diarrhea which is supposed to fall into the latter bucket but usually it's a disaster. do the cleanup. wash hands. leave mess for nurses to observe and flush. push pole back to bedside, plug in, get into bed without wrapping self in tubing, wrap pulsoximeter around finger, hide hand under pillow to diffuse the bright red pulsoximeter light, get comfy, sleep again.

2 hours later my lovely nurse wakes me up for vital signs and starts chatting about her weekend, and i want to kill her. finally i am back snuggled into sleep. and then the bad dreams come. dreams of escaping animals or men, dreams of my mother, dreams of being angry and yelling but no one hearing me, dreams of my ex-husband, dreams of not being able to find oliver. i wake up crying. forgetting that earlier in the evening the nurse had disconnected my tubes and rendered me a free woman, i pull the pole behind me, arrange the cords, disconnect the pulsoximeter (beep beep beep), put on my shoes, and begin pushing the pole to the bathroom. the nurse comes in and says "honey, leave the pole behind. you aren't connected." i laugh at my automaton self and fly to the bathroom, only weighted down by a full bladder and a troubled mind.

i awoke this morning feeling the familiar dip of the spirit, the panic at the pain in my chest, the weight of another day. i know i should get right out of bed as soon as i wake up; it is that early morning time that is so difficult for me to navigate. being ill has robbed me of my life purpose; i have defined myself by how much i accomplish in a day. the new struggle is how to feel okay about NOT doing, creating, caring for, cooking, sugaring, gardening, foraging, raising animals and bees. i remember the year my friend opted out of gardening and then started a support group for people not gardening! there is such competitive pride in our determination to be self-sufficient here in rural vermont. i read the emails from my sisters: "the work you are doing now is as valuable as any work you've ever done" one of them writes. another tells me "you are healing, you are breathing, you are loving, you are navigating hell, you are helping your children feel their way through this devastating time. let that be your purpose." so i get out of bed, make myself eat eggs and toast, load the skis into the car, and head to the cross-country ski trails that a local saint grooms and opens his land to the community. we park at a friend's sugarhouse where he was preparing for tonight's boil, and headed across the old orchard, past the restored farmhouse with doors painted red, over gentle hills, down down down through the little break in the stone wall, across the brook. as i was saying a silent prayer of gratitude to the land owner he gracefully skated by on his skis.

today I painted one of the living room walls orange. why the fuck not?

i find myself thinking a lot about my childhood and my marriage. growing up with my father was like being in an army boot camp, and then i married a man who worked from sunup until 8 PM logging, driving a tractor, fixing rigs, plowing snow, shoveling. . . . i have a phd. in hard labor and i don't know how to turn off my body and sit. sitting still makes my skin itch. but i don't stop trying. i try to sit and meditate frequently but it works better to do it when i hike my daily 3 miles. a kind of meditation anyway. i talk out loud to myself as i slap my boots along the mud roads and paths. i talk to my parents. i talk to myself about my dissolved marriage—i can't seem to get over the guilt and the anger. i worry out loud about my health. i talk to my children—i make lists of things i want to do for them. i know, i know, you're not supposed to think of the future. so i concentrate really hard on my maggie-liz blood cells; i see them before my eyes, those lovely stem cells in a salmon serum stew. i give them intense healing energy, protective energy. i blanket them with love. I hike to a big rock outcropping, and sit in the early spring sun and work on not thinking at all.

the pants wetting history of the lesser girls: my first memory is of liz, making me laugh so hard i peed as i skied down the mountain, first thing in the morning. it felt good in my boots the first 20 seconds. then, disgusting, cold, no change of clothing. i spent the day miserable and barefoot in the ski lodge. i remember trying to make our mother laugh as she was driving the car—the goal was to get her to wet her pants. sometimes it worked. and i ▶

remember countless other times, collapsing on the floor of the kitchen yelling to whichever sister was making me laugh, STOP! I AM WETTING MY PANTS! Liz sent me this poem after the transplant, about the salmon colored stem cells.

if salmon can wet their pants
that's what they are doing
laughing their way home
to the marrow deep within.
they are so excited to be
in the bloodstream of the girl
they have always loved
sometimes from afar,
in the days when we were not one.

i walk the frozen muddy ruts early each morning, down to the mailbox and back, looking for those thin, milky slices of ice between the ruts. i love to shatter them, to feel and hear the crunch under my boot. my kids say walking with me is like taking a 5-year-old for a walk—i aim for the puddles, the ice, i stop to poke and pick up things, and stuff treasures into my pockets.

i don't understand the grand scheme of being human. why do despotic murderers and religious zealots kill, rape, and grab land and power? why do good people die young? why do criminal businessmen make 1200 time more than the mcdonalds $8-an-hour employees and fucking get away with it? they make 24 million a year! it's beyond garishly disgusting, as these single moms struggle. why why why? but i love this life even though it's grossly unfair, and even though it ends, even though last night was probably the last of sugaring this season—and, for me, probably the last time ever. maybe i love sugaring more than anything else because it is a metaphor for my life; a long, dark winter finally morphing through dramatic upheaval into sweetness and warmth. i love it because it is the ultimate reward for hard work, and i don't mean the syrup as reward. i mean the deep friendships that are forged during the long hours of tapping and then boiling. when it is over, when we no longer drive the truck through mud to the sugarhouse as dusk falls, i am always sad, but also relieved. it takes a few days to reorient ourselves. but there is life after sugaring; last night driving home in the first cold spring rain i said to oliver," the salamanders are going to start crossing," and in a few minutes we came upon a sign," CAREFUL, SALAMANDERS CROSSING." and there was our neighbor, flashlight in hand, shepherding spotted salamanders across the road. i could hear the very first peepers of the year screaming nearby, and a few early frogs burping and croaking. now there are gardens to plant. and lambs arriving, and 25 meat bird chicks, and bees, and a dozen fruit trees to plant, and a greenhouse exploding with vegetable and flower seedlings. so the end of the sugar season marks the birth of true spring. tonight there is a steady cold rain, watering the brown fields and thirsty raspberry plants. the rhubarb is up 4 inches, the garlic is peeking up through the straw mulch, and it's not too early to plant peas. tomorrow. i still do have tomorrow.

i rest in the window seat and watch the clouds race across the sky. they cover the sun and then the sun wins and breaks through the tall clouds with dramatic streaks of light. marcia called these "jesus clouds." i've been watching those breaks in the clouds. the golden hue bursting through. i've been thinking death might just be like that—breaking through the clouds. going somewhere different. going into that golden hue. i will be ready. in the meantime, i am living while leaving.

Reading Group Guide:
Discussion Questions for *Marrow*

1. Lesser explains a wish to write about authenticity, "a truer self, an essential self, a core, a soul . . . a fullness of being." How do you define authenticity? Why is it important to Lesser? What is the role of authenticity in communication and connection? Why might something so important be so elusive?

2. KaLiMaJo, the four Lesser sisters, each took on archetypal roles in the family. How and why does this happen with siblings? What is potentially valuable or limiting about the roles we assume during childhood? What role to you have in your own family? How would your parents or siblings describe you? Do their descriptions line up with how you see yourself now?

3. What was Maggie like as a girl? How was she different from her sisters? How did she change over the course of the book? Think about the arc of your own life: for better or worse, what have you kept of your childhood identity?

4. Lesser explains that "conditions of worth" when growing up can be a healthy form of encouragement, but can also "squelch the uniqueness right out of a kid." How did this apply to her and her sisters? What were conditions of worth in your family? If you are raising a family now, how might you instill a value system in your children that leaves room for uniqueness, personality quirks, and self-expression?

5. As she begins to reconnect with Maggie, Lesser is reminded "how little we know about the deepest heart of those closest to us." Think of your own primary relationships: What obstacles do you think prevent us from truly knowing one another?

6. Lesser shares the Greek myth of Elpis (hope) who stayed behind when all other gods and spirits escaped from Pandora's jar. Why do you think she shares this story? What is the role of hope in everyday life? What role does it play for Maggie during her illness? In what way might hope be problematic?

7. Lesser presents the body's interaction with donor cells as a metaphor for the way humans "interpret difference as danger and, in covert or obvious ways . . . reject or attack otherness." Why is this so? Why does Lesser believe such instincts must be overcome? How is this possible?

8. When considering supportive therapy with Maggie, Lesser acknowledges that "being brave one-on-one with another person . . . takes the most courage." What are the potential rewards for being courageous in this way? What are the challenges to such focused intimacy?

9. Consider the insight offered by one of Lesser's heroes, Gerda Lerner, who says that women have a particular challenge to overcome, culturally generated "deep-seated resistance" to accepting themselves and their knowledge. What are some of the sources of these cultural limitations? How do they manifest in Lesser and Maggie? How do they confront and change them? What cultural limitations do you see in your own life and how do they impact you?

10. Quoting Adrienne Rich, Lesser observes: "An honorable human relationship . . . is . . . a process of refining the truths . . . [and] it is important because we can count on so few people to go that hard way with us." What does Rich mean by "refining the truths"? What else is necessary for an "honorable human relationship"? Why is something so important seemingly so rare?

11. What do Maggie's field notes add to your understanding of her experience? How might her completed version of the story have been different from Lesser's version?

12. Lesser spends a great deal of time and energy trying to deeply understand the relationship between herself and the stem cells taken from her for Maggie. What is the relationship between the mind and the body? What are the limitations and possibilities of healing the body with the mind? What is value do you see in the physical and psychological melding that results in Maggie-Liz?

13. At the center of Lesser and Maggie's journey is Friedrich Nietzsche's idea of amor fati. What is amor fati? Why is it so important to Lesser? What role does it play in both of their lives during Maggie's illness? ▶

Reading Group Guide *(continued)*

14. What is valuable about mindfulness and meditation? How might one begin to incorporate these qualities and behaviors into daily living? If you already have a mindfulness practice, what impact do you feel it has in your life?

15. Of all the sisters, Lesser seems "the logical choice as a guide through illness." What qualities and abilities make her such a good guide? What are some ways she must change to fulfill the role well? If someone is sick or suffering in your life, how might you be a source of comfort for them?

16. What important role does Maggie's art play in her experience with illness? What role might art play in healthy living?

17. After her long battle with cancer, Maggie elects to exercise Vermont's death with dignity law. How do you feel about the right to die after a terminal diagnosis? What role did this choice have in Maggie's ability to live well and to die well?

18. Why did Maggie consider a year of such suffering and difficulty "the best year of her life?" What experiences, in health or in illness, are essential to a good, satisfying life? How are those elements present in Maggie's year?

19. Are there people in your life with whom you would like to go deeper into the "marrow" of your relationship? Are there people you should avoid doing this with? Why? How might you get started on this journey?